The Schlager Anthology of Hispanic America

A Student's Guide to Essential Primary Sources

The Schlager Anthology of Hispanic America

A Student's Guide to Essential Primary Sources

Aaron E. Sánchez
Editor in Chief

Dallas, TX

The Schlager Anthology of Hispanic America:
A Student's Guide to Essential Primary Sources

Copyright © 2023 by Schlager Group Inc.

All rights reserved. No part of this book may be reproduced or utilized in any form or by any means, electronic or mechanical, including photocopying, recording, or by any information storage or retrieval systems, without permission in writing from the publisher. For information, contact:

Schlager Group Inc.
10228 E. Northwest HWY, STE 1151
Dallas, TX 75238
USA
(888) 416-5727
info@schlagergroup.com

You can find Schlager Group online at https://www.schlagergroup.com

For Schlager Group:
Vice President, Editorial: Sarah Robertson
Vice President, Operations and Strategy: Benjamin Painter
Founder and President: Neil Schlager

Printed in the United States of America 10 9 8 7 6 5 4 3 2 1
Print ISBN: 9781935306849
eBook: 9781935306856

Library of Congress Control Number: 2023931711

Contents

Reader's Guide..ix

Contributors...xi

Acknowledgments...xii

Introduction...xiii

Volume 1

Chapter 1: Pre-Contact...3
Popol Vuh..7
Hopi Creation Myth..12
Codex Boturini..16
Codex Mendoza...20
Origin Myth of the Acoma..25

Chapter 2: Contact with the Spanish (1492–1598)...29
Christopher Columbus: Columbus Reports on His First Voyage..33
Columbus Meets the Taíno..36
A Universal Cosmography according to the Tradition of Ptolomy
and the Surveys of America Vespucci and Others..38
Requerimiento..40
Hernán Cortés: Second Letter to Charles V..44
Álvar Núñez Cabeza de Vaca: *The Journey of Álvar Núñez Cabeza de Vaca*............................47
A Franciscan Friar Describes the Land and the People of New Mexico.....................................50
Bartolomé de las Casas: *A Short Account of the Destruction of the Indies*................................54
Philip II: Spain Asserts Control over the Indians of Nueva Galicia...57
Bernal Díaz: *The True History of the Conquest of New Spain*...60
Juan de Oñate: Letter about a Settlement in New Mexico..64
Fray Antonio de la Ascension: *A Brief Report of the Discovery in New Spain*...........................67
Tzacoalco (Jalisco): Concerns about a Marriage..70
Our Lady of Guadalupe: "The Apparitions and the Miracle"..73

Chapter 3: The Spanish Borderlands and the Mexican North (1600–1840s).......................77
Pedro Naranjo: The Pueblo Indians Call for War...81
Casta Paintings..85
Bishop Pedro Tamarón y Romeral Visits New Mexico..88
Friar Junípero Serra: Response to the Revolt and Destruction of Mission San Diego.................91
Manuel Mier y Terán: Reports on the Divisions in Texas...95
José Antonio Saco: "The Color Line"...99
Richard Henry Dana Jr.: *Two Years Before the Mast*..102
Guadalupe Vallejo Reminisces about the Rancho Period...105

Chapter 4: U.S. Expansion: Internal and External Colonization (1830s–1898)..................109
Stephen F. Austin: Letter to George Fisher Describing the Occurrences in Texas.......................113
Lorenzo de Zavala: *Journey to the United States of North America*...116

Stephen F. Austin: A Letter Describing the Texas Cause...119

Antonio López de Santa Anna: Message to the Inhabitants of Texas...122

Juan Nepomuceno Seguín: A Tejano Leader Calls for Support of the Texas Revolution....................125

John L. O'Sullivan: "Great Nation of Futurity"..127

John G. F. Wurdemann: A Physician's Notes on Cuba..130

Joint Resolution on the Annexation of Texas..133

Treaty of Guadalupe Hidalgo...137

Alexander von Humboldt: *The Island of Cuba*..141

Elisha M. Pease: Letter to Texas Legislature on the "Cart War"...145

Juan Seguín: *Personal Memoirs*...148

Juan Nepomuceno Cortina: Proclamation to Texans, September 1859..151

Juan Nepomuceno Cortina: Proclamation to the Mexicans of Texas, November 1859.........................155

"Proclamation of Las Gorras Blancas"...159

José Martí: "Our America"..163

Louis Dalrymple: "School Begins"..166

Marian M. George: *A Little Journey to Puerto Rico*...169

Platt Amendment...173

Chapter 5: Expansion and Migration...**175**

"Corrido de Kiansis"...179

"The National Boundary Line at Nogales"...182

"El Corrido Pensilvanio"...184

"The Ballad of Gregorio Cortez"...187

"Los Padrinos en los Funerales de Don Pedrito"...190

"Los Sediciosos"..192

Manuel Gamio: Interview with Isidro Osorio...195

Manuel Gamio: Interview with Anastacio Torres..199

Excerpts from the 1930 U.S. Census...202

Chapter 6: Revolution and Reform...**205**

Francisco Madero: Plan de San Luis Potosí..209

Plan de Ayala...213

"The Plan of San Diego"..217

José Vasconcelos: *The Cosmic Race/La raza cósmica*...220

Aims and Purposes of the Latin-American Citizens League...224

Constitution of the League of United Latin American Citizens...227

Pedro Albizu Campos: "Puerto Rican Nationalism"...231

"Resolution on Racial Discrimination"..235

Emma Tenayuca and Homer Brooks: "The Mexican Question in the Southwest"...............................238

Luisa Moreno: "Caravans of Sorrow" Speech..242

Vernon D. Northrop: Letter to Secretary of State Regarding Puerto Rico...246

Fidel Castro: "History Will Absolve Me"...250

Fidel Castro: Speech at Presidential Palace..254

Chapter 7: Cultural Negotiation—Acculturation and Assimilation...**259**

Robert N. McLean: Protestant Religious Work among the Mexicans...262

Manuel Gamio: Interview with Juan Berzunzolo..265

Manuel Gamio: Interview with Elías Garza..269

Manuel Gamio: Interview with Juana de Hidalgo..273

vi   The Schlager Anthology of Hispanic America

Manuel Gamio: Interview with Elisa Silva..276
Daniel Venegas: *The Adventures of Don Chipote; or, When Parrots Breast Feed*..............279
Paul S. Taylor: Sociological Observations of Mexican Americans in Nueces County, Texas.........283
Paul S. Taylor: Interviews with Mexican Americans in Nueces County, Texas....................287
Américo Paredes: "The Mexico-Texan"..291
Américo Paredes: "Alma pocha"...294
Jesús Colón: "Greetings from Washington" (from *A Puerto Rican in New York*)..............297

Volume 2

Chapter 8: The Great Depression and Postwar Years..**303**
Elsie Chavez Chilton: Working with the Civilian Conservation Corps near Las Cruces 306
Susan Archuleta Looks Back at Jobs with the CCC and the
National Youth Administration in Northern New Mexico..309
U.S. Commissioner General of Immigration Reports on Mexican Immigration.......................312
Franklin D. Roosevelt: First Inaugural Address..315
Memorandum by the American Ambassador in Mexico of a
Conversation with the Mexican Minister for Foreign Affairs....................................319
Works Progress Administration Interviews with Hispanic Women in New Mexico, 1936–39.........322
Américo Paredes: *George Washington Gómez: A Mexicotexan Novel*....................................326
Selden C. Menefee and Orin C. Cassmore: *The Pecan Shellers of San Antonio*........................331
Raúl Morín Discusses Mexican Americans in Military Service......................................335
Photograph of Mexican Agricultural Laborers..339
"Youth Gangs Leading Cause of Delinquencies"..341
"Zoot Suiters Lined Up outside Los Angeles Jail"..345

Chapter 9: Early Civil Rights and American Liberalism..**347**
Report of the Joint Fact-Finding Committee to the Fifty-Fifth California Legislature...........349
Mendez v. Westminster...354
Delgado v. Bastrop..358
Hernandez v. Texas..361
José Antonio Villarreal: *Pocho*..365
Lyndon B. Johnson: Remarks at a Reception Honoring Henry González................................369
Henry B. González: Speech against the Chicano Movement..373

Chapter 10: Civil Rights and Liberation..**377**
César Chávez: Plan de Delano..380
Rodolfo "Corky" Gonzales: "I Am Joaquín"..384
Piri Thomas: "Brothers Under the Skin" (from *Down These Mean Streets*)...........................389
Reies López Tijerina: Interview after Martin Luther King's Assassination.........................393
Patricio Paiz: "En memoria de Arturo Tijerina"..397
Staff Report: Demographic, Economic, and Social Characteristics of the Spanish Surname
Population of the Five Southwestern States—U.S. Civil Rights Commission, San Antonio, TX.........401
Staff Report: A Study of Equality of Educational Opportunity for Mexican Americans in
Nine School Districts of the San Antonio Area—U.S. Civil Rights Commission, San Antonio, TX.....404
Staff Report: Farm Workers—U.S. Civil Rights Commission, San Antonio, TX.........................408
Father Ruiz: Statement before the U.S. Commission on Civil Rights................................411
Young Lords Party 13-Point Program and Platform..415

Contents   vii

East LA Walkout Demands...419

Alurista and Rodolfo Gonzales: "El Plan Espiritual de Aztlan"...423

José Angel Gutiérrez: "The Thirty-Ninth MAYO Walkout: A Diary"..428

Crystal City Walkout Demands...432

El Plan de Santa Barbara: A Chicano Plan for Higher Education...435

Rodolfo "Corky" Gonzales: Arizona State University Speech..439

Mexican American Marines in Vietnam..443

Luis Valdez: "Pensamiento Serpentino: A Chicano Approach to the Theater of Reality"..............................445

Sandra María Esteves: "Blanket Weaver"...451

Chapter 11: "The Decade of the Hispanic" and Hispanic Politics in the 1980s..**455**

Cuban Adjustment Act...458

Serna v. Portales...461

Gerald Ford: Address to the Republican National Hispanic Assembly..465

Plyler v. Doe..468

Virginia Escalante, Nancy Rivera, and Victor Valle: "Inside the World of Latinas".....................................472

David Reyes: "In Pursuit of the Latino American Dream"...477

Frank Sotomayor: "Latinos: A Diverse Group Tied by Ethnicity"...481

Ronald Reagan: Address to the Nation on United States Policy in Central America.......................................485

Tato Laviera: "AmeRícan"...489

Reyes Cárdenas: "If We Praise the Aztecs"...493

Frank del Olmo: "Latino 'Decade' Moves into '90s"...495

"The Decade of the Hispanic: An Economic Retrospective"...499

Chapter 12: Latinos in Modern Politics...**501**

Linda Chávez: "Toward a New Politics of Hispanic Assimilation"..504

Proposition 187..508

Lionel Sosa: The Americano Dream: How Latinos Can Achieve Success in Business and in Life.....................512

DREAM Act..514

Sonia Sotomayor: "A Latina Judge's Voice"...518

Samuel P. Huntington: "The Hispanic Challenge"...522

Herman Badillo: "From Kennedy Democrat to Giuliani Republican"...526

Leslie Sanchez: "The Emerging Latino Republican Majority"..529

Lorna Dee Cervantes: "Coffee"..533

Bill Richardson: Democratic National Convention Speech...538

Sonia Sotomayor: Supreme Court Nomination Speech..542

Barack Obama: Speech at the National Council of La Raza...545

Barack Obama: Speech Announcing DACA...548

Marco Rubio: Presidential Campaign Launch Speech..552

Denice Frohman: "Abuela's Dance"..556

Manuel Pastor: "Latinos and the New American Majority"..559

Donald Trump: Speech on Immigration..563

Donald Trump: State of the Union Address..568

Alexandria Ocasio-Cortez: Response to Being Accosted by Ted Yoho...572

"Latinx LGBT Adults in the U.S."..575

Latino GDP Report for 2021..579

List of Documents by Category...583

Index...589

viii   The Schlager Anthology of Hispanic America

The Schlager Anthology of Hispanic America

A Student's Guide to Essential Primary Sources

Chapter 8

The Great Depression and Postwar Years

As the Great Depression set in for the United States and the rest of the world in the 1930s, many Americans found themselves hit with harsh economic and social struggles. America's once-booming economy essentially collapsed upon the ruins of post-World War I Europe. For many Mexicans living in the United States, likewise, the Great Depression was a period of great angst and anxiety. As whites headed west from hard hit areas like Oklahoma and Kansas in search of work in the agricultural fields of California, they displaced many Mexican workers, as American businesses were often quick to hire whites over those deemed of color. This led to tensions in these areas. For the first time, America saw new immigration laws and practices that targeted Mexican nationals living within the United States.

Mass Deportations of Mexican Workers

Beginning in the 1930s, thousands of Mexicans voluntarily returned home to Mexico, as fears began to grow that the U.S. government would begin to execute increased raids to arrest and deport Mexican nationals deemed to be in the United States illegally. In 1931, for example, 389 individuals who were determined to be in the United States illegally (269 of which were from Mexico) were rounded up during a series of raids in Los Angeles County. These raids were initiated by the Bureau of Immigration (later the Immigration and Naturalization Service) and resulted in thousands of official deportation cases in the United States from 1930 to 1939. In addition, however, there were also many instances in which Mexican immigrants were deported from the country through more local and state-based raids. In 1933, for example, the state of Michigan deported 1,500 Mexican nationals suspected of being in the country illegally. These efforts, combined with an economic push from large employers like U.S. Steel, Ford Motor Company, and the Southern Pacific Railroad to drive Mexican workers out and replace them with now jobless whites, would ultimately result in what some historians estimate would be over one million Mexican nationals leaving the United States in the period of 1929–1939. Despite these mass deportations, including of many who had been born American citizens but lacked proper documentation to prove their citizenship, many remained behind to try and survive in a nation reeling in economic turmoil.

The Great Depression and Postwar Years

As President Herbert Hoover's policies were replaced by incoming President Franklin Roosevelt's New Deal policies, Mexican Americans began to find themselves the benefactors of some economic relief. The U.S. Farm Security Administration (FSA) developed migrant work camps for Mexicans, which provided the necessities for agricultural workers in the southwest as well as some protection from con men who sought to take advantage of Mexican workers in their weakened economic state. Many of these camps served as the first communities of Mexicans who would come together around the issues of labor and open the door to later movements such as those of César Chávez and Dolores Huerta. As the economy slowly began to improve, new work opportunities opened up in cities like San Antonio, Los Angeles, and Detroit. Suddenly, Mexican Americans were no longer just a rural population but rather also an urban one competing for jobs alongside their white counterparts.

With the onset of World War II, many Hispanics rallied with African American and white counterparts to join and fight against the Japanese and Germans. Unlike their Japanese American and Black comrades, Hispanics were often integrated into military units and served with great distinction during the war both in Europe and the Pacific, with thirteen Medal of Honor recipients during the course of the war (seventeen would ultimately be bestowed the honor after four more received medals in 2014). Despite the mistreatment of many Hispanics in the decade prior, many fought proudly defending their nation, often alongside the same men who would have sought their deportation only a decade prior.

The Bracero Program

While many fought overseas, many more stayed home to work in the factories doing jobs left by the men who went off to war, including some estimated 125,000 workers who crossed the southern border as part of the Bracero Program. This program, also known as the Mexican Farm Labor Program, permitted Mexican men to legally work in the United States on short contracts in an effort to augment the depleted workforce, particularly in agricultural areas. In an effort to protect these workers from becoming a new form of slave labor, the Mexican government negotiated terms on behalf of the workers to ensure fair wages and limit discrimination. Despite these efforts, many found themselves subject to de facto company policies that shortchanged them for their work through frivolous pay deductions. The program would bring an estimated 4.5 million workers to the United States between 1942 and 1964, many of which would remain in the country even after the program closed.

The Zoot Suit Riots

One side effect of the urbanization of Latin Americans in the United States was the development of a unique youth culture that blended the fashion, slang, and music of Mexico with American cultural traditions. This rebellious subculture sought to fight against both nations by blending traditions that angered many conservatives from both the United States and Mexico. The *Pachucos,* as they were coined, were seen as the equivalent of a gang and became the target of frequent harassment due to the long dress coats and baggy pants that defined their counterculture movement. While seemingly minor from a modern perspective, in a time of war when citizens were rationing cloth, leather, and even food and oil, this baggy clothing was viewed as excessive and therefore showing a lack of patriotism for the war effort. These tensions came to a boiling point in 1943, when an altercation broke out between U.S. sailors on leave in Los Angeles and some young Latino males. The incident resulted in the targeting of anybody wearing the so-called Zoot Suits that represented the *Pachuco* style. After two nights of unrest, the Zoot Suit riots came to an end with numerous arrests and fights between whites and young Latinos, further exposing the inequities of America's racial problems.

Further Reading

Books

Hoffman, Abraham. *Unwanted Mexican Americans in the Great Depression: Repatriation Pressures, 1929–1939*. Tucson: University of Arizona Press, 1974.

Mize, Ronald L. *The Invisible Workers of the U.S-Mexico Bracero Program: Obreros Olvidados*. Washington, DC: Lexington Books, 2016.

Articles

Gratton, Brian, and Emily Merchant. "Immigration, Repatriation, and Deportation: The Mexican-Origin Population in the United States, 1920–1950." *International Migration Review* 47, no. 4 (2013): 944–75.

Heyman, Josiah McC. "Uprooting and Transformations at the Border, 1929–1967." In *Life and Labor on the Border: Working People of Northeastern Sonora, Mexico, 1886–1986*. Tucson: University of Arizona Press, 1991: 110–61.

Mitchell, Don. "*La Casa de Esclavos Modernos*: Exposing the Architecture of Exploitation." *Journal of the Society of Architectural Historians* 71, no. 4 (2012): 451–61.

Websites

"America's Forgotten History of Mexican-American 'Repatriation'." NPR website, September 10, 2015, https://www.npr.org/2015/09/10/439114563/americas-forgotten-history-of-mexican-american-repatriation.

"Moving to the Cities: Mexican Immigration and Relocation in U.S. History: Classroom Materials at the Library of Congress." Library of Congress website, accessed December 13, 2022, https://www.loc.gov/classroom-materials/immigration/mexican/moving-to-the-cities/.

The Great Depression and Postwar Years

Elsie Chavez Chilton: Working with the Civilian Conservation Corps near Las Cruces

Author
Elsie Chavez Chilton

Date
1930s, recorded in 1991

Document Type
Essays, Reports, Manifestos

Significance
Demonstrates both the poverty of the Hispanic families living in New Mexico during the Great Depression and the positive impact the New Deal government programs had on them

Overview

Elsie Chavez Chilton was a resident of Las Cruces, New Mexico, in the 1930s and 1940s. She grew up in an area of the city called Chiva Town, also known as Goat Hill. That region, now part of Las Cruces' Mesquite Historic District, had long been noted for its goat herders. Local farmers, many of them Hispanic, raised goats in the high ground surrounding the Las Cruces Arroyo. Goatherds harvested milk from the goats, made cheese from it, and sold the cheese around the city's neighborhoods.

Much of Chilton's account revolves around the impact the New Deal had on the area, in particular the work some of her relatives performed for the CCC, or Civilian Conservation Corps. The CCC was created by President Franklin D. Roosevelt in 1933 to relieve unemployment or underemployment among young people, especially teenagers. Young men signed up for service and were put to work on government projects, often in very rural areas. They built campsites in national forests and national parks, planted trees in areas that had been deforested, and constructed wildlife refuges and animal shelters. Some of their work survives and is still in use today.

The National Youth Administration (NYA) was one of several programs of the Works Progress Administration, an umbrella organization established in 1935 as a way of providing jobs in areas where other relief organizations did not operate. The NYA was notable as one of the first government organizations that provided assistance to people of color as well as white people.

306   The Schlager Anthology of Hispanic America

Civilian Conservation Corps workers (National Archives and Records Administration)

Document Text

At that time there was a lot of bartering. That was pre-depression and I was such a small child I don't remember too much about it, but I know they got along just fine. When the depression hit we were already living in town. We had no money to lose because we had no money in the bank. We did have hard times—especially the families whose fathers didn't have a steady income. I had uncles who had steady incomes. They were ditch riders. One was at Leasburg Dam and one at Mesilla Dam.... No matter how small it was, if it was a steady income it meant a lot. Since my father was self-employed that was worse. We managed somehow. Also there was the NYA [National Youth Administration] and the WPA [Works Progress Administration]....

We had a lot of boys... working in the CCC camps around here.... We had a lot of work done by the CCC camp boys—Jornada Range was one area.... I would go over there and have dinner where the officials had dinner. My friend showed me all the fence that they had built. I don't know what they were fencing in but they built miles and miles of fence. I remember my brother went to Vista Viento in California. He got himself into a CCC camp and we were delighted. My folks got $25 a month that summer as a result of his working in the camp.... For a short time, my father worked as a "pusher" at a camp in Radium Springs. Can you imagine that! That's what the boys used to call him. In the camps they called the supervisors that because they used to push the boys to do the work. That was soon over and he had to resort to his other jobs.

Glossary

Jornada Range: This is now the Jornada Experimental Range, located northeast of Las Cruces, New Mexico. It is part of the Jornada Basin, which lies at the northernmost part of the Chihuahuan Desert, the largest warm-climate desert in North America.

Leasburg Dam: An irrigation dam constructed in 1908 on the Rio Grande in New Mexico. It is currently part of the Leasburg Dam State Park, located about half an hour's drive from Las Cruces.

Mesilla Dam: Another irrigation dam on the Rio Grande in New Mexico. This one is located about six miles south of Las Cruces.

Radium Springs: A resort community near Albany, Georgia. It is considered a hot spring site because its water temperature remains at 68 degrees Fahrenheit throughout the year. The water also contains trace amounts of radium.

Short-Answer Questions

1. What does Chilton say was the most important type of income for a family to have? Why would this be?

2. How far apart were the work areas where Chilton says her extended family and friends worked?

3. Chilton begins her account of the Great Depression's impact on her family with a statement about bartering—exchanging products for other products without the use of money. What other indications do you see that her family was very poor?

Susan Archuleta Looks Back at Jobs with the CCC and the National Youth Administration in Northern New Mexico

Author
Susana Archuleta, speaker, and Nan Elsasser, recorder

Date
1930s; recorded 1980

Document Type
Essays, Reports, Manifestos

Significance
Looks at how the New Deal impacted Hispanic youths during the Great Depression of the 1930s

Overview

In the early years of the Great Depression, Susana Archuleta lived in the town of Rock Springs, a mining community in southern Wyoming not far from the New Mexican border. Her father, a miner, had moved his family to the area looking for work in the mines. Her father's death left the family destitute when the Depression hit. However, the creation of the Civilian Conservation Corps (CCC) and the National Youth Administration (NYA) brought more revenue streams to the family. Archuleta worked for the NYA at her school, performing secretarial tasks like filing in addition to homework and assisting in her mother's laundry business.

Archuleta's NYA work shows the extent to which jobs like hers helped alleviate poverty among Hispanic families that other forms of assistance missed. Young women were hired as well as young men, and the work they performed was designed to give them skills they could use to find employment when the job market improved. In addition, NYA opportunities were open to people of color, including young Hispanic women like Archuleta.

National Youth Administration worker
(National Archives and Records Administration)

Document Text

During the Depression, things got bad. My dad passed away when I was about twelve, leaving my mother with eight children and no means of support. . . . My mother took in washings to make a living, and our job was to pick up the washings on the way home from school. We'd pick up clothes from the schoolteachers, the attorney, and what-have-you. Then, at night, we'd help iron them and fold them. . . .

When I was a teenager, the Depression began to take a turn. Franklin Roosevelt was elected, and the works projects started. The boys and young men who'd been laid off at the mines went to the CCC camps, and the girls joined the NYA. . . .

They paid us about twenty-one dollars a month. Out of that we got five and the other sixteen was directly issued to our parents. The same was true of the boys working in the camps. They got about thirty dollars a month. They were allowed to keep five of it. The rest was sent to their families. All of us were hired according to our family income. If a man with a lot of children was unemployed, he was given preference over someone who had less children. . . . Those programs were great. Everybody got a chance to work.

Glossary

CCC: Civilian Conservation Corps, created in 1933 through executive order by President Franklin Delano Roosevelt to put young people to work, mostly in rural areas, as a way of improving federal lands and extending work opportunities to a chronically underemployed part of the population

NYA: National Youth Administration, created in 1935 as a subcategory of the Work Progress Administration (WPA); one of the few federal agencies that extended benefits to young men and women of color

what-have-you: an informal expression that means something like "those sorts of things"

Short-Answer Questions

1. Archuleta states that "things got bad" during the Depression. When does she indicate that her economic situation began to improve?

2. Who received the majority of the income earned by the young men in the CCC and the young women in the NYA? What is your opinion of this practice?

3. Why, according to Archuleta, were programs like the CCC and the NYA "great"?

U.S. Commissioner General of Immigration Reports on Mexican Immigration

Author
Harry E. Hull, U.S. Commissioner General of Immigration

Date
1931

Document Type
Essays, Reports, Manifestos

Significance
Demonstrated the impact the Great Depression had on Hispanic American immigration to the United States

Overview

The report on immigration excerpted here was released by the U.S. government in June 1931, at the height of the Great Depression. Although the report gives interesting statistics on the movement of Mexican Americans into and out of the United States, it is just as interesting for what it does not say. At least half the story lies in the context of the document.

Commissioner General of Immigration Harry E. Hull was a businessman from Iowa. A former member of Congress, he represented an Iowa district as a Republican for ten years, from 1915 to 1925. When his reelection effort failed, President Calvin Coolidge, also a Republican, appointed him to the immigration post. Hull remained commissioner general of immigration until 1933, when Franklin Delano Roosevelt was inaugurated president. Hull retired and lived in Washington until his death in 1938.

Hull does not appear sympathetic toward Mexican American immigrants in this document. That may have been because part of his job would have been to report on the success of a law passed in 1929 designed specifically to limit immigration from Mexico: the Undesirable Aliens Act, a piece of legislation designed by white supremacist members of Congress to discriminate against Mexicans. The act made the first illegal entry into the United States a misdemeanor and a subsequent attempt into a felony, which would bar the immigrant from U.S. citizenship permanently. In addition, the act was enforced through a Mexican repatriation program that threatened immigrants with fines and jail time if they could not prove they were in the country legally. With that in mind, Hull's claim that the drop in Mexican American immigration was due to immigrants not finding work seems baseless at best.

Harry E. Hull (Library of Congress)

Document Text

During the year [1931] but 7,715 aliens were admitted at the various ports of entry on the southern border. . . . This will cover transactions in three immigration districts, San Antonio, El Paso, and Los Angeles. The number admitted as immigrants is a great decrease from the 12,122 so admitted in the preceding year. . . . Mexicans . . . comprise practically all these 7,715 aliens admitted over the southern land border. . . . during the same. 17,733 Mexican aliens were recorded as leaving the United States, practically all going to Mexico. . . . The net decrease of this race to the alien population of the United States for the year just ended . . . was 11,769, as compared with an increase of 5,390 in the previous year. . . .

From numerous sources it has been reported that the departures of Mexicans to their own country in the past year . . . have reached large proportions. Communities in the Far West and Southwest have aided in this repatriation to relieve their charity burdens, but from many parts of the country Mexicans and their families have gone back because of continued lack of employment in this country, the attraction of home ties, and the belief that they can . . . obtain assistance from their relatives or others.

Glossary

aliens: refers here to people who are not U.S. citizens

repatriation: refers to non-U.S. citizens returning to their native lands

transactions: number of U.S. border crossings, whether entering the country or leaving it

Short-Answer Questions

1. What are the reasons Commissioner General Hull gives for Mexican Americans leaving the United States in 1931?

2. What are the reactions of communities with Mexican American immigrant populations to the loss of jobs in the Great Depression?

3. Based on what the commissioner general says, are Mexican American immigrants given the same treatment as other groups during the Great Depression?

Franklin D. Roosevelt: First Inaugural Address

Author
Franklin D. Roosevelt

Date
1933

Document Type
Speeches/Addresses; Presidential/Executive

Significance
Pledged that the United States would adopt a new foreign policy that did not intervene in the affairs of other nations

Overview

When he was elected president in 1932, Franklin D. Roosevelt faced significant challenges both at home and abroad. The United States was the midst of the Great Depression, with millions of Americans out of work and the economy stalled. Meanwhile, the United States was unpopular with many of its neighbors in Latin America and the Caribbean because of U.S. military interventions. Between 1899 and 1932, the United Sates deployed troops or naval vessels to Cuba, the Dominican Republic, El Salvador, Guatemala, Haiti, Honduras, Mexico, Nicaragua, and Panama. On the eve of his inauguration, U.S. Army troops and Marines were deployed in Haiti (where they had been since 1914) and Nicaragua (since 1912). The military interventions were usually to support pro-American regimes or to protect U.S. economic interests. Often the U.S. military was used to maintain dictators who were friendly toward the United States.

In his first inaugural address on May 4, 1933, Roosevelt told a nation battered by the Depression that "the only thing we have to fear is fear itself" and asserted that if everyone worked together, they could overcome the obstacles confronting the nation. Unemployment could be reduced by having people work for the government and by encouraging Americans to move away from areas with few jobs or opportunities. Meanwhile, the government would better regulate banks and financial institutions.

The new president argued that one way for the nation to overcome its economic problems was for the United States to improve trade. More significantly, Roosevelt asserted that the United States had to behave like a "good neighbor." It had to respect the rights and authority of other nations and end the pattern of military interventions. This change in the way the United States dealt with other countries would not only make the nation more popular with those states, but it would also increase trade opportunities. Finally, the United States would also reduce its military spending by eliminating foreign deployments and occupations.

Portrait of Franklin D. Roosevelt
(FDR Presidential Library & Museum)

Document Text

I am certain that my fellow Americans expect that on my induction into the Presidency I will address them with a candor and a decision which the present situation of our Nation impels. This is pre-eminently the time to speak the truth, the whole truth, frankly and boldly. Nor need we shrink from honestly facing conditions in our country today. This great Nation will endure as it has endured, will revive and will prosper. So, first of all, let me assert my firm belief that the only thing we have to fear is fear itself—nameless, unreasoning, unjustified terror which paralyzes needed efforts to convert retreat into advance. In every dark hour of our national life a leadership of frankness and vigor has met with that understanding and support of the people themselves which is essential to victory. I am convinced that you will again give that support to leadership in these critical days....

Our greatest primary task is to put people to work. This is no unsolvable problem if we face it wisely and courageously. It can be accomplished in part by direct recruiting by the Government itself, treating the task as we would treat the emergency of a war, but at the same time, through this employment, accomplishing greatly needed projects to stimulate and reorganize the use of our natural resources.

Hand in hand with this we must frankly recognize the overbalance of population in our industrial centers and, by engaging on a national scale in a redistribution, endeavor to provide a better use of the land for those best fitted for the land. The task can be helped by definite efforts to raise the values of agricultural products and with this the power to purchase the output of our cities. It can be helped by preventing realistically the tragedy of the growing loss through foreclosure of our small homes and our farms. It can be helped by insistence that the Federal, State, and local governments act forthwith on the demand that their cost be drastically reduced. It can be helped by the unifying of relief activities which today are often scattered, uneconomical, and unequal. It can be helped by national planning for and supervision of all forms of transportation and of communications and other utilities which have a definitely public character. There are many ways in which it can be helped, but it can never be helped merely by talking about it. We must act and act quickly.

Finally, in our progress toward a resumption of work we require two safeguards against a return of the evils of the old order: there must be a strict supervision of all banking and credits and investments, so that there will be an end to speculation with other people's money; and there must be provision for an adequate but sound currency....

Through this program of action we address ourselves to putting our own national house in order and making income balance outgo. Our international trade relations, though vastly important, are in point of time and necessity secondary to the establishment of a sound national economy. I favor as a practical policy the putting of first things first. I shall spare no effort to restore world trade by international economic readjustment, but the emergency at home cannot wait on that accomplishment.

The basic thought that guides these specific means of national recovery is not narrowly nationalistic. It is the insistence, as a first consideration, upon the interdependence of the various elements in all parts of the United States—a recognition of the old and permanently important manifestation of the American spirit of the pioneer. It is the way to recovery. It is the immediate way. It is the strongest assurance that the recovery will endure.

In the field of world policy I would dedicate this Nation to the policy of the good neighbor—the neighbor who resolutely respects himself and, because he does so, respects the rights of others—the neighbor who respects his obligations and respects the sanctity of his agreements in and with a world of neighbors.

If I read the temper of our people correctly, we now realize as we have never realized before our interdependence on each other; that we cannot merely take but we must give as well; that if we are to go forward, we must move as a trained and loyal army willing to sacrifice for the good of a common discipline, because without such discipline no progress is made, no leadership becomes effective. We are,

I know, ready and willing to submit our lives and property to such discipline, because it makes possible a leadership which aims at a larger good. This I propose to offer, pledging that the larger purposes will bind upon us all as a sacred obligation with a unity of duty hitherto evoked only in time of armed strife.

With this pledge taken, I assume unhesitatingly the leadership of this great army of our people dedicated to a disciplined attack upon our common problems. . . .

For the trust reposed in me I will return the courage and the devotion that befit the time. I can do no less.

We face the arduous days that lie before us in the warm courage of the national unity; with the clear consciousness of seeking old and precious moral values; with the clean satisfaction that comes from the stern performance of duty by old and young alike. We aim at the assurance of a rounded and permanent national life.

We do not distrust the future of essential democracy. The people of the United States have not failed. In their need they have registered a mandate that they want direct, vigorous action. They have asked for discipline and direction under leadership. They have made me the present instrument of their wishes. In the spirit of the gift I take it. . . .

Glossary

arduous: difficult; hard to accomplish

dictator: a person who rules without oversight by the people

inaugural address: a speech given at the beginning of a leader's term in office

military intervention: the deployment of soldiers or sailors in a foreign country

Short-Answer Questions

1. Why did Roosevelt state that "the only thing we have to fear is fear itself"? What message was he trying to convey to the American people?

2. Why did Roosevelt call for the United States to adopt a "good neighbor" policy? How would this mark a change in U.S. foreign policy?

3. What benefits could the United States gain from changing its foreign policy? What would be some ways the "good neighbor policy" would help the U.S. economy recover from the Great Depression?

Memorandum by the American Ambassador in Mexico of a Conversation with the Mexican Minister for Foreign Affairs

Author
Josephus Daniels

Date
1933

Document Type
Essays, Reports, Manifestos

Significance
Reported that Chinese immigrants were entering the United States from Mexico and sought assistance from the Mexican government to stop the migrants from crossing the border

Overview

The United States has always been a nation of immigrants. However, by the late 1800s, the federal government and various state governments began to enact rules to restrict immigration. Some people in the United States feared that immigrants caused increased competition for jobs, while others opposed new immigrants because of racism. In 1882, the U.S. Congress enacted, and President Chester A. Arthur signed, the Chinese Exclusion Act, which banned new immigration from China for ten years, with some exceptions for students, teachers, and merchants. In 1892, the law was made permanent. The Immigration Act of 1924 placed further restrictions on immigrants from East Asia and set a quota system for migrants from the region, and it created the Border Patrol to enforce immigration laws. Like other migrants to the United States, most Chinese were fleeing repression or seeking economic opportunities.

These new laws against immigration led many Chinese to seek to enter the United States from Mexico. There were no restrictions on Chinese immigration to Mexico. There were also few obstacles to prevent people from crossing the border between Mexico and the United States. Indeed, there was already a pattern of agricultural workers from Mexico traveling to the United States to work during harvesting seasons and then returning home.

The onset of the Great Depression in the 1930s led the United States to attempt to better enforce immigration laws to reduce the number of people seeking jobs. In this memorandum, the U.S. ambassador to Mexico, Josephus Daniels, notes that over the two-year period from 1931 to 1933, more than 2,600 Chinese immigrants had been apprehended and sent back to China at considerable cost. Daniels also makes a false claim that some Chinese were traveling to the United States to gain a free trip back to their homeland. The ambassador seeks assistance from the Mexican government to reduce the number of Chinese migrants.

The Chinese Exclusion Act was eventually repealed in 1943 during World War II, while China was an ally of the United States.

U.S. ambassador to Mexico Josephus Daniels
(Library of Congress)

Document Text

Under date of May 8, 1933, Ambassador [Josephus] Daniels informed His Excellency the Minister for Foreign Affairs, Doctor Puig Casauranc, that according to information received from official sources the United States immigration authorities at Nogales, Arizona, had apprehended two hundred ninety-seven Chinese nationals at that city during the month of March, 1933.

Since the delivery of Mr. Daniels' note, further information has been received regarding this situation.

It appears that from September, 1931, to the end of February, 1933, two thousand six hundred seventy-six Chinese nationals were deported from that district of the United States Department of Labor having headquarters at El Paso, at a total cost to the immigration appropriation of about three hundred sixty thousand dollars.

It is stated that, although few Chinese still remain in the State of Sonora, the volume of Chinese illegally entering the United States continues, and that many of the Chinese now arriving as refugees in the United States are in fact able to pay their passage to China and are, strictly speaking, not refugees, but come from south of Sonora, taking advantage of the situation to secure a free trip to China.

It has been suggested that if the Chinese are in fact not refugees and are not forced to leave Mexico, the Mexican authorities may be willing to cooperate by refusing to permit these Chinese nationals to proceed to the border, unless they are in possession of documents visaed by American Consular Officers, this being the procedure which was previously adopted in the case of European aliens.

It has been suggested that Mr. William P. Blocker, present American Consul at Ciudad Juárez, be detailed to cooperate with the Mexican authorities in this matter, provided the Mexican Government has no objection.

Glossary

consul: a diplomatic representative of a foreign country

deported: the process whereby someone is forced by the government to leave a country

immigrant: a person who moves permanently to a new country

immigration: the process of permanently moving to a new country

visaed: receiving official permission to travel to another country

Short-Answer Questions

1. Why did the U.S. government seek to limit immigration to the United States in the late 1800s and early 1900s? Were its reasons justified?

2. Why was the United States seeking cooperation from Mexico to enforce its immigration laws? How did the cost of dealing with unlawful immigration factor into the U.S. request?

3. What happened to Chinese immigrants who were caught trying to illegally enter the United States? Was this an appropriate response? Why or why not?

Works Progress Administration Interviews with Hispanic Women in New Mexico, 1936–39

Author
Edith Crawford (interviewer), Lorencita Miranda (interviewee)

Date
1939

Document Type
Essays, Reports, Manifestos

Significance
Recollects the hardships and challenges of a Latina pioneer in New Mexico in the late 1800s

Overview

During the 1930s, the Works Progress Administration, a federal program that provided jobs for Americans, conducted thousands of interviews with Americans to document their experiences and life histories. On May 5, 1939, Edith Crawford of the WPA sat down with seventy-seven-year-old Lorencita Miranda in Lincoln, New Mexico, to record her memories of her early life.

Miranda's story highlights the difficulties faced by settlers during the era. For instance, she and her husband had to walk five miles to a church to get married. She briefly describes the founding of Lincoln County and the establishment of some of its towns as the Hispanic culture of the region was replaced by the incoming Anglo settlers. The very name of the town of Las Placitas, for example, was changed to Lincoln.

Violence was a common theme throughout her life. Miranda's father was killed just after she was born, and her aunt disappeared during the bloody Lincoln County War of 1878. This conflict involved two rival groups who engaged in attacks on each other and a series of revenge killings that left at least twenty-three people dead and more than twenty wounded. The gunfighter Billy the Kid was one of the participants in the fighting. Miranda met the infamous Billy the Kid, who came to her home to drink coffee on several occasions. She recounts how her family tried to avoid becoming involved in the fighting, even when the home of Alexander McSween (a leader of the faction that included Billy the Kid) was burned down.

Miranda's life was tragic in many ways; her husband died before her, as did seven of her eight children. However, her story underscores the resilience of the settlers of the region as they faced the hardships of the frontier.

WPA worker in New Mexico (Library of Congress)

Document Text

I was born August 10, 1861, in the town of Las Placitas, New Mexico, in Socorro County, New Mexico. (Las Placitas is now the town of Lincoln, and is in Lincoln County, New Mexico.) My father Gregorio Herrera married my mother Gerelda Torres in Manzano, New Mexico, about the year 1860. They moved to Las Placitas New Mexico, and I was born there. On August 18th, 1861, about ten days after I was born, my father was killed in a drunken row, in Las Placitas. Another man was killed at the same time and we never were sure who did kill my father. After Father's death my mother went back to Manzano to live with her people. My mother gave me to one of my aunts, Trinidad Herrera, (who was nick-named Chinita) who, with my mother moved back to Las Placitas when I was about two years old.

I have lived the rest of my life in Lincoln County. I will soon be 78 years old.

In the year 1869, when I was eight years old, all of the territory lying east of the Mal Pais, was created into Lincoln County, and the county seat was established at Las Placitas and the name was changed to Lincoln.

I was married to Jose Delbros Miranda in January 1877. We were married in the Catholic Church at the Torres Ranch, by Father Sambrano Tafoya of Manzano, New Mexico. This church is about six miles west of Lincoln, New Mexico. I remember that we had to walk about five miles to the church to get married.

Works Progress Administration Interviews with Hispanic Women in New Mexico, 1936–39

My husband had a two roomed adobe house built for us to live in. It had a dirt floor. We had no stove and I had to cook on the fireplace. All eight of my children were born in Lincoln. Seven of them are dead and buried there. My youngest son, Emelio Miranda, is married and has twelve children. He lives in Lincoln and is the post-master there. One **of my grandsons lives with me on my little farm, a** half mile west of the town of Lincoln. I raise a few chickens and a small garden which helps to keep me busy.

The house where I was born in Las Placitas (now Lincoln) stood on the site of the old Laws Sanitarium. The place then belonged to Sabino Gonzales, who was one of the men that helped build the old Torreon in 1855. My father-in-law Felipe Miranda also helped to build the Torreos. This old Torreon was rebuilt and dedicated in 1935, by the Chaves County Archaeological and Historical Society.

My husband and I were living on our farm just above Lincoln, New Mexico, all during the Lincoln County War. We liked both factions so we never took any part in the war. I remember the day the McSween home was burned. We could see the flames and smoke from our house but we stayed at home for we were scared to death to stick our heads out of the house. We could also hear some of the shooting. Billy the Kid came to our house several times and drank coffee with us. We liked him for he was always nice to the Spanish people **and they all liked him.**

My Aunt, Chinits Herrera, started to walk to Socorro, New Mexico, to see her brother. (I do not remember the year.) She was seen on the road to Socorro by Mrs. Susan McSween Barber who gave her a drink of water and some food. She was not far from a ranch house and Mrs. Barber thought she would got along all right, but my aunt was never seen or heard of again. We never did know what become of her.

My mother married a man by the name of Octaviano Salas, and lived in Lincoln, New Mexico, until her death in September 1926.

My husband Jose Deloros Miranda died October 28, 1928, in Lincoln and was buried here.

Glossary

Billy the Kid: infamous American gunfighter, born Henry McCarty and also known as William H. Bonney, orphaned at fifteen and killed when he was twenty-one

McSween: Alexander McSween, a leader of the warring faction that included Billy the Kid

row: a quarrel or fight

Torreon: a tower or turret on a building

Short-Answer Questions

1. Why did Miranda like Billy the Kid?

2. What were conditions like for Miranda after she got married? What were some of the hardships she faced?

3. Why did Miranda and her family try to avoid involvement in the Lincoln County War? What might have happened if they did choose one of the sides?

Works Progress Administration Interviews with Hispanic Women
in New Mexico, 1936–39

Américo Paredes:
George Washington Gómez: A Mexicotexan Novel

Author
Américo Paredes

Date
1940; 1990

Document Type
Poems, Plays, Fiction

Significance
A look at the struggles of the Mexican American worker in the United States in the 1930s

---

Overview

During the 1930s, the Great Depression ravaged America's economy, particularly the rural parts of the United States. American immigration policy had been particularly lenient toward Mexican immigrants to appease the high demand of agricultural labor in the South, but following the collapse of the stock market and the advent of the Dust Bowl, many white Americans began heading into the southwest in the hopes of finding work, including working in the fields. As work became increasingly scarce, this created difficulties for Mexican migrant workers, many of whom had come to the United States during World War I and then remained. The lack of codified immigration law in the United States exacerbated issues as many local law enforcement agencies created arbitrary immigration laws and arrested and deported those who had come across at a time when there had been no policy regarding Mexican immigration. In many cases, this resulted in the separation of families or even the unlawful deportation of U.S. citizens solely because they lacked evidence that they had been born in the United States.

Making the situation worse was a lack of unity among Mexican Americans. While African Americans would develop the National Association for the Advancement of Colored People (NAACP) and similar organizations aimed at aiding each other with legal defense and even petitioning for change, the first major Latin American organization, the League of United Latin American Citizens (LULAC), wasn't founded until 1929, and much of its early efforts were stunted by the Great Depression. This meant that many citizens who found themselves being targeted for racial persecution were left to their own devices, fighting a battle many could not win.

In this novel about a young Mexican American in the early twentieth century, completed in 1940 but not published until 1990, Américo Paredes addresses these issues while illustrating the identity, cultural, and legal conflicts of life near the Texas-Mexico border during the Great Depression.

Family in Texas in the early 1940s (Library of Congress)

Document Text

And in due time the Depression came. La Chilla, Mexicans called it. The Squeal. Or perhaps a euphemism for that most useful of Mexican expressions: *La Chingada. Estamos la gran chi-i-illa, compadre.* La Chilla. Sugar is two cents a pound and men are two cents a dozen, Mexicans half-price. Flour costs a quarter a sack, and a quarter costs all of a man's efforts and the little pride he has left. La Chilla. Long lines of men sitting in the employment offices with a gloomy hope in their eyes. Long lines of women standing in the street before relief agencies, hunger and humility on their faces. Little groups of children playing in the sun, dirtier, skinnier, quieter than ever before.

Help wanted. Young white man to help with farm. That red-faced Gringo will get it. No matter. That's old man Lilly's farm and he's an anti-Mexican *sanavabiche*. Wanted. Nursemaid for children two and five years old. Must be English-speaking. No chance for the old women there, not a chance. Wanted. White woman to keep old lady company. Wanted, dependable, hard-working white man.

The Mexicotexan has a conveniently dual personality. When he is called upon to do his duty for his country he is an American. When benefits are passed around he is a Mexican and always last in line. And he has nobody to help him because he cannot help himself. In the United States he is not the only racial group that often finds the going hard. But while there are rich Negroes and poor Negroes, rich Jews and poor Jews, rich Italians and Poles and poor Italians and Poles, there are in Texas only poor Mexicans. Spanish-speaking people in the Southwest are divided into two categories: poor Mexicans and rich Spaniards. So while rich Negroes often help poor Negroes and rich Jews help poor Jews, the Texas-Mexican has to shift for himself.

Now the Great Depression has arrived. Jobs are few and the Mexican gets few of those available. Relief rations are limited, and the Mexican gets more dirty looks than groceries at the RFC, the *ora sí*, as he calls it, the "Now's the Time." For one decent meal at least. . . .

—Give your name, references, work you've been doing.

—Eusebio Pérez. Just out of high school. Haven't done much except pick some cotton, I guess. But I can type and know some bookkeeping.

—Yusibio Pérez. Cotton picker.

—How about my schooling? Aren't you going to put that down?

—I don't think we need to mention that. Next! . . . That one there was too good for picking cotton. I don't see why we waste tax money on sending them to school. Taking the bread out of white people's mouths, these damn cheap politicians. Anything for a vote. . . .

La Chilla. La Chilla. Rows of vacant store buildings, their empty windows looking like eye-glasses on rows of skulls. And on the sidewalks, in the little lobbies formed by store entrances, groups of dark-skinned men, waiting, waiting. For nothing.

A shiny car stops, and a heavy sweaty man with a pistol belt around his middle lumbers down. A younger officer in a khaki uniform follows. They go directly to the group of men and single out one of them.

—You Juventino Grajales?

—*Sí, señor.*

—**Where were you born?**

—Oaxaca.

—How long you been over on this side?

—Since 1915.

—Immigration paid?

—Immigration?

—I thought so. Get in the car.

—Get in the car? What for, *señor*? I haven't done anything. I am a peaceful man. . . .

—Don't you know it's illegal to enter the United States of America without paying immigration and getting your papers?

—I swear I didn't know, *señor*. Nobody ever told me. Mister Estrong himself, he went with a truck and got us from Morelos back in 1915 to pick his cotton in Alice, and we just stayed around. Nobody said for us to go home and nobody took us. Is that a crime?

—Sure is, and ignorance of the law is no excuse. But since this your first time we'll just take your fingerprints and put you across the river. And don't you try coming back a second time if you what's good for you.

—But *señor*, my wife. She's a Texan, my children were born here.

—Listen. We enforce the law. We don't mix up in your family affairs. Come on. . . .

Juventino Grajales, 42, was sentenced to three years at the FTI today on a charge of habitual violation of American immigration laws. The FTI, still another alphabetical term, is the Farm Type Institution. There is one at La Tuna built especially to take care of habitual violators of the immigration laws.

Grajales contended that he crossed the river illegally to see his wife, children and one grandchild which he had never seen. His record shows a number of deportations, as well as three penitentiary sentences of one year, 15 months, and 18 months in Leavenworth on immigration charges. Grajales, through his counsel, had promised previously that he would not return any more, even for short visits.

The court also heard a complaint filed by Sr. Nestor Martinez, lawyer for the Mexican consulate, that Grajales had been slugged and otherwise mistreated at the hands of the arresting officers. Officers contend Grajales resisted arrest. Charges brought by Sr. Martinez were dropped for lack of sufficient evidence.

Glossary

bookkeeping: accounting work

consulate: a diplomatic mission to represent and protect the nation's people and interests

deportations: forcible evictions to one's country of origin

FTI: "farm type institution"; a large farm where convicts would work in the fields; common in rural parts of the United States

Leavenworth: a federal prison in Kansas

Mexicotexan: somebody of Mexican ancestry who resides in Texas

nursemaid: a woman employed to look after young children

Short-Answer Questions

1. How did opportunities for work compare for Mexican Americans and Mexican migrants compared to other U.S. citizens and immigrants? How did the Great Depression complicate this situation?

2. The author speaks of wealthy minorities assisting other wealthy minorities, yet he draws a marked difference between wealthy Mexican Americans and poor Mexican Americans. How did this reflect a lack of unity in the identity of the Mexicotexan that he describes elsewhere in the passage? How might this have made it difficult to effect change in Texas and other border states?

3. The experience of Juventino Grajales reflects a common experience for Mexican migrant workers in the United States during the Great Depression. How did a clear lack of federal statutes regarding Mexican migrant workers impact the ability of migrant workers to remain in Texas? How was the treatment of his family, who were of similar descent and color, different based solely on their location of birth? What effect did this have on the unification of Mexican Americans in the early twentieth century?

Selden C. Menefee and Orin C. Cassmore:
The Pecan Shellers of San Antonio

Authors
Selden C. Menefee and Orin C. Cassmore

Date
1940

Document Type
Essays, Reports, Manifestos

Significance
Documented and analyzed the deplorable working conditions of Mexican American pecan shellers in San Antonino, Texas, in the 1930s

Overview

Throughout the twentieth and twenty-first centuries, farms and agricultural companies in the United States hired large numbers of Mexicans and Mexican Americans as seasonal workers. In the 1930s, the pecan industry developed a contract system whereby farms hired companies to shell the pecans, which were then sold to other businesses or consumers. The contractors who owned pecan-shelling plants found it less expensive to employ temporary laborers than to use machines to do the work. Because of high unemployment and the Great Depression, a period of especially high unemployment and low economic productivity worldwide, workers were willing to accept low wages since there were few jobs available.

As part of an effort improve working conditions across the United States in the 1930s, the federal government's Works Progress Administration documented problems with various businesses and industries. A published report about the pecan industry, *The Pecan Shellers of San Antonio: The Problem of Underpaid and Unemployed Mexican Labor*, was written by Selden C. Menefee and

Orin C. Cassmore and detailed the problems faced by Hispanic workers who shelled pecans.

The working conditions were horrible. Contractors did not want to spend money to provide even the most basic of necessities for their employees. Business owners knew that workers could be easily replaced. The report highlighted many of the worst abuses in the industry, including a lack of sanitation and dangerous working conditions. It also noted the economic difficulties of the temporary workers, who often faced long periods of unemployment. The pecan plants were overcrowded and poorly ventilated. Changes in local laws helped improve conditions somewhat in the late 1930s.

The system was especially difficult for Hispanic women, who were usually expected to take care of children, prepare meals, and perform other housework in addition to the work they did as pecan shellers. It was also common for children as young as ten years old to work in the plants.

Pecan shellers in San Antonio (Library of Congress)

Document Text

Under the contract system the working force in the industry was somewhat disorganized. The Mexicans looked upon pecan shelling as a last resort, and worked at it only when other work was not available. Often the pickers would leave a plant where the nuts were small or running heavily to shell, and go to other plants where the nuts were reported to be better. Women would come to work for a few hours while their children were in school, returning home to prepare lunch and dinner for their families. Old men and women, cripples, and even children worked in the shelling plants to earn enough to pay the rent or buy food. An NRA investigator found children from 10 to 15 years of age at work in several San Antonio plants.

Working conditions in the hand shelling plants were (and are) bad. Often as many as a hundred pickers sat at their stalls around long tables in a room perhaps 25 by 40 feet, wielding their picking knives with quick, deft movements. Illumination was poor. There was no ventilation, except for open doors or windows in warm weather, and the fine, brown dust from the pecans hung in the air. (Many pecan workers believe that this dust causes some of the tuberculosis that is so prevalent among the Mexicans, and some think that is it harmful to the eyes, but medical finding are not available on these points.)

In a majority of the shelling plants, particularly the smaller ones, sanitary facilities were completely lacking for many years. There were no inside flush toilets and no washbowls for the workers. (In October 1936 this was partly corrected when the city amended its health ordinance to require that all shelling plants have running water and sanitary facilities. In many plants, however, there was still only one toilet for a large number of workers of both sexes in 1938; and lighting and ventilation were still very poor.)

The number of contractors dropped to about 300 in 1935, but the number of workers at the peak season remained high. This was due partly to the large amount of shelling in this period, especially during the 1935–36 season, following the bumper crop of 1935. In 1936 two things happened to reduce further the number of contractors. First, there was a very small pecan crop that year; and second, contractors were required to improve working conditions and homework was outlawed by the health ordinance mentioned above.

After the passage of this ordinance, many of the small establishments closed down. The maximum number of plants was 204 in 1936, and 191 in 1937, according to the San Antonio Department of Health, which issued health certificates to pecan workers. Early in January of 1938 health department records showed that over 12,000 workers were registered as employed in 110 different plants, nearly all of which were operated by contractors.

. . . Pecan shelling was marked by wide seasonal variations in activity. A few of the larger compa-nies operated throughout the year, but many of the small ones customarily closed down during the summer, operating only from October or November until some time in May. The peak of employment came about the end of November, with the number of employees then remaining almost stationary until March. The low point of employment occurred in midsummer, when thousands of shellers had left San Antonio for the cotton and beet fields. The number of employees varied from a usual peak of 10,000 or more in the late fall to a minimum of a few hundred in August and early September of slack years, according to officials of the San Antonio Department of Health.

Seasonal agricultural work and other types of seasonal employment dovetailed to some extent with pecan shelling to furnish fairly regular employment for some Mexicans. But even when other work was found in the summer to supplement pecan shelling, the pecan workers often lost considerable time between jobs and during periods of layoff. Out of 1,160 workers in the families of the 512 pecan workers interviewed, only 15 percent had steady employment throughout 1938. Of the balance, 21 percent were unemployed for 150 days or more during the year. The modal length of unemployment among all worker was 60 to 89 days, which fact was accounted for mainly by the shutdown of most shelling plants from October to December.

Glossary

bumper crop: a very large or fruitful harvest

NRA: National Recovery Administration; from 1933 to 1935, a federal agency that oversaw efforts to improve workers' pay and employment conditions while also regulating businesses

tuberculosis: a deadly respiratory disease

Short-Answer Questions

1. Why did pecan contractors use laborers instead of machines to shell pecans? What impact did the Great Depression have on the pecan shelling industry?

2. Describe the working conditions for the pecan shellers. What led to improvements in the pecan factories?

3. Why did the pecan shellers often have to seek other employment? Were they usually able to find other jobs? Why or why not?

Raúl Morín Discusses Mexican Americans in Military Service

Author
Raúl Morín

Date
1942

Document Type
Essays, Reports, Manifestos

Significance
Gave an overview of Mexican American participation in the U.S. armed forces during World War II

Overview

Raúl Morín (1913–1967) was a U.S. veteran of World War II who became a civil rights activist in the 1950s and 1960s. Morín was born in Texas, but he moved to California in the 1930s and set up his own business as a sign painter in East Los Angeles before World War II broke out. He enlisted in the U.S. Army in 1944 and served with the 79th Infantry in the European theater. During the Battle of the Bulge (December 1944–January 1945), he was wounded in action and was sent home to recuperate. It was during that time that he conceived the idea to produce a book to highlight the contributions of Mexican Americans

veterans—who were often treated with hostility and discrimination—in World War II.

Morín's book, *Among the Valiant: Mexican Americans in WWII and Korea* (1963), discusses the contributions of Hispanic Americans in the wars of the mid-twentieth century. It was based on interviews and news stories that he collected over the course of more than a decade of research. When the volume finally saw print, almost two decades after Morín began his own military service, its introduction was written by a fellow Texan, Lyndon B. Johnson, at the time the U.S. vice president.

Mexican American military service member Francisco Mercado Jr., right (Library of Congress)

Document Text

The first [Mexican American] volunteers were those who joined the regular army before World War II. They enlisted during peacetime at military centers such as: Fort Sam Houston, Fort Bliss, Fort McArthur, and the Presidio at San Francisco. . . .

On October 29, 1941, Pedro Aguilar Despart of Los Angeles was the holder of number 158 in the national draft lottery, . . . and thus became the first Angelino to be drafted for selective service in World War II.

On December 8th of the same year, the National Guard was federalized. . . . Many civilian members who had signed up in the guard . . . suddenly found themselves in the role of real soldiers in many National Guard Divisions.

After the bombing of Pearl Harbor, the draft boards set up the machinery to send a steady stream of selectees into the Armed Forces. . . . Even alien non-citizens living in the United States were . . . drafted into the service. . . .

In June, 1942, Mexico . . . joined other Latin-America countries in declaring war on the Axis. Soon many young Mexican nationals crossed the border . . . to volunteer for service with the United States.

Other volunteers here in the States were . . . young high school students who, upon reaching the age of 18 (or 17 with their parents' permission), immediately signed up before being drafted . . . to . . . go into the Navy, Marines or Air Force. . . .

The draft boards in Los Angeles, Nogales, Albuquerque, San Antonio, El Paso, Corpus Christi, and the Lower Rio Grande Valley of Texas . . . were loaded with Spanish names on their files; and very few were ever exempted, reclassified, or found too essential to be drafted. Local rural youths were being drafted so fast . . . that . . . owners of large farms and ranches . . . voiced stern protests with the local draft boards.

Where They Came From

. . . They came from farms, from large cities, from small villages, from the back woods, and from the hills—from all parts of the United States and from . . . Mexico.

They had been laborers, small businessmen, farmers, truck drivers, craftsmen, students. . . . While the majority of the Spanish-speaking recruits . . . were from the . . . cities of the . . . Southwest, the names most often-repeated . . . were . . . of the . . . small *barrios* (neighborhoods). . . .

Besides being from . . . towns in the Southwest, many of the Mexican-Americans . . . hailed from . . . North Platte, Nebraska; Garden City, Kansas; Cheyenne, Wyoming; . . . Chester, Pennsylvania; . . . Gary, Indiana; Detroit, Michigan; Lorraine, Ohio; St. Louis, Missouri; and Oklahoma City, Oklahoma.

One could always tell where they came from by their manner of speech . . . the fast-English-speaking Angelenos [or] the slow-Spanish-speaking Texan or New Mexican. The *Caló* talk (slang words) of the . . . habitant from El Paso . . . was in contrast to the home-spun Spanish of the Coloradan or Arizonan. Those that originated from far away localities . . . preferred the English language. . . .
A study of this particular group will give an idea of

. . . the different kinds of "Mexicans" that were to be found in the Army.

First, we had the American-born of Mexican parents. . . . Born, raised, and educated in the United States, this type still clung to many of the Mexican customs and traditions. . . . Their speech was more Spanish than English, sometimes a mixture of both. . . .

Quite different were those born and raised in Mexico. Some had left there since early childhood, others more recently, although all had become naturalized citizens. . . .

Undoubtedly, the largest group were those born in the United States whose parental lineage ran back to the original settlers and the early immigrants of the Southwest. In this group were the Spanish-Americans from New Mexico and Colorado, the *Tejanos* from Texas, and the *Pochos* from California. Those belonging to this group were definitely more "American." . . . They enjoyed Spanish songs, Latin rhythms, and the Mexican *mariachis*, but also were also very "hep" to the latest American songs, dances, and the latest "craze" . . . of our modern-day youths. . . .

Among them were many . . . Mexican-Italians, Mexican-Filipinos, Mexican-Negroes, Spanish-Mexicans, French-Mexicans, Irish-Mexicans, Mexican-Germans, and English-Mexicans. . . .

. . . The GI's of Mexican descent were not too different. The only difference . . . was in what they called themselves, or . . . what they were accustomed to being called by the people back home.

The so-called "Spanish" were in many instances accused of being ashamed of the term "Mexican." Being native-born and raised Americans, they never felt any sentiment for Mexico; . . . they had never lived there. . . .

Then came the "Spanish-Americans" or Hispanos. Most of these were from New Mexico or Southern

Colorado. They had been told long ago that only the people from south of the border were Mexican. . . .

Next came the so-called "Latin-Americans." Most of these lived in Texas; a few came from the northern or middle-western states. They had struggled for many years to prove to everyone that they were from this country and not Mexicans from Mexico. . . .

Last, were . . . the proudest of all our groups, those boasting of being "*chicano,*" or *mejicano.* They had nothing but scorn for those who denied their racial ties or pretended not to understand Spanish. . . . Most had been raised in predominantly "Mexican" surroundings along the border towns and in southern Texas or southern Arizona. . . .

Native Californians were known as *Pochos*; New Mexicans as *Manitos.* Others were called just plain *Chicanos* or Tejanos. . . .

All the different terms to describe the Spanish-speaking people . . . have stemmed from the attempts by these groups to be set apart from the aliens. The futility of it all is noted by the small impression made on the other Americans. . . . We would always be referred to as "those Mexicans." . . .

For this reason we have made the term "Mexican-American" our choice. We then imply that we are proud to be Americans, and at the same time are not trying to deny our Mexican ancestry.

Glossary

federalized: brought under the control of the U.S. government; federalizing the National Guard gave the president the authority to call up servicemen at short notice if they were needed

GI: an initialism for "Government Issue" that came to mean a general serviceperson

hep: 1940s-era slang for knowledgeable, "in the know"

Short-Answer Questions

1. How many different terms were there during the 1940s for Hispanic groups?

2. How does Morín differentiate between Mexican-Americans born in Mexico and those born in the United States?

3. Morín points out that many Mexican Americans who worked as rural laborers were drafted in the armed forces and were unable to get a deferment, which would have excused them from the draft. What other forms of discrimination can you see in his account?

Photograph of Mexican Agricultural Laborers

Creator
Marjory Collins

Date
1943

Document Type
Cartoons, Images, Artwork

Significance
Illustrates Mexican farm laborers near Stockton, California, in 1943, during the period of the Bracero Program

Overview

The entry of the United States into World War II on December 7, 1941, created a shortage of workers as American men and women joined the military and support services and left their civilian jobs. To support the agricultural, railroad, and other industries, the U.S. government began negotiations with the Mexican government to create a guest worker program to allow Mexican citizens to work temporarily in the United States.

For decades, Mexicans had entered the United States to find temporary employment as workers in agriculture or other industries. Many of the workers would send their pay back to their families in the form of remittances, or money transfers, and return home periodically after time spent in the United States. However, the Mexicans often faced discrimination, low pay, and abuse. On occasions, employers withheld their pay and had them sent forcibly back to Mexico.

In an attempt to end these problems, the United States and Mexico signed the Mexican Farm Labor Agreement on August 4, 1942. The accord served as the basis for the Bracero Program. The word *bracero* simply means worker or laborer, and the Bracero Program granted seasonal work permits for temporary laborers to work in the United States. The braceros were promised better living and working conditions, including a minimum wage of 30 cents per hour (equal to about $5.50 in 2022). Workers had individual contracts that specified pay, hours, housing, and other employment conditions. Mexicans were employed not just as farm laborers but also as railway workers and in other occupations. On average, about 200,000 to 250,000 Mexicans were part of the program each year. This image of Mexican farm laborers was taken by photojournalist Marjory Collins (1912–1985) near Stockton, California, in May 1943, during the era of the Bracero Program.

The program did not end all mistreatment of guest workers, but it did improve the conditions for most. Discrimination still occurred. Texas was even suspended from the arrangement because of widespread mistreatment of braceros.

Opposition to the Bracero Program in the United States grew after World War II. Some Americans argued that the initiative encouraged illicit migration, while other contended that it led to lower wages for American workers. By the late 1950s, the growing use of technology reduced the need for agricultural workers. These factors led to the end of the program in 1964.

Document Image

Photograph of Mexican Agricultural Laborers (Library of Congress)

Short-Answer Questions

1. Why was the Bracero Program created? What role did World War II play in creating a need for the initiative?

2. Why was the Bracero Program stopped?

3. How did the program benefit Mexican workers? Did it end discrimination and abuse of workers? Why or why not?

"Youth Gangs Leading Cause of Delinquencies"

Author
Gene Sherman

Date
1943

Document Type
Essays, Reports, Manifestos

Significance
Commented on the supposedly delinquent habits of Mexican American youth on the eve of the so-called Zoot Suit Riots

Overview

Among the contemporaneous news articles surrounding the issue of delinquency and its relation to 1940s Mexican American zoot-suit, or *pachuco*, culture, this one in the *Los Angeles Times*, by Gene Sherman, stands out for having been published a day before the start of the so-called Zoot Suit Riots of June 3–8, 1943, and for highlighting "language variance in the home" as "a serious factor of delinquency." Sherman begins by reminding readers of events that occurred the year prior and the growing problem with wayward youth in the city. His audience would have recalled the tragic events of August 2, 1942, in which a young Mexican American man, José Gallardo Díaz, was killed in an altercation at a party. Consequently, many members of the 38th Street gang were arrested, seventeen of whom were eventually convicted for the murder in January of 1943. After numerous appeals by their families, community members, and civil rights activists who charged that the trial had been racially motivated, they were all acquitted and freed in 1944.

The riots of June 1943 marked a halfway point during this contentious period and almost sparked an international incident after the Mexican Embassy lodged a formal complaint with the U.S. State Department. The governor of California, Earl Warren, ordered an investigation, which found that racism was the root cause of the aggression. While it is true that some *pachucos* were not the most upstanding citizens, most of the violence during the riot was instigated by U.S. servicemembers, mainly sailors on offshore leave, as well as police officers and white civilians, who attacked, beat, and stripped the clothes off Mexican Americans. World War II was underway, and tensions ran high as people rationed food and raw materials. The zoot suit was flamboyant, used a lot of cloth during a time of rationing, and made *pachucos* stand out. Although the suit was popular among many ethnic groups, including Filipinos, Italians, Irish, and African Americans, anti-Mexican sentiment incited by the press led to violence against *pachucos* in several American cities.

Photograph of men wearing zoot suits
(National Archives and Records Administration)

Document Text

Fresh in the memory of Los Angeles is last year's surge of gang violence that made the "zoot suit" a badge of delinquency.

Public indignation seethed as warfare among organized bands of marauders, prowling the streets at night, brought a wave of assaults, finally murders.

Gang activities constitute an important part of the juvenile delinquent problem in Los Angeles. Next to "desire for adventure and employment" the Police Department lists gangs as the chief cause of delinquency.

Many Over 18 in Gangs

There are, however, two exceedingly important things to remember when dealing with gangs—a large group of the membership of gangs comprises youths over 18 years of age and although many gang members wear "zoot suits," thousands of "zoot suit" wearers are non-delinquents.

At the beginning of the year it was estimated that there were 30 gangs in the country, including approximately 750 juvenile boys.

This estimate is at variance, however, with the police statistics which blame gang activity for the booking of 811 juveniles last year and the investigation (without booking) of 115 more.

Mark of "Distinction"

Although "zoot suits" became a uniform of delinquency because of their popularity among the gangs, their adoption by some of the city's youth was more a bid for recognition, a way of being "different," in the opinion of Heman G. Stark, County Protection Office chief of delinquency prevention.

Stark and Superior Judge Robert H. Scott of Juvenile Court concur in the belief that the formation of gangs was an outgrowth of a feeling of inferiority on the part of minority groups.

Whitfeiffer, executive-secretary of the Council of Social Agencies, points out that, between native-born youths of native-born parents and native-born youths of foreign-born parents, the latter always poses the greater delinquency problem.

Language Marks Difference

Juvenile files repeated show that a language variance in the home—where the parents speak no English and cling to past culture—is a serious factor of delinquency. Parents in such a home lack control over their offspring.

Motives for gang warfare are ridiculous in adult eyes but sometimes lead to planned and bloody fighting. One youth rallied his gang when a member of another East Side band made disparaging remarks about his automobile. A knife fight almost resulted when a member of one gang bumped into a member of another on Main St.

Many of the gang fights reported in newspapers have been planned conflicts with clubs, rods, lengths of pipe, knives and even guns—planned much like a football contest would be.

Detective Work Started

Using the gang idea, much has been done to direct the energies of groups of idle boys into constructive channels.

A plumber on Third Street not long ago was troubled by boys who broke his windows and raided other stores in the block. The plumber corralled the leader of the group, invited the whole group to have dinner with him, planned the organization of a club and personally raised money for athletic equipment.

Window-breaking ceased and the merchants had the fun of backing a winning softball team!

The gang theory is used to superlative advantage in the Boy Scouts, Wood-craft Rangers, Campfire Girls and other youth organizations. Juvenile officers report instances where whole gangs, engaged in assorted depredations, have been formed into merit-badge-winning Scout troops. . . .

Glossary

flamboyant: tending to attract attention due to exuberance, confidence, and stylishness

pachuco/pachuca: a young Mexican American who was part of a countercultural style that emerged in El Paso, Texas, in the late 1930s. Followers of the style wore zoot-suit fashion, listened to jazz and swing music, and had their own distinct lingo known as caló. Often maligned by the press as gang members, they regarded themselves as resisting assimilation into Anglo-American society through acts of self-empowerment and defiance.

zoot suit: a flashy suit made up of high-waisted, wide-legged, tight-cuffed, and pegged trousers; a long coat with wide lapels and wide padded shoulders; and a fedora hat, a knee-length long chained pocket watch, and French-style pointed shoes

"Youth Gangs Leading Cause of Delinquencies"

Short-Answer Questions

1. In his article "Youth Gangs," Gene Sherman tried to explain to readers the growing problem of juvenile delinquency associated with young people who wore zoot suits. Does the article present the issue in an objective and even-handed way? Please explain.

2. Sherman offers some sociological explanations surrounding the home lives and generational background of the Mexican American youth he perceives as troublesome. What are some of these observations, and what is the point he is trying to make?

3. It is noteworthy that Sherman's article was published a day before the rioting began. Do you think the press and pieces like this one influenced public opinion about young people who stood out and belonged to ethnic minorities. If so, to what extent?

"Zoot Suiters Lined Up outside Los Angeles Jail"

Author
Acme Newspapers, Inc.

Date
1943

Document Type
Cartoons, Images, Artwork

Significance
Illustrates Mexican American men under arrest after being attacked by white U.S. service members during a series of confrontations known as the Zoot Suit Riots

Overview

Zoot suits were a type of men's clothing that originated among African American entertainers in the 1930s. By the 1940s, the style had become very popular among African Americans, Hispanics, and some Asian Americans, especially in California. A zoot suit included a long, oversize jacket that sometimes hung to the knees and had padded shoulders. The trousers were baggy, fastened above the waist, and tapered around the ankles.

Among Mexican American youths in Los Angeles, California, the zoot suit emerged as more than a fashion. It became a part of their identity and a symbol of their culture. For a community wracked by poverty, the zoot suit conveyed status and pride. The suits also became the dress of several Mexican gangs in Los Angeles, including the Clanton 14 and the 38th Street Boys.

Some whites in Los Angeles and other California communities began to associate zoot suits with criminals and criminal activity. Many Hispanics males who wore

zoot suits found themselves questioned or harassed by the police. When the United States entered World War II, a backlash arose against the style. Many saw zoot suits as extravagant and wasteful at a time that Americans were being asked to conserve resources, including materials for clothing, for the war effort.

During the week of June 3–8, 1943, Anglo Americans instigated a series of race riots that came to be called the Zoot Suit Riots in Los Angeles and other areas of Southern California. White Californians and U.S. service members, mainly sailors, attacked Mexican Americans and other people of color wearing zoot suits, beating them with clubs and other weapons and ripping off their clothes. More than 150 people were injured in the violence, and police officers arrested more than 500 people, mainly Mexican Americans. In response, the Los Angeles City Council banned zoot suits. However, the style survived as a symbol of Mexican American pride and would influence future civil rights activists.

Document Image

Zoot suiters lined up outside Los Angeles jail (Library of Congress)

Short-Answer Questions

1. What is a zoot suit? How did the style originate?

2. Why did some people have a negative view of zoot suits? Were those perceptions justified?

3. Who caused the Zoot Suit Riots? How did authorities react to the violence?

Chapter 9
Early Civil Rights and American Liberalism

Following the end of World War II, America went through a significant social change, as the experiences of the war redefined the new racial norm in the United States. Segregation remained a part of America's military forces. However, racial norms had started to change as a result of the experiences of those who had not only fought overseas, but also worked in the defense factories at home, where Blacks and whites worked alongside one another. Though racial tensions still remained high, conversations around desegregation began to become increasingly common, especially after the armed forces desegregated in 1948 and the year prior when Jackie Robinson broke the color barrier in Major League Baseball. Segregation still occurred in many parts of the United States, particularly for Hispanics living in the South and Southwest. Nonetheless, the first steps towards gaining equality could be seen brewing in America's judicial system.

School Segregation in California

In the 1940s children of Latin American families were often sent to schools segregated from their white peers, and those schools were often underfunded and under-staffed. Latinos found themselves in the difficult position of being classified as "white" but not subjected to the same rules (and privileges) as whites. Schools were therefore able to claim that Hispanic children needed to be sent to separate facilities because of a language deficiency. In California, Hispanic children were subjected to subpar instruction on this basis for decades. In 1946, however, the Mendez family brought forth a case against the California schools arguing that these practices violated the Fourteenth Amendment guarantee of due process. The courts agreed, and the schools in California were ordered to desegregate. While the case of *Brown v. Board of Education* in 1954 would garner much more attention and historical significance as it applied to all schools in the country, the *Mendez* case opened the door for educational equality for all students, regardless of not just race but ethnic background and language as well.

Hernandez v. Texas

Hispanics accused of crimes also saw some racial progress in the 1950s, as courts began to reexamine the idea of race and the rights of the criminally accused under the Fourteenth Amendment. The Supreme Court allowed a South Carolina law to stand in the case of *Brownfield v. South Carolina* (1903), which allowed Blacks to be tried by an all-white jury even when the majority of the county was African American. Though Justice Oliver Wendall

Holmes acknowledged that the "case involves questions of the gravest character," the Court could only consider the constitutional issue at hand of whether the trial by jury required the jury to be of the same race. This decision allowed for many states, including Texas, to maintain their own discriminatory practices in their court systems against those of Hispanic heritage, allowing only those who were deemed as "white" to serve on juries. For many Latinos, this meant that any trip to the criminal court system was likely to result in a trial by race rather than one based on the evidence. In 1954, however, the Supreme Court ruled in *Hernandez v. Texas* that a criminal jury composed of only whites in a case involving a Mexican American was not representative of the county's demographics and was therefore not a trial by peers as defined by the Constitution. This case would have a significant impact on the beginning of the civil rights efforts of the 1950s.

LULAC and the American GI Forum Make Progress

Organizations like the League of United Latin American Citizens (LULAC) increased their efforts through-out the postwar years to help mobilize Latin Americans to participate more in politics. The goal was to create a voting bloc that even the most conservative of politicians could not ignore. While progress was relatively slow, their most significant contribution was the unification of Latin Americans that had previously been difficult to achieve in the 1920s and 1930s. The American GI Forum, led by Hector P. Garcia, helped to bring attention to the inequities Hispanic veterans faced on their return home from the Second World War. In 1949 the remains of Felix Longoria (who had died in 1945 in the Philippines) were returned to his home town in Three Rivers, Texas. However, he was refused a proper wake owing to his ethnicity. Garcia petitioned Texas Senator Lyndon Baines Johnson to intervene, and Longoria's body was interred in Arlington National Cemetery with full military honors. The efforts of LULAC and the American GI Forum had succeeded in bringing the Latino experience to the national spotlight. This opened the door for the movement to gain momentum not just in the southwest but across the United States at the same time as the growing call for desegregation and equal rights for African Americans.

Further Reading

Books

Orozco, Cynthia E. *Pioneer of Mexican-American Civil Rights: Alonso S. Perales.* Houston, TX: Arte Publico Press, 2020.

Rosales, F. Arturo, *Chicano! The History of the Mexican American Civil Rights Movement.* Houston, TX: Arte Publico Press, 1997.

Websites

Allsup, V Carl. "Felix Longoria Affair." TSHA website, June 1, 1995, https://www.tshaonline.org/handbook/entries/felix-longoria-affair.

"History." LULAC website, accessed December 14, 2022, https://lulac.org/about/history/.

Report of the Joint Fact-Finding Committee to the Fifty-Fifth California Legislature

Author
Joint Fact-Finding Committee on Un-American Activities in California, California Legislature, 55th Session

Date
1943

Document Type
Essays, Reports, Manifestos

Significance
An example of how anti-fascist and anti-communist sentiment was used to reinforce discrimination against Hispanics in California during World War II

Overview

Following the entry of the United States into World War II in 1941, there were widespread but unfounded concerns that fascist and communist groups were actively working to undermine the war effort of the country. In 1941, the California legislature created a committee to investigate what were termed "un-American activities" by different organizations. Its 1943 report described some of its findings of active fascist and communist groups in the state.

The report traced the rise of the fascist Sinarquist movement in Mexico and its subsequent emergence in California. The committee's members wrote that the group rejected the importance of democracy and instead embraced totalitarianism, a belief in total government control, and adopted their uniforms and rituals from the Nazi Party of Adolf Hitler. The Sinarquistas were reported to be made up primarily of middle-class Mexicans but were attempting to recruit members from the poorer areas of East Los Angeles.

Communists and fascists were staunch enemies. The committee's report notes that the communists had waged a long campaign in newspapers and other publications against the Sinarquistas. During World War II, the United States was allied with the Soviet Union, a communist country. However, communists were viewed with suspicion by many in the United States because their beliefs clashed with capitalist views on the economy and individual freedom.

The report speculates that some crimes committed by young Mexican Americans, known as members of the "Zoot-Suit Gang" because of the way they dressed, were the result of conflict between communists and fascists. However, communist publications argued that these crimes were often caused by poverty and that the police unfairly provoked the Zoot-Suiters.

Sinarquistas at a meeting (Wikimedia Commons)

Document Text

Anti-Communist movements, unchecked, uncontrolled and in irresponsible hands gravitate rapidly into Fascist organizations. If history has taught us anything during the last decade, it has taught us this. Mussolini's Black Shirts were anti-Communist and Hitler's crusade in Germany was directed against the Communists. Just as the Socialism of Karl Marx seems to demand a dictator and a ruthless totalitarian government for its progress and achievement, anti-Communist movements likewise, wittingly or unwittingly, move toward a totalitarian dictatorship for the crushing of Communism.

BACKGROUND AND HISTORY

Your committee is in possession of several confidential reports on the history of *Sinarquism* in Mexico, its origin, leaders and objectives. The committee is also in possession of some of the publications of the movement, both in Mexico and in the southwestern United States and California. . . .

Many of the Communist articles are obviously vehicles for subtle libel of the Catholic Church. Certain facts appear to be well established. The leader of the *Sinarquismo* in Mexico is Salvador Abascal.

He is reported to be a man about 32 years of age. He is a lawyer and was a district judge in a village in the State of Guerrero.

In 1936 a German engineer by the name of Oscar Schreiter, teaching at a college in the State of Guanaguato, is reported to have organized a movement called the *Centro Anti-Communista.*

Abascal and two of his lawyer friends, Manuel Zeremeno and Jose Urquizu, joined Schreiter's *Centra Anti-Communista.* In 1937 *Centra Anti-Communista* became the Union National *Sinarchista.* Jose Urquizu became the first Chief—*El Jefe.* It is reported that Urquizu was killed in a running gun-battle with a government man. Manuel Zeremeno succeeded Urquizu and Abascal finally succeeded Zeremeno August 15, 1940.

As far back as the Summer of 1941, the Communist press in the United States asserted that the *Sinarquist* movement was being financed by the Nazis. The German origin of the movement appears to lend some authority to this statement. . . .

The organization is reported to have been semi-military from its inception. The Communist press charges that the military instructor of the organization in Mexico is a Spaniard, a member of the Falange, by the name of Bilbao. The *Sinarquist* uniform is described as very similar to the one worn by Nazi storm-troopers. An armband worn on the left sleeve of the uniform is said to be red bearing a white circle in which is contained a green map of the country of Mexico. The flag of the organization is said to be a red banner with a white circle, also containing the green map of Mexico. The salute of the *Sinarquistas* is made by crossing the left arm diagonally over the chest.

The *Sinarquistas* in Mexico are reported as proclaiming: "Our leader is chosen by God; this is the keystone of our unity and discipline." The official organ of the movement, *El Sinarquista,* in its issue of November 7, 1940, declares: "The *Sinarquists* carry firmly engraved this truth because it is the cornerstone of our unity and of our discipline: the *Jefe* is imposed by God."

The proof of the Fascist tendencies of the *Sinarquistas* is expressed in *El Sinarquista* for September 28, 1939: "The members of the same trade or professions unite, constituting corporative groups. Above these professional groups or corporations there must exist a superior power charged with ordering their mutual relations and direct them to the good of the collectivity. Similar professional corporations must unite among themselves and must submit to a supreme authority which is incorporated in the political structure of the Nation." Certainly, there is a close similarity in this language of *Sinarquism* with Mussolini's *corporate State.*

Authoritarianism is indicated in the following, from *El Sinarquista* of June 18, 1940: "Among ourselves we do not discuss about what to do with our strength. Take away our discipline, take away our loyalty to the *Jefe,* and *Sinarquism* is nothing." . . .

We have learned that the organization contains branches at San Fernando, Oxnard, San Bernardino, Ontario, Azusa, Pomona, La Verne, Pacoima, and Watts. The general membership is apparently made up of middle-class Mexicans. . . .

The Communist Party press and its members began an intensive agitation against the *Sinarquistas* in Los Angeles in the Fall of 1942. A number of Mexican boys had been arrested and charged with various crimes, including murder, and because of their peculiar manner of dressing, became known as the "Zoot-Suit Gang." This appellation was suggested by the style of dress effected by certain of the Mexican colony's boys and some of the Negroes in the eastern part of the City of Los Angeles. It consists, generally, of more or less baggy trousers, drawn tightly and cuffed at the ankles. When coats are worn they are of an extremely long cut, closely fitted at the hips and reaching in many extreme cases to the knees. A pomaded hair dress with the hair grown long and brushed toward the back forms what has become known as the "duck tail" hairdress.

The first publications of any consequence regarding the Mexican situation in Los Angeles consisted in a series of articles run in the *People's Daily World*, Communist West Coast publication, signed by Tom Cullen. The first of these articles appeared in the issue of October 3, 1942. Cullen quotes Guy T. Nunn as stating that the *Sinarquista's* principal weapon against Democracy "is to discourage all war efforts in every way. Their seeds are sown in fertile soil among the boys and girls brought up on the east side of Los Angeles." . . .

In the issue of the *People's Daily World* for October 5, 1942, Carey McWilliams is reported to have stated that the Mexican boy gangs are the result of an economic situation and he accuses police officers of attaching razor blades to sticks for the purpose of ripping the peg-top trousers and "zoot-suit" coats off the Mexican boys.

Glossary

authoritarianism: a government that emphasizes obedience over personal freedom

Black Shirts: an Italian anti-communist movement that seized power in 1922

Centro Anti-Communista: the Anti-Communist Center

communism: a far-left political ideology in which there is collective ownership of property and government control of the economy with the objective of a classless society

corporate state: a political system in which the government controls large segments of the economy

el Jefe: the Boss

Falange: a Spanish fascist organization that seized power in Spain in 1937

fascism: a far-right political ideology based on rule by one person, anti-communism, and government control

libel: deliberately false written statements meant to harm reputations

Nazi Party: a fascist political party led by Adolf Hitler that ruled Germany in the 1930s and 1940s

Negroes: old-fashioned term for Black or African American; often considered offensive today

Sinarquist: a Mexican fascist organization

Glossary

socialism: a leftwing political ideology based on public ownership of property and resources

totalitarianism: a political ideology based on government control of all aspects of a country's culture, economy, and society

Short-Answer Questions

1. Why did the California legislature establish the Un-American Activities Committee?

2. What was the Sinarquist movement? What was its relationship with the Nazis?

3. What was the "Zoot-Suit Gang"? Why were they targeted by the police?

Report of the Joint Fact-Finding Committee to the
Fifty-Fifth California Legislature

Mendez v. Westminster

Author
U.S. Court of Appeals for the Ninth Circuit

Date
1947

Document Type
Legal

Significance
The first case to declare that school segregation is unconstitutional and violates the Fourteenth Amendment

Overview

In March of 1945, five families in Orange County, California, brought a class-action lawsuit against four school districts on behalf of their own children and five thousand other children who were forced to attend segregated schools for Mexican children. The lawsuit was filed as *Mendez et al. v. Westminster et al.* and represented five families: the Estradas, the Guzmans, the Mendezes, the Palominos, and the Ramirezes. On their behalf, attorney David C. Marcus challenged the existence of Mexican remedial schools in four districts of Orange County, California. The United States Court of Appeals for the Ninth Circuit ruled in an *en banc* decision that the forced segregation of Mexican American students into separate "Mexican schools" was unconstitutional. In contrast to the *Brown v. Board of Education* case eight years later (1954), the Mexican American families did not pursue a racial discrimination approach. Under the Treaty of Guadalupe Hidalgo (1848)—which ended the U.S. War with Mexico and extended the boundaries of the United States by over 525,000 square miles—Mexican Americans were considered legally white since, at the time, only two racial categories were recognized: Black and white. The families instead claimed discrimination based on ethnic background and a perceived "language deficiency." Thus, they charged that segregation of the kind practiced by Orange County schools denied their children equal protection under the Fourteenth Amendment, which granted citizenship to all persons born or naturalized in the United States and provided all citizens with equal protection under the law. Judge Paul McCormick ruled in favor of the plaintiffs on March 18, 1946. He argued that Mexican American students suffered socially and psychologically under segregation and that the associated pedagogical costs were detrimental to their education. Claiming that the federal courts did not have jurisdiction in matters of education, the school districts launched an unsuccessful appeal that was decided on April 14, 1947. Ultimately, *Mendez* is important as a precedent for later school court cases, such as *Brown*, but especially for being one example of many in which Mexican Americans prevailed in their own long civil rights struggle.

Sylvia Mendez in 2011 (Flickr)

Document Text

The evidence clearly shows that Spanish-speaking children are retarded in learning English by lack of exposure to its use because of segregation, and that commingling of the entire student body instills and develops a common cultural attitude among the school children which is imperative for the perpetuation of American institutions and ideals. It is also established by the record that the methods of segregation prevalent in the defendant school districts foster antagonisms in the children and suggest inferiority among them where none exists. One of the flagrant examples of the discriminatory results of segregation in two of the schools involved in this case is shown by the record. In the district under consideration there are two schools, the Lincoln and the Roosevelt, located approximately 120 yards apart on the same school grounds, hours of opening and closing, as well as recess periods, are not uniform. No credible language test is given to the children of Mexican ancestry upon entering the first grade in Lincoln School. This school has an enrollment of 249 so-called Spanish-speaking pupils, and no so-called English-speaking pupils; while the Roosevelt, (the other) school, has 83 so-called English-speaking pupils and 25 so-called Spanish-speaking pupils. Standardized tests as to mental ability are given to the respective classes in the two schools and the same curricula are pursued in both schools and, of course, in the English language as required by State law. Section 8251, Education Code. In the last school year the students in the seventh grade of the

Lincoln were superior scholarly to the same grade in the Roosevelt School and to any group in the seventh grade in either of the schools in the past. It further appears that not only did the class as a group have such mental superiority but that certain pupils in the group were also outstanding in the class itself. Notwithstanding this showing, the **pupils of such excellence were kept in the Lincoln School.** It is true that there is no evidence in the record before us that shows that any of the members of this exemplary class requested transfer to the other so-called intermingled school, but the record does show without contradiction that another class had protested against the segregation policies and practices in the schools of this El Modeno district without avail.

The study of American institutions and ideals in all schools located within the State of California is required by Section 10051, Education Code.

While the pattern or ideal of segregating the school children of Mexican ancestry from the rest of the school attendance permeates and is practiced in all of the four defendant districts, there are procedural deviations among the school administrative agencies in effectuating the general plan.

In Garden Grove Elementary School District the segregation extends only through the fifth grade. Beyond, all pupils in such district, regardless of their ancestry or linguistic proficiency, are housed, instructed and associate in the same school facility.

This arrangement conclusively refutes the reasonableness or advisability of any segregation of children of Mexican ancestry beyond the fifth grade in any of the defendant school districts in view of the standardized and uniform curricular requirements in the elementary schools of Orange County.

But the admitted practice and long established custom in this school district whereby all elementary public school children of Mexican descent are required to attend one specified school (the Hoover) until they attain the sixth grade, while all other pupils of the same grade are permitted to and do attend two other elementary schools of this district, notwithstanding that some of such pupils live within the Hoover School division of the district, clearly establishes an unfair and arbitrary class distinction in the system of public education operative in the Garden Grove Elementary **School District.**

The long-standing discriminatory custom prevalent in this district is aggravated by the fact shown by the record that although there are approximately 25 children of Mexican descent living in the vicinity of the Lincoln School, none of them attend that school, but all are peremptorily assigned by the school authorities to the Hoover School, although the evidence shows that there are no school zones territorially established in the district. . . .

There could have been no arbitrary discrimination claimed by plaintiffs by the action of the school authorities if the same official course had been applied to the 35 other so-called English-speaking pupils exactly situated as were the approximate 26 children of Mexican lineage, but the record is clear that the requirement of the Board of Education was intended for and directed exclusively to the specified pupils of Mexican ancestry and if carried out becomes operative solely against such group of children.

It should be stated in fairness to the Superintendent of the Santa Ana City Schools that he testified he would recommend to the Board of Education that the children of those who protested the action requiring transfer from the Franklin School be allowed to remain there because of long attendance and family tradition. However, there was no official recantation shown of the action of the Board of Education reflected by the letters of the Secretary and sent only to the parents of the children of Mexican ancestry.

The natural operation and effect of the Board's official action manifests a clear purpose to arbitrarily discriminate against the pupils of Mexican ancestry and to deny to them the equal protection of the laws.

The court may not exercise legislative or administrative functions in this case to save such discriminatory act from inoperativeness.

There are other discriminatory customs, shown by the evidence, existing in the defendant school districts as to pupils of Mexican descent and ex- traction, but we deem it unnecessary to discuss them in this memorandum.

We conclude by holding that the allegations of the complaint (petition) have been established sufficiently to justify injunctive relief against all defendants, restraining further discriminatory practices against the pupils of Mexican descent in the public schools of defendant school districts.

Glossary

commingling: blending

injunctive: legally ordered

retarded: inhibited; slowed

segregation: separation, especially by race, class, language, or ethnic group

---

Short-Answer Questions

1. The desegregation case *Mendez v. Westminster* was argued and decided eight years prior to the landmark case of *Brown v. Board of Education*, which ruled that U.S. state laws establishing racial segregation in public schools are unconstitutional, even if the segregated schools are otherwise equal in quality. What accounts for the fact that *Mendez* is not as well-known or celebrated as *Brown*?

2. Both *Mendez* and *Brown* are federal court cases that successfully paved the way for the eventual dismantling of school segregation. While similar in nature, what are some key differences between the two, and how do they compare in terms of strengths and weaknesses?

3. A common refrain has been that all ethnic minorities in the United States have benefited from and followed in the footsteps of African American civil rights activism. How might the *Mendez* case challenge that belief and help amend the prevailing view?

Delgado v. Bastrop

Author	Significance
Ben H. Rice Jr.	Struck down a statewide policy on segregating Mexican American schoolchildren from white schoolchildren in Texas ostensibly based on English proficiency and attendance
Date	
1948	
Document Type	
Legal	

Overview

Mexican American parents and their children secured a major legal victory in 1930 with the course case *Salvatierra v. Del Rio Independent School District*. The case, filed in a Texas district court by the League of United Latin American Citizens (LULAC) on behalf of Mexican American parents whose children attended a public elementary school in Del Rio, Texas, challenged the state's existing "separate but equal" policy that allowed for distinct facilities for white and Mexican American students. Supporters of segregation contended that the Mexican American students' comparatively weak grasp of English and below-average attendance records justified the policy, but District Court Judge Joseph Jones decreed that schools should be desegregated. The Texas Court of Appeals subsequently overturned Jones's ruling, contending that the separation was based not on the students' ethnicity but on their specific needs in the classroom.

The Supreme Court decided not the review the case, but the issue resurfaced sixteen years later, this time in California's federal courts. A U.S. District Court judge heard another case regarding the segregation of Mexican American children, *Mendez v. Westminster*, and decided it violated both state law and the equal protection of the law clause of the Fourteenth Amendment. The U.S. Court of Appeals for the Ninth Circuit upheld the lower court's decision, which inspired Mexican American activists in Texas to resume the fight against segregation in their state. Renewed efforts supported by LULAC and several Mexican American parents led to legal challenges to the segregation policies in five public school districts. In the case of *Delgado et al. v. Bastrop Independent School District et al.*, attorneys for the parents successfully argued that the districts were in violation of the Fourteenth Amendment by barring Mexican American students from attending public school with white children.

358   The Schlager Anthology of Hispanic America

LULAC filed Delgado v. Bastrop *in a Texas district court.*
(Wikimedia Commons)

Document Text

IT IS THEREFORE ORDERED, ADJUDGED, AND DECREED that:

1. This action by plaintiffs is a representative class action on behalf of themselves and of all pupils of Mexican or other Latin American descent, and the action has been properly brought as such class action pursuant to law.

2. The regulations, customs, usages, and practices of the defendants, Bastrop Independent School District of Bastrop County, et al., and each of them in so far as they or any of them have segregated pupils of Mexican or other Latin American descent in separate classes and schools within the respective school districts of the defendant school districts heretofore set forth are, and each of them is, arbitrary and discriminatory and in violation of plaintiff's constitutional rights as guaranteed by the Fourteenth Amendment to the Constitution of the United States, and are illegal.

3. The defendants, Bastrop Independent School District of Bastrop County, Texas, and the above-named trustees and superintendent of said district, the Elgin Independent School District of Bastrop County, Texas, and the above-named trustees and superintendent of said district, the Martindale Independent School District of Caldwell County, Texas, and the above-named trustees and superintendent of said district, and the Travis County Board of School Trustees above-named, and each of them are hereby permanently restrained and enjoined from segregating pupils of Mexican or other Latin American descent in separate schools or classes within the respective school districts of said defendant and each of them and from denying said pupils use of the same facilities and services enjoyed by other children of the same ages or grades; provided, however, that this injunction shall not prevent said defendant school districts or their trustees, officers, and agents from providing for and maintaining, separate classes on the same campus in the first grade only, solely for instructional purposes, for pupils in their initial scholastic year in the first grade, or who have not accumulated attendance substantially equivalent to a scholastic year, clearly demonstrate, as a result of scientific and standardized tests, equally given and applied to all pupils, that they do not possess a sufficient familiarity with the English language to understand substantially classroom instruction in first-grade subject matters.

4. If in any school district obedience to this decree renders it practically necessary, in the discretion of the school district, that additional school buildings be provided or moved from one campus to another, then a reasonable time is hereby allowed for compliance, but in no event beyond September 1949.

5. The defendant, L. A. Woods, as State Superintendent of Public Instruction, is hereby permanently restrained and enjoined from in any manner, directly or indirectly, participating in the custom, usage or practice of segregating pupils of Mexican or other Latin American descent in separate schools or classes.

6. The motion of the State Board of Education and the members thereof to be dropped as parties hereto is sustained, and they are hereby dropped and dismissed from this suit with their costs.

Dates at Austin, Texas, this 15th day of June, 1948.

(Ben H. Rice, Jr.)
United States District Judge

Glossary

adjudged: ruled, decided

class action: a lawsuit brought forth by a group

enjoined: ordered, commanded

Fourteenth Amendment: provides equal legal and civil rights to all U.S. citizens

heretofore: up to now

Short-Answer Questions

1. In what ways might this decision have influenced other court cases that followed? How can this case be considered within the larger framework of the civil rights movement?

2. What events transpired between 1930 and 1946 that might have proved instrumental in convincing district courts in Texas to reverse their decision regarding the segregation of schools?

3. How might the policy of segregation have informed Mexican American schoolchildren's perception of themselves?

Hernandez v. Texas

Author	**Significance**
Chief Justice Earl Warren	Ruled that the exclusion of Mexican Americans from juries was a violation of the Fourteenth Amendment and therefore unconstitutional, and marked the first time that Mexican American lawyers argued before the Supreme Court
Date	
1954	
Document Type	
Legal	

Overview

In 1951, Pete Hernandez, a Mexican American, was charged with murder by an all-white grand jury in Jackson County, Texas, and then convicted by another all-white jury. He appealed his conviction by arguing that he had not been tried by a jury of his peers since Mexican Americans were excluded from service on juries in Jackson County and at least 69 other counties in Texas. The U.S. Supreme Court reviewed Hernandez's appeal in January 1954.

Lawyers representing Hernandez asserted that the jury commissions that picked potential jurors in Texas had a pattern of excluding Mexican Americans. Indeed, no Mexican American had served on a jury commission in Texas. In addition, although they made up more than 10 percent of the population, no Mexican Americans or people with Hispanic last names, had served on a jury in more than two decades. Hernandez's lawyers contended

that this violated the Fourteenth Amendment, which mandated that all groups had to be treated equally.

Lawyers representing Jackson County argued before the Court that there was no explicit law that banned Mexican Americans from serving on juries. In addition, they asserted that the Fourteenth Amendment had been used to extend legal protections specifically for African Americans. Since Mexican Americans were considered white at the time, the Fourteenth Amendment did not apply in the case.

The Supreme Court ruled in favor of Hernandez on May 3, 1954, and ordered that he have a new trial with a jury that included Mexican Americans. Chief Justice Earl Warren wrote in a unanimous opinion that although the Texas system might not explicitly discriminate against Mexican Americans, the system had re sulted in discrimination. The court cited the percentage of Mexican Americans in the county and the history of past discrimination against the community in its ruling. It also noted that groups other than African Americans faced discrimination, and therefore the Fourteenth Amendment could be applied to other racial minorities. This permanently changed the way the amendment was applied. The case was the first time that Mexican American lawyers argued before the Supreme Court.

Chief Justice Earl Warren wrote the unanimous opinion in **Hernandez v. Texas.**
(Library of Congress)

Document Text

The petitioner, Pete Hernandez, was indicted for the murder of one Joe Espinosa by a grand jury in Jackson County, Texas. He was convicted and sentenced to life imprisonment. The Texas Court of Criminal Appeals affirmed the judgment of the trial court. . . . Prior to the trial, the petitioner, by his counsel, offered timely motions to quash the indictment and the jury panel. He alleged that persons of Mexican descent were systematically excluded from service as jury commissioners, . . . grand jurors, and petit jurors, although there were such persons fully qualified to serve residing in Jackson County. The petitioner asserted that exclusion of this class deprived him, as a member of the class, of the equal protection of the laws guaranteed by the Fourteenth Amendment of the Constitution. After a hearing, the trial court denied the motions. At the trial, the motions were renewed, further evidence taken, and the motions again denied. An allegation that the trial court erred in denying the motions was the sole basis of petitioner's appeal. In affirming the judgment of the trial court, the Texas Court of Criminal Appeals considered and passed upon the substantial federal question raised by the petitioner. . . .

In numerous decisions, this Court has held that it is a denial of the equal protection of the laws to try a defendant of a particular race or color under an indictment issued by a grand jury, or before a petit jury, from which all persons of his race or color have, solely because of that race or color, been excluded by the State, whether acting through its legislature, its courts, or its executive or administrative officers. . . . Although the Court has had little occasion to rule on the question directly, it has been recognized . . . that the exclusion of a class of persons from jury service on grounds other than race or color may also deprive a defendant who is a member of that class of the constitutional guarantee of equal protection of the laws. . . . The State of Texas would have us hold that there are only two classes—white and Negro—within the contemplation of the Fourteenth Amendment. The decisions of this Court do not support that view. . . .

Throughout our history, differences in race and color have defined easily identifiable groups which have at times required the aid of the courts in securing equal treatment under the laws. But community prejudices are not static, and, from time to time, other differences from the community norm may define other groups which need the same protection. Whether such a group exists within a community is a question of fact. When the existence of a distinct class is demonstrated, and it is further shown that the laws, as written or as applied, single out that class for different treatment not based on some reasonable classification, the guarantees of the Constitution have been violated. The Fourteenth Amendment is not directed solely against discrimination due to a "two-class theory." . . .

As the petitioner acknowledges, the Texas system of selecting grand and petit jurors by the use of jury commissions is fair on its face and capable of being utilized without discrimination. . . . But, as this Court has held, the system is susceptible to abuse, and can be employed in a discriminatory manner. . . . The exclusion of otherwise eligible persons from jury service solely because of their ancestry or national origin is discrimination prohibited by the Fourteenth Amendment. The Texas statute makes no such discrimination, but the petitioner alleges that those administering the law do. . . .

The petitioner established that 14% of the population of Jackson County were persons with Mex-

ican or Latin American surnames, and that 11% of the males over 21 bore such names. . . . The County Tax Assessor testified that 6 or 7 percent of the freeholders on the tax rolls of the County were persons of Mexican descent. The State of Texas stipulated that "for the last twenty-five years there is no record of any person with a Mexican or Latin American name having served on a jury commission, grand jury or petit jury in Jackson County." The parties also stipulated that "there are some male persons of Mexican or Latin American descent in Jackson County who, by virtue of being citizens, freeholders, and having all other legal prerequisites to jury service, are eligible to serve as members of a jury commission, grand jury and/or petit jury." . . .

To say that this decision revives the rejected contention that the Fourteenth Amendment requires proportional representation of all the component ethnic groups of the community on every jury ignores the facts. The petitioner did not seek proportional representation. . . . His only claim is the right to be indicted and tried by juries from which all members of his class are not systematically excluded—juries selected from among all qualified persons regardless of national origin or descent. To this much, he is entitled by the Constitution.

Glossary

appeal: a request that a higher court examine the ruling of a lower court

Fourteenth Amendment: an 1868 amendment to the U.S. Constitution that, among other things, guarantees equal protection for all citizens and requires due process before certain rights may be limited

grand jury: a special jury that determines whether there is enough evidence to charge a person with a crime

indictment: an official accusation of a crime

jury commission: a panel of officials that makes decisions about who may serve on a jury

Hernandez v. Texas

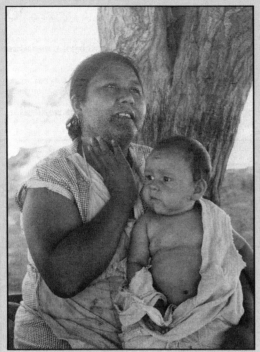

Pocho *is set in Depression-era California.*
(Dorothea Lange)

Document Text

"This is my brother's daughter from Cholula, don Juan," said Cirilo as Juan Rubio and his son Richard entered his house.

"Much pleasure in knowing you," said Juan Rubio, taking her hand. "Juan Rubio at your command."

"Equally," replied the young girl. "Pilar Ramírez, to serve you."

She turned to Richard, and they exchanged the introduction in the same manner. She was not shy, but appeared so because she was a woman from México. Not since he was a child and his family followed the crops had he seen a woman act like she acted. He was seeing his mother as she had been long ago. She spoke only if directly addressed, and he talked to her. She was from Cholula, in the state of México, she said, and her father was dead and so she was here. He said he had never known anyone from that far south, and she said she was sixteen years old. Once, she giggled as he spoke and he flushed, for he knew she was laughing at his Spanish, which was a California-Mexican American Castilian.

"I am a Pocho," he said, "and we speak like this because here in California we make Castilian words out of English words. But I can read and write in the Spanish, and I taught myself from the time I had but eight years."

"It matters not," she said. "I understand you perfectly well."

She was slight, yet breasty, with good legs, and very dark. And he thought her pretty, because to a Mexican swarthiness means beauty.

The others talked among themselves, so Richard and Pilar were allowed to enjoy their conversation until it was time to leave. He would come back, he thought, for she was interesting and pleasant, and he liked her. She could tell him about the México of today, not that of twenty years ago, which his parents knew.

He never saw her again, but his father did, and occasionally brought back word that she had asked for him, and, in fact, he kidded him about his "admirer." It did not occur to Richard that his father had his eye on her.

Then, one early morning, Richard came home from being with Zelda, to find his house ablaze with lights and his father in a rage. He had never seen him so angry. His face was livid, and when he spoke, saliva sprayed with his words and some trickled down the corner of his mouth.

"My daughters will not behave like whores!" he shouted.

"If I am a whore, it is having your blood that makes me one!" Luz stood up to him, shouting back.

"What hour is this—three o'clock in the morning—for a decent girl to be coming home?" he asked. "Where were you?"

"That is no concern of yours," she replied. "What I do is my business!"

The children were huddled against a wall, the smaller ones crying. Consuelo, in a soiled robe, also shrank back, she alone knowing what wrath could drive her husband to do.

"Tell me where you were!" he insisted. "This is still my house, and as long as you are in it, you answer to me!"

"Wake up!" screamed Luz, and her face was ugly. "This *your* house!" She laughed shrilly. "This is our house, and if we want, we can have you put out! Tell him, Mamá. He put the house in your name, in case something happened to him you would have no trouble! *Tell him, Mamá!*" she screamed. "Tell him something has happened to him!"

Juan Rubio hit her with the back of his hand, and she bounced off the wall but she did not fall. Again she screamed to Consuelo, and Consuelo, given courage by the utterance of that which she had lately been telling her daughters, lost her head and stepped forward, screeching, "Do not dare to touch her again, you brute!" She took hold of his arm, and he spun toward her, the force of his movement knocking her off balance, so she stumbled crazily through the door and landed on her face in the kitchen.

Richard stood on the opposite side, transfixed

by the grotesque masque that was taking place before his eyes. A masque it surely was, for he did not know any of these people. In his mind, he was not sure any of it was real. Horrified and in anguish, he thought, *A bad dream! A real bad dream or a Goddamn dumb show!*

His sister brought him out of shock. "Stand there! Just stand there, you weak bastard, and watch this son of a bitch hit your mother!" She leaped at Juan Rubio's face with her hands, and very deliberately he hit her in the face with his fist. She did not get up.

Juan Rubio rushed out the door and down into the cellar. From his tool closet he took an axe, and began first on the wine barrels and then on the shelves upon shelves of preserves, and when he was done destroying everything he had built or accumulated with his own hands, he walked into the house, a specter drenched in wine, purple and ominous. "Out!" he shouted. "Out, everyone, for I am going to destroy this cancer!" But his family was incapable of moving, their fear was so great, and as he walked toward the cupboard, Richard tackled him from behind. Crying, tears streaming down his face, he pleaded, "No, Papá! No, Papá! It is worth nothing—all this!" And all the time he held on to the kicking legs of his father, and when he was shaken off and they were both on their feet, his father hit him a chopping blow with his great hand, and once more turned to what was now a duty. Richard came back again, dripping blood from his nose and mouth, and this time he jumped on his father's back, only to slip off, and as he fell his head struck the floor, knocking him unconscious.

José Antonio Villarreal: *Pocho*

Glossary

Castilian: the standard Spanish dialect spoken throughout Hispanophone America and originating in the province of Castile, Spanish

patriarchy: a societal or governmental system in which the father or eldest male is head of the family and descent is traced through the male line

pocho: label used to describe ethnic Mexicans who have assimilated and adopted U.S. customs and attitudes; historically used in a derogatory way

stereotype: an oversimplified image of a particular type of person or group of people; when used to characterize groups, it can lead to negative or less than ideal representations

Short-Answer Questions

1. When Villarreal wrote *Pocho*, the scant literature relating ethnic Mexican experiences in the United States was not widely accessible. Had those texts been available for him to draw from, would the character dynamics and subject matter of the novel have been different?

2. Villarreal always maintained that *Pocho* was not an autobiography, but readers assumed that he had based the novel on his personal life. Assuming his family did inspire the fictional story, what does the excerpt tell us about Mexican American home life at the time?

3. During the Chicano Movement, critics accused Villarreal of not being in step with the political trend toward social justice and cultural nationalism. Despite their disdain of his personal convictions, what might explain the recognition of *Pocho* as the first Chicano novel?

Lyndon B. Johnson:
Remarks at a Reception Honoring Henry González

Author
Lyndon B. Johnson

Date
1965

Document Type
Speeches/Addresses; Presidential/Executive

Significance
A speech by President Lyndon B. Johnson in support of Henry B. Gonzáles, a member of the House of Representatives who was running for reelection

Overview

In 1965, President Lyndon B. Johnson, a Democrat, remained a popular figure in U.S. politics. He had won election in November 1964 with 61.1 percent of the vote, the highest percentage of any presidential candidate since 1820. A native of Texas, Johnson returned there in November 1965 to campaign for fellow Democrat Henry B. González in his reelection campaign ahead of the 1966 vote.

In remarks at San Antonio, Johnson spoke of his background in Texas and his experiences with the Mexican American community. He listed some of his jobs and elected positions in the state as a way of establishing his links to the region. He emphasized his understanding of the issues facing the Mexican American community, especially poverty. The president also discussed his friendship with famous Mexican comedian Cantinflas (Mario Moreno) as a way of further identifying with the voters. Johnson and Cantinflas had both campaigned for González when he was first elected to Congress in 1961. González

was the first Mexican American elected to Congress from Texas.

The core of Johnson's speech praised Gonzáles and described him as someone who had devoted his life to public service. The president further spoke of the qualities that made the United States a great country. Many of things mentioned were part of Johnson's "War on Poverty," a range of new or expanded programs that the president introduced in 1964 to help the poor and disadvantaged groups. Johnson applauded González for supporting his programs and thanked the Texas congressman, along with Senator Ralph Yarborough (Democrat) from the state.

Johnson closed his address by referring to former President John F. Kennedy. Kennedy had been assassinated in November 1963 but remained highly popular. Johnson concluded with an invitation for the people of San Antonio to join him in a memorial service for the fallen president.

Photograph of President Lyndon B. Johnson
(Lyndon Baines Johnson Presidential Library and Museum)

Document Text

Thirty-one years ago last week I came to this beautiful city of San Antonio in an attempt—and it was a successful attempt—to find a bride. We were married here, with the help of Postmaster Dan Quill, in the Episcopal Church.

Four years ago, with the help of "Pepe" [Mario Moreno, also known as Cantinflas, a noted Mexican comedian], we came here to San Antonio to campaign for Henry González for the United States Congress.

For me, that election had a very special meaning. That meaning was the love and the respect that I had developed over many years for Americans of Mexican descent.

As a young teacher in a Mexican school in Cotulla I came to know what it meant to many of your children not only to be poor, but to be poor without hope.

As a young assistant to the Congressman from this very district, I came to know your dreams and **your ambitions.**

As a State Director of the National Youth Administration during the great depression, I came to know your dignity and your dogged determination.

As a Congressman for 12 years, and later as a Senator for 12 years, I came to know your great loyalty.

And that is why I had such a very special interest in your election 4 years ago—and that is why I have come back here to San Antonio today. This is part of my home. You are part of my people. You have never, never deserted me throughout my long career in public life—and that has been for more than 34 years—and I hope that it can always be said that I never deserted you.

With us on that memorable day here in this same place in November 1961, was a very old and very dear friend of mine and a good friend of yours: Cantinflas. He spent the weekend with me and in my home last night, and he came here today to join us again in this reunion. All the world knows Cantinflas as one of the greatest and one of the best loved comedians of all times. But we know him best as a man whose heart always goes out to his fellow man. We know him as a man who believes in human dignity. We know him as a man who has done more to further good relations between the United States and our neighbor to the south, Mexico, than most professional statesmen have done.

But we came here today for another purpose. Henry González is a man of the people who is devoting his life to the cause of people. I can pay him no higher tribute than that.

For to me, that is what America is all about.

America's greatness is guaranteeing to every child all the education that he or she can take.

America's greatness is bringing the miracle of modern medicine to every humble citizen of this land.

America's greatness is equality of race, respect of religion, and blindness of color.

America's greatness is food for hungry people.

America's greatness is the helping hand to the child of the slum.

America's greatness is training for the unemployed.

America's greatness is willingness to lend a helping hand to our neighbors from other lands who seek freedom here in our shores.

And in the search for that greatness, we search also for a real and lasting peace. We want to help build a world where reason will replace rockets. We want to build a world where trust will replace terror.

All these goals are possible. They are possible because we believe in them. And if we believe in them, and we unite ourselves, then we can do them.

And that is what American greatness means to me. And that is what it means to this great Congressman, Henry B. González.

There is no man in the House of Representatives who has supported your people and your President more loyally than your Congressman, Henry B. González.

And I can take great pride in saying the same thing: There is no man in the United States Senate that has supported the program of the people of this country or the program of the President of this country more than the senior Senator from Texas, your able Senator and my friend, Ralph Yarborough.

By sending Henry González to the Congress to speak your voice and to vote your purpose, you have helped to share and to shape America's greatness. For a long time I have felt deeply in the debt of the good people of San Antonio and Bexar County, and I came here this afternoon to again express to you the appreciation and the gratitude that I feel for your loyalty and for your friendship and for your patriotism throughout the years.

To those of you who would feel at home if I said, *Buenas tardes, mis amigos*, I would say this, that I know that you are glad that you are American citizens, but you are also, and you can always be very proud that you have Mexican blood in your veins.

It was 2 years ago this afternoon that we came here to this friendly city with the great President of the United States, our late beloved leader, John Fitzgerald Kennedy. You met him with cordiality and with hospitality. You opened your arms to him, and you received him, not knowing that just one day removed, he would no longer be with us.

But tomorrow at noon, we will go to a little Catholic church in Fredericksburg where we will be led by the priest and by ministers of other denominations in a memorial church service, a memorial to our late beloved President John Fitzgerald Kennedy.

We would like to ask each of you that might care to, to join us in that service tomorrow, if you have the time and you feel that you could come. We would be glad to have you in the Catholic Church at Fredericksburg.

This afternoon though, before closing, I think that each of you would want to join with all of us in standing and bowing our heads in respect and in memory to our great leader, John Fitzgerald Kennedy, who was here with us in San Antonio 2 years ago today.

Glossary

Buenas tardes, mis amigos: "Good afternoon, my friends," in Spanish

cordiality: polite affection or kindness

National Youth Administration: a federal program, from 1935 to 1943, to provide employment and educational opportunities for young Americans

Short-Answer Questions

1. Why did President Johnson discuss his background in Texas at the beginning of his remarks? What did he seek to accomplish?

2. What were some of the things that the president cited as part of "America's greatness"? Are these the qualities that make a nation great? What other features are there as well?

3. Why did Johnson invoke President John F. Kennedy in his address? How could mentioning Kennedy help González get reelected?

Henry B. González:
Speech against the Chicano Movement

Author
Henry B. González

Date
1969

Document Type
Speeches/Addresses; Legislative

Significance
Argued against Hispanic groups that promoted division and instead called for unity to combat existing social injustices

Overview

Henry B. González (1916–2000) was a Mexican American Democratic congressman from Texas who served in the U.S. House of Representatives from 1961 to 1999. González was known as a prominent liberal and staunch supporter of civil rights. He surprised many of his fellow Democrats and progressives on April 22, 1969, when he delivered a speech that was highly critical of some groups and strategies that were emerging in the late 1960s as part of a growing movement for Hispanic rights and self-empowerment. The period was marked by the emergence of organizations that sought economic, political, and social equality for Hispanics.

González began his address by discussing the difficulties faced by Mexican Americans who often found themselves trapped between two cultures—the dominant Anglo culture of the United States versus the traditions and heritage of Mexico and the broader Southwest. The congressman went on to assert that Mexican Americans were confronted by a fundamental question over what the community wanted. González stated that he sought "justice," which he equated with equality—equality in employment and wages, education, and legal matters, among other areas. The congressman from Texas emphasized that he shared many of the goals of the new organizations but differed in how to achieve those objectives. For González, the path to equality "requires work and vigilance." The congressman's remarks made it clear that he did not believe his sentiments were shared by the new groups.

González criticized the rise of new Mexican American organizations and groups he described as promoting divisions and tensions to advance their own interests. The congressman implied that some groups simply sought to increase their size and resources, and others were just tools for political leaders to advance their careers. One central problem among some of the emerging organizations, he suggested, was their use of "hate" in response to racial and ethnic discrimination. González argued that little was accomplished by these tactics.

Henry B. González (Library of Congress)

Document Text

I, and many other residents of my part of Texas and other Southwestern States, happen to be what is commonly referred to as a Mexican American. . . . What is he to be? Mexican? American? Both? How can he choose? Should he have pride and joy in his heritage, or bear it as a shame and sorrow? Should he live in one world or another, or attempt to bridge them both?

There is comfort in remaining in the closed walls of a minority society, but this means making certain sacrifices; but it sometimes seems disloyal to abandon old ideas and old friends; you never know whether you will be accepted or rejected in the larger world, or whether your old friends will despise you for making a wrong choice. For a member of this minority, like any other, life begins with making hard choices about personal identity. These lonely conflicts are magnified in the social crises so clearly evident all over the Southwest today. There are some groups who demand brown power, some who display a curious chauvinism, and some who effect the other extreme. There is furious debate about what one should be and what one should do. . . . I understand all this, but I am profoundly distressed by what I see happening today. . . . Mr. Speaker, the issue at hand in this minority group today is hate, and my purpose in addressing the House is to state where I stand: I am against hate and against the spreaders of hate; I am for justice, and for honest tactics in obtaining justice.

The question facing the Mexican-American people today is what do we want, and how do we get it? What I want is justice. By justice I mean decent work at decent wages for all who want work; decent support for those who cannot support themselves; full and equal opportunity in employment, in education, in schools; I mean by justice the full, fair, and impartial protection of the law for every man; I mean by justice decent homes; adequate streets and public services. . . .

I do not believe that justice comes only to those who want it; I am not so foolish as to believe that good will alone achieves good works. I believe that justice requires work and vigilance, and I am willing to do that work and maintain that vigilance. . . . It may well be that I agree with the goals stated by militants; but whether I agree or disagree, I do not now, nor have I ever believed that the end justifies the means, and I condemn those who do. I cannot accept the belief that racism in reverse is the answer for racism and discrimination; I cannot accept the belief that simple, blind, and stupid hatred is an adequate response to simple, blind, and stupid hatred; I cannot accept the belief that playing at revolution produces anything beyond an excited imagination; and I cannot accept the belief that imitation leadership is a substitute for the real thing. Developments over the past few months indicate that there are those who believe that the best answer for hate is hate in reverse, and that the best leadership is that which is loudest and most arrogant; but my observation is that arrogance is no cure for emptiness.

All over the Southwest new organizations are springing up; some promote pride in heritage, which is good, but others promote chauvinism, which is not; some promote community organization, which is good, but some promote race tension and hatred, which is not good; some seek redress of just grievances, which is good, but others seek only opportunities for self aggrandizement, which is not good. . . .

Unfortunately it seems that in the face of rising hopes and expectations among Mexican Americans there are more leaders with political ambitions at heart than there are with the interests of the poor at heart; they do not care what is accomplished in fact, as long as they can create and ride the winds of protest as far as possible. Thus we have those who play at revolution, those who make speeches but do not work, and those who imitate what they have seen others do, but lack the initiative and imagination to set forth actual programs for progress. . . .

Not long after the Southwest Council of La Raza opened for business, it gave $110,000 to the Mexican-American Unity Council of San Antonio; this group was apparently invented for the purpose of receiving the grant. Whatever the purposes of this group may be, thus far it has not given any assistance that I know of to bring anybody together; rather it has freely dispensed funds to people who promote the rather odd and I might say generally unaccepted and unpopular views of its directors.

The Mexican-American Unity Council appears to specialize in creating still other organizations and equipping them with quarters, mimeograph machines and other essentials of life. Thus, the "unity council" has created a parents' association in a poor school district, a neighborhood council, a group known as the barrios unidos—or roughly, united neighborhoods—a committee on voter registration and has given funds to the militant Mexican-American Youth Organization—MAYO; it has also created a vague entity known as the "Universidad de los Barrios" which is a local gang operation. Now assuredly all these efforts may be well intended; however it is questionable to my mind that a very young and inexperienced man can prescribe the social and political organizations of a complex and troubled community; there is no reason whatever to believe that for all the money this group has spent, there is any understanding of what it is actually being spent for, except to employ friends of the director and advance his preconceived notions. The people who are to be united apparently don't get much say in what the "unity council" is up to. . . .

Militant groups like MAYO regularly distribute literature that I can only describe as hate sheets, designed to inflame passions and reinforce old wounds or open new ones; these sheets spew forth racism and hatred designed to do no man good. The practice is defended as one that will build race pride, but I never heard of pride being built on spleen. . . .

Glossary

chauvinism: unfounded pride in oneself or one's group

militants: someone who excessively supports a cause or idea

preconceived: opinions that are formed or held before facts are examined

Glossary

progressives: political liberals who support significant changes in a country's social and economic systems

self aggrandizement: promoting oneself in an inappropriate way

spleen: spite; or an inappropriate disposition

Short-Answer Questions

1. Why did González's speech surprise many of his political allies and supporters? Should the congressman have been more moderate in his speech, or was his tone necessary to convey his message? Why?

2. When González spoke about justice, what did he mean? What did he suggest were the ways to achieve justice? Why?

3. What were the congressman's main criticism about some of the newly formed Hispanic groups? What evidence did González present to support his arguments?

Chapter 10

Civil Rights and Liberation

The Civil Rights Movement is often associated historically with the push for African American equality in the United States and liberation from a socio-economic norm of suppression for Blacks around the country. The movement also had a significant impact on Latinos living in the United States at the time as well who also benefitted from the achievements of civil rights leaders like Martin Luther King Jr. For Mexican Americans living in the United States however, they still found themselves in a difficult position of being non-white and thus still targets of discrimination and oppression. As a result, the struggle to remove themselves from the political and economic oppression would require a separate campaign to effect change for Hispanics in the United States.

Hispanic Workers Strike

The Delano Grape Workers strike in 1965 was initiated by the Agriculture Workers Organizing Committee (AWOC) in response to poor wages that were paid to Filipino agricultural workers in the fields north of Bakersfield. As a thousand Filipino workers went on strike, the growers sought to hire migrant and poor Mexican workers to replace them. The growers also hoped they would serve as strike breakers in order to coerce the Filipino workers back to the line. The plan backfired when the National Farm Workers of America (NFWA) led by César Chávez intervened and unified the Mexican workers to work with the Filipinos rather than against them.

The strike lasted five years and cost ranchers millions of dollars as they used force and intimidation to try and compel the workers to return to the fields. These tactics had been successful in America's past (such as the Pullman and Homestead Strikes), but were difficult to maintain in an era powered by television which connected Americans to the plights of the workers. The workers also garnered support from groups like the Student Nonviolent Coordination Committee (SNCC) and the Congress of Racial Equality (CORE), which were actively coordinating efforts to bring about change and equality for Blacks as well. The strikes, combined with large scale boycotts around the Southwest led the movement to evolve from just a

Civil Rights and Liberation

simple labor dispute to a civil rights battle that drew national headlines. The movement called attention to the struggles of Latinos in the United States and sparked conversations about change.

The Cold War and Vietnam War

The change did not occur in a vacuum however, and much like the efforts of Martin Luther King Jr. and Malcolm X, the call for change was hastened in part as a result of international events occurring around the world. The Cold War had started as a struggle between two nuclear superpowers focused on dominating the world. By the 1960s, some began to question whether America could really "win" the Cold War if it accused communism of oppressing its people while America simultaneously oppressed those of color. With the onset of the Vietnam War, the question about being the moral victor of a cold war became increasingly debated as the demographics of the war were revealed. During the Vietnam War for example, Hispanics accounted for roughly ten percent of the American population yet suffered nearly twenty percent of deaths during the war from military action.

The Chicano Movement and Aztlán

The Chicano Movement that evolved during this time period in response to the growing frustration with an oppressive socio-economic system emphasized the historical connection to Aztec roots by declaring that they now lived in the land of Aztlán, the name of the original home of the Mexica in the eleventh century. While historians and geographers disagree about the actual location of this historical land, most agree that it likely encompassed some part of the southwestern United States where most Mexican Americans now lived.

The symbolism became a key component of the movement with some activists arguing that like their ancestors, the modern Chicano needed to rise and claim the land as their own. Authors like Rodolfo "Corky" Gonzales wrote about the need to change the perception of America's history. He pointed to George Washington, arguing that Washington should be taught not as America's great hero, but rather as the chief exploiter. Essentially, for the Hispanic American, the narrative needed to change from one of subjugation to one of independence, at least from an academic and economic point of view. When combined with the movements like those seen in Delano, California, against big businesses that exploited minority workers, the movement was powerful enough to increase the political power and influence among many Hispanic youths. The renewed call for the creation of a nation of Aztlán by some leaders also helped give a sense of cultural identity for a new generation.

Further Reading

Books

Araiza, Lauren. *To March for Others: The Black Freedom Struggle and the United Farm Workers*. Philadelphia: University of Pennsylvania Press, 2014.

Jenkins, J. Craig. *The Politics of Insurgency: The Farm Worker Movement in the 1960s*. New York, NY: Columbia University Press, 1985

Levy, Jacques E., and César Chávez. *César Chávez: Autobiography of La Causa*. New York, NY: Norton, 1975.

Articles

Escobar, Edward J. "The Unintended Consequences of the Carceral State: Chicana/o Political Mobilization in Post–World War II America." *Journal of American History* 102, no. 1 (2015): 174–84.

Ontiveros, Randy. "No Golden Age: Television News and the Chicano Civil Rights Movement." *American Quarterly* 62, no. 4 (2010): 897–923.

Websites

"EPublications at Regis University," accessed December 18, 2022, https://epublications.regis.edu/chicano_vietnam/.

"Workers United: The Delano Grape Strike and Boycott (U.S. National Park Service)." National Parks Service, U.S. Department of the Interior, accessed December 18, 2022, https://www.nps.gov/articles/000/workers-united-the-delano-grape-strike-and-boycott.htm.

César Chávez:
Plan de Delano

Author
César Chávez

Date
1965

Document Type
Essays, Reports, Manifestos

Significance
Outlines a nonviolent, multinational approach to counter abusive and exploitive farm labor practices that would lend further voices to the growing American civil rights movement

Overview

In early September 1965 the Filipino-dominated Agricultural Workers Organizing Committee (AWOC) called for a general strike after its members were denied a pay raise after relocating nearly 300 miles north to pick table grapes. The growers informed the AWOC that they would not negotiate as their labor was easily replaceable. The AWOC workers chose to strike, and the growers used a tried-and-true tactic of hiring Mexican laborers to cross strike lines to replace the AWOC members. AWOC leaders sought out César Chávez, the leader of the Mexican-dominated National Farm Workers Association (NFWA). Although Chávez was uncertain if his NFWA could support the strike, he opened the issue to debate by the NFWA members. Eight days after the strike started, the AWOC picket lines were joined by

their NFWA counterparts. The next day, on March 17, 1966, Chávez began a 300-mile walk from Delano, California, north to Sacramento to inspire political and popular pressure on the growers. News of the strike spread, and by late fall, farm workers across the state of California had gone on strike. Representatives of the striking workers had convinced longshoremen, greengrocers, and the average Californian to boycott non-union-picked grapes, and the boycott soon spread throughout the country. The AWOC and NFWA merged to form the United Farm Workers (UFW) labor union and joined the powerful AFL-CIO labor federation in 1967. The grape strike would finally conclude in July 1970 when growers signed labor contracts guaranteeing timed pay increases, health coverage, and other benefits.

César Chávez (Library of Congress)

Document Text

PLAN for the liberation of the Farm Workers associated with the Delano Grape Strike in the State of California, seeking social justice in farm labor with those reforms that they believe necessary for their well-being as workers in these United States.

We, the undersigned, gathered in Pilgrimage to the capital of the State in Sacramento in penance for all the failings of Farm Workers as free and sovereign men, do solemnly declare before the civilized world which judges our actions, and before the nation to which we belong, the propositions we have formulated to end the injustice that oppresses us.

We are conscious of the historical significance of our Pilgrimage. . . . Our sweat and our blood have fallen on this land to make other men rich. This Pilgrimage is a witness to the suffering we have seen for generations. The Penance we accept symbolizes the suffering we shall have in order to bring justice to these same towns, to this same valley. The Pilgrimage we make symbolizes the long historical road we have traveled in this valley alone, and the long road we have yet to travel, with much penance, in order to bring about the Revolution we need, and for which we present the propositions in the following PLAN:

1. This is the beginning of a social movement in fact and not in pronouncements. We seek our basic, God-given rights as human beings. . . . We are ready to give up everything, even our lives, in our fight for social justice. We shall do it without violence because that is our destiny. To the ranchers, and to all those who oppose us, we say, in the words of Benito Juarez, "EL RESPETO AL DERECHO AJENO ES LA PAZ."

2. We seek the support of all political groups and protection of the government, which is also our government, in our struggle. For too many years we have been treated like the lowest of the low. Our wages and working conditions have been determined from above, because irresponsible legislators who could have helped us, have supported the rancher's argument that the plight of the Farm Worker was a "special case." They saw the obvious effects of an unjust system, starvation wages, contractors, day hauls, forced migration, sickness, illiteracy, camps and sub-human living conditions, and acted is if they were irremediable causes. The farm worker has been abandoned to his own fate—without representation, without power—subject to the mercy and caprice of the rancher. We are tired of words, of betrayals, of indifference. . . . From this movement shall spring leaders who shall understand us, lead us, be faithful to us, and we shall elect them to represent us. WE SHALL BE HEARD.

3. We seek, and have, the support of the Church in what we do. At the head of the Pilgrimage we carry LA VIRGEN DE LA GUADALUPE because she is ours, all ours, Patroness of the Mexican people.

We also carry the Sacred Cross and the Star of David because we are not sectarians, and because we ask the help and prayers of all religions. All men are brothers—sons of the same God; that is why we say to all men of good will, in the words of Pope Leo XIII, "Everyone's first duty is to protect the workers from the greed of speculators who use human beings as instruments to provide themselves with money. It is neither just nor human to oppress men with excessive work to the point where their minds become enfeebled and their bodies worn out." GOD SHALL NOT ABANDON US.

4. We are suffering. We have suffered, and we are not afraid to suffer in order to win our cause. We have suffered unnumbered ills and . . . also suffered the desperation of knowing that that system caters to the greed of callous men and not to our needs. Now we will suffer for the purpose of ending the poverty, the misery, and the injustice, with the hope that our children will not be exploited as we have been. They have imposed hungers on us, and now we hunger for justice. We draw our strength from the very despair in which we have been forced to live. WE SHALL ENDURE.

5. We shall unite. We have learned the meaning of UNITY. We know why these United States are just that—united. The strength of the poor is also in union. We know that the poverty of the Mexican or Filipino worker in California is the same as that of all farm workers across the country, the Negroes and poor whites, the Puerto Ricans, Japanese, and Arabians. . . . The ranchers want to keep us divided in order to keep us weak. . . . That is why we must get together and bargain collectively. We must use the only strength that we have, the force of our numbers. The ranchers are few; we are many. UNITED WE SHALL STAND.

6. We shall strike. We shall pursue the REVOLUTION we have proposed. We are sons of the Mexican Revolution, a revolution of the poor seeking bread and justice. Our revolution will not be armed, but we want the existing social order to dissolve; we want a new social order. We are poor, we are humble, and our only choice is to strike in those ranches where we are not treated with the respect we deserve as working men, where our rights as free and sovereign men are not recognized. We do not want the paternalism of the rancher; we do not want the contractor; we do not want charity at the price of our dignity. We want to be equal with all the working men in the nation; we want a just wage, better working conditions, a decent future for our children. To those who oppose us, be they ranchers, police, politicians, or speculators, we say that we are going to continue fighting until we die, or we win. WE SHALL OVERCOME. . . .

History is on our side.

MAY THE STRIKE GO ON!

VIVA LA CAUSA!

Glossary

"El respeto al derecho ajeno es la paz": "Respect for the right of others is peace," a phrase that was part of a manifesto released by President of the United Mexican States Benito Juárez after the popular overthrow of French shadow governance of the Second Mexican Empire in 1867

La Virgen de la Guadalupe/Virgin of Guadalupe: a statue or image of Mary, the mother of Jesus, in remembrance of a series of five appearances of Mary in the Basilica of Our Lady of Guadalupe in Mexico City in December 1531; the icon of the Virgin of Guadalupe became a cultural symbol of Mexican nationalism

paternalism: the practice of extending authority to artificially limit the responsibilities or freedoms from a subordinate for the "best interests" of the subordinate, as a father might do for a young child

"Viva la causa!": "Long live the cause!"

Short-Answer Questions

1. Filipinos and Mexicans hold a common history through Spanish colonization. What themes of common cultural heritage does Chávez use in his plan?

2. Chávez suspects that a piecemeal solution will be offered to lure workers back to the farms. What evidence is there to support this assertion in the text?

3. From Chávez's writing, does he believe that politicians will be the solution to the labor issues faced by the workers? Why or why not?

César Chávez: Plan de Delano

Rodolfo "Corky" Gonzales: "I Am Joaquín"

Author
Rodolfo "Corky" Gonzales

Date
1967

Document Type
Poems, Plays, Fiction

Significance
Narrates the economic struggles, social inequality, and overall injustice that Chicanos experienced as ethnic minorities in the United States

Overview

The poem "I Am Joaquín" by Rodolfo "Corky" Gonzales is credited with setting the foundation for the Chicano poetry literary genre. Published in 1967, Gonzales's epic poem made a profound impact on the emerging Chicano Movement. This was a socio-cultural and civil rights movement in which activists relentlessly pursued substantial political representation, increased economic possibilities, and improved educational prospects for Mexican Americans by removing them from generational poverty, marginalization, and powerlessness. This was a time when information circulated primarily through print media, and like many documents that later became instrumental for the burgeoning Mexican American civil rights movement of the 1960s and 1970s, the poem was mimeographed and widely distributed at rallies and meetings. The poem's impact is attributed to its reliance on the oral and visual idiosyncrasies of Mexican American culture, which made it an instant source of inspiration for young Chicanos.

One of the biggest cultural contributions of "I Am Joaquín" was its normalization of the term *Chicano*, which prior to 1967 served as a term of slight or as a form of in-group diminutive name-calling. From then on, young Mexican Americans adopted it and took pride in the term as a personal and collective identity. Gonzales's work is also significant in that it marked the first time a Chicano published a poem for Chicanos. "I Am Joaquín" narrated their history in a way that captured the sentiment of pride that Chicanos felt. It chronicles Chicano history vicariously through major figures from Mexican and Mexican American history. The poem highlights the strengths and weaknesses of Chicanos through a searing commentary on the cultural genocide, social castration, and psychological wounds experienced by the people. The grievances are contrasted with words of encouragement, self-determination, and resilience. More significantly, by repeating the phrase "I am Joaquín," the poem connects with its intended audience through the literary device of repetition. In doing so, Gonzales effectively transforms the subjective "I" into the collective "we," thereby making the figure of "Joaquín" a symbolic stand in for all Chicanos.

In the epic poem, Gonzales traces his ancestry to both the conquistadors and the Aztecs.
(Biblioteca Museu Víctor Balaguer)

Document Text

Yo soy Joaquín,
perdido en un mundo de confusión:

I am Joaquín, lost in a world of confusion,
caught up in the whirl of a gringo society,
confused by the rules,
scorned by attitudes,
suppressed by manipulation,
and destroyed by modern society.

My fathers
have lost the economic battle
and won the struggle of cultural survival.

And now! I must choose between the paradox of
victory of the spirit,
despite physical hunger,
or to exist in the grasp of American social neurosis,
sterilization of the soul and a full stomach.

Yes, I have come a long way to nowhere,
unwillingly dragged by that monstrous,
technical, industrial giant called Progress and Anglo success....
I look at myself.

I watch my brothers.
I shed tears of sorrow.
I sow seeds of hate.

I withdraw to the safety within the circle of life—
MY OWN PEOPLE

I am Cuauhtémoc, proud and noble,
leader of men, king of an empire civilized
beyond the dreams
of the gachupín Cortés,
who also is the blood, the image of myself.

I am the Maya prince.
I am Nezahualcóyotl, great leader of the Chichimecas.

I am the sword and flame of Cortes the despot
And I am the eagle and serpent of the Aztec civilization.

I owned the land as far as the eye could see under the Crown of Spain,
and I toiled on my Earth and gave my Indian sweat and blood
for the Spanish master who ruled with tyranny over man and
beast and all that he could trample But . . .

THE GROUND WAS MINE.

I was both tyrant and slave.

As the Christian church took its place in God's name,
to take and use my virgin strength and trusting faith,

Rodolfo "Corky" Gonzales: "I Am Joaquín"

the priests, both good and bad, took—
but gave a lasting truth that Spaniard Indian Mestizo
were all God's children.

And from these words grew men who prayed and fought
for their own worth as human beings, for that
GOLDEN MOMENT of FREEDOM.

I was part in blood and spirit of that courageous village priest
Hidalgo who in the year eighteen hundred and ten
rang the bell of independence and gave out that lasting cry—
El Grito de Dolores
"Que mueran los gachupines y que viva la Virgen de Guadalupe. . . ."

I sentenced him who was me I excommunicated him, my blood.
I drove him from the pulpit to lead a bloody revolution for him and me. . . .

I killed him.

His head, which is mine and of all those
who have come this way,
I placed on that fortress wall
to wait for independence. Morelos! Matamoros! Guerrero!
all companeros in the act, STOOD AGAINST THAT WALL OF INFAMY
to feel the hot gouge of lead which my hands made.

I died with them . . . I lived with them . . . I lived
to see our country free.
Free from Spanish rule in eighteen-hundred-twenty-one.
Mexico was free??

The crown was gone but all its parasites remained,
and ruled, and taught, with gun and flame and mystic power.

I worked, I sweated, I bled, I prayed,

and waited silently for life to begin again.
I fought and died for Don Benito Juarez, guardian of the Constitution.
I was he on dusty roads on barren land as he protected his archives
as Moses did his sacraments.

He held his Mexico in his hand on
the most desolate and remote ground which was his country.
And this giant little Zapotec gave not one palm's breadth
of his country's land to kings or monarchs or presidents of foreign powers.

I am Joaquín.
I rode with Pancho Villa,
crude and warm, a tornado at full strength,
nourished and inspired by the passion and the fire
of all his earthy people.

I am Emiliano Zapata.
"This land, this earth is OURS."

The villages, the mountains, the streams
belong to Zapatistas.

Our life or yours is the only trade for soft brown earth and maize.

All of which is our reward,
a creed that formed a constitution
for all who dare live free!

"This land is ours . . .
Father, I give it back to you.
Mexico must be free. . . ."

I ride with revolutionists
against myself.
I am the Rurales,
coarse and brutal,
I am the mountain Indian,
superior over all.

The thundering hoof beats are my horses.

The chattering machine guns are death to all of
me:
Yaqui
Tarahumara
Chamala
Zapotec
Mestizo
Español.

. . .

I am Joaquín.

I must fight
and win this struggle
for my sons, and they
must know from me
who I am.

Part of the blood that runs deep in me
could not be vanquished by the Moors.

I defeated them after five hundred years,
and I have endured.

Part of the blood that is mine
has labored endlessly four hundred
years under the heel of lustful
Europeans.

I am still here!

I have endured in the rugged mountains
Of our country
I have survived the toils and slavery of the fields.

I have existed
In the barrios of the city
In the suburbs of bigotry
In the mines of social snobbery
In the prisons of dejection
In the muck of exploitation
And
In the fierce heat of racial hatred.

And now the trumpet sounds,

The music of the people stirs the
Revolution.

Like a sleeping giant it slowly
Rears its head
To the sound of
Tramping feet
Clamoring voices
Mariachi strains
Fiery tequila explosions
The smell of chile verde and
Soft brown eyes of expectation for a
Better life.

And in all the fertile farmlands,
the barren plains,
the mountain villages,
smoke-smeared cities,
we start to MOVE.

La raza!
Méjicano!
Español!
Latino!
Chicano!
Or whatever I call myself,
I look the same
I feel the same
I cry
And
Sing the same.

I am the masses of my people and
I refuse to be absorbed.

I am Joaquín.

The odds are great
But my spirit is strong,
My faith unbreakable,
My blood is pure.

I am Aztec prince and Christian Christ.

I SHALL ENDURE!

I WILL ENDURE!

Rodolfo "Corky" Gonzales: "I Am Joaquín"

Glossary

Chicano: often used as a synonym for Mexican American, especially one with a socio-political and cultural consciousness; although the meaning of this identity is open to debate, it has a clear origin that dates to the late nineteenth to the early twentieth centuries as a shortening of "mexicano," from the Nahuatl "Mexica" (Aztec)

exploitation: the action or fact of treating someone unfairly to benefit from their work

gachupín: disparaging term for Spanish settler in the Americas

Moors: a term generally used by Europeans to describe the Muslim people of North Africa and the Iberian Peninsula during the Middle Ages

Short-Answer Questions

1. The poem "I Am Joaquín" is the first work written by a Chicano for Chicanos, making it foundational in the literary genre that it helped create. Which lines from the excerpt point to this being a uniquely Chicano piece and not simply a Mexican American one?

2. As with other documents from the Chicano Movement, "I Am Joaquín" makes references to indigenous figures and themes to advance a specific position about identity and place. What is that position? Does Gonzales effectively communicate it to his audience?

3. Through the rhetorical device of the collective "I," "Joaquín" transforms into the Chicano everyman/woman who is "lost in a world of confusion." How does Gonzales describe that confusion? Does he offer a resolution to the chaos? Explain your answer.

Piri Thomas: "Brothers Under the Skin" (from *Down These Mean Streets*)

Author Piri Thomas **Date** 1967 **Document Type** Essays, Reports, Manifestos	**Significance** Illustrated the particular identity struggles of mixed-race Latino families in the United States

Overview

Piri Thomas was a Black Latino of Puerto Rican and Cuban descent who grew up in the Spanish Harlem neighborhood of New York City. His writings anticipated the Nuyorican movement, a flourishing of artistic expression beginning in the late 1960s and 1970s by Puerto Ricans in New York. His memoir *Down These Mean Streets* became a bestseller in the United States. In this excerpt, the author wrestles with what it means to have dark skin in a mostly light-skinned family and illustrates how difficult it was for him to find his identity in a family that refused to acknowledge his African heritage.

Document Text

My daydreaming was splintered by my brother José kicking at the door in sheer panic. "Hey, who's in there?" he yelled. . . .

"I'm goin' down South."

"Where?"

"Down South."

"What for?"

"Don't know all the way," I said, "except I'm tryin' to find somethin' out."

"Down South!" He said it like I was nuts.

Thomas's book begins with his childhood in the 1940s in New York City. (Library of Congress)

"*Sí.* I want to see what a *moyeto*'s worth and the paddy's weight on him," I said.

"Whatta ya talking about?" . . .

"I'm a Negro."

"You ain't no n*****," José said.

"I ain't?"

"No. You're a Puerto Rican."

"I am, huh?" I looked at José and said, "Course, you gotta say that. 'Cause if I'm a Negro, then you and James is one too. And that ain't leavin' out Sis and Poppa. Only Momma's an exception. She don't care what she is." . . .

"We're Puerto Ricans and that's different from being *moyetos*." . . .

"That's what I've been wanting to believe all along, José," I said. . . . "But only pure white Puerto Ricans are white." . . .

"I don't give a good shit what you say, Piri. We're Puerto Ricans, and that makes us different from Black people." . . .

I said, "José, that's what the white man's been telling the Negro all along, that 'cause he's white he's different from the Negro; that he's better'n the Negro or anyone that's not white. . . . Poppa's a Negro and, even if Momma's *blanca*, Poppa's blood carries more weight." . . .

"I'm not Black, no matter what you say, Piri." . . .

"Maybe not outside, José," I said. "But you're sure that way inside."

"I ain't Black, damn you! Look at my hair. It's almost blond. My eyes are blue, my nose is straight. . . . My skin is white."

"So what . . . am I? . . . Am I your brother or ain't I?"

"Yeah, you're my brother, and James an' Sis." . . .

"Boy, you, Poppa and James sure are sold on that white kick. Poppa thinks that marrying a white woman made him white. He's wrong. It's just another n***** marrying a white woman and making her as Black as him. That's the way the paddy looks at it. The Negro just stays Black. Period. Dig it?"

José's face got whiter and his voice angrier at my attempt to take away his white status. . . .

"Like I said, man, that shit-ass poison I've been living with is on its way out. It's a played-out lie about me—us—being white. There ain't nobody in this . . . house can lay any claim to bein' paddy exceptin' Momma, and she's never made it a mountain of fever like we have. You and James are like houses—painted white outside, and Blacker'n a mother inside. An' I'm close to being like Poppa—trying to be white on both sides."

José looked at me. . . . "I don't know how you come to be my brother, but I love you like one. I've busted my ass, both me and James, trying to explain to people how come you so dark and how

come your hair is so curly an'—"

I said, "You and James hadda make excuses for *me*? Like for me being *un Negrito*?" I looked at the paddy in front of me. "Who to?" I said. "Paddies?"

Lights began to jump into my head and tears blurred out that this was my brother before me. . . . I felt the shock run up my arm as my fists went up the side of his head. I felt one fist hit his mouth. . . .

I heard myself screaming, "You bastard! Dig it, you bastard. You're bleeding, and the blood is like anybody else's—red!" . . .

"Goddamn you for beating your brother like that. My God!—"

I twisted my head and saw Poppa. And somewhere, far off, I heard a voice that sounded like Momma crying, "What's it all about? What's it all about? Why do brothers do this to each other?" . . .

I looked at Poppa. "'Cause, Poppa," I said, "him, you and James think you're white, and I'm the only one that's found out I'm not. . . . Poppa," I added, "what's wrong with not being white? What's so wrong with being *tregeño*?" . . .

I said, "I'm proud to be a Puerto Rican, but being Puerto Rican don't make the color." . . .

Momma put her hand on me and she asked, "Why does it hurt you so to be *un Negrito*?"

I shook my head and kept walking. I wished she could see inside me. I wished she could see it didn't hurt—so much.

Glossary

blanca: Spanish word meaning "white female"

moyeta/moyeto: Spanish term for a Black person

Negrito: Spanish word meaning "Black person"

paddy: racially insensitive term for an Irishman; used in this context for anyone who is white

tregeño: Spanish term for a non-white person

Short-Answer Questions

1. Why does Piri Thomas's brother José persist that he is Puerto Rican and refuse to acknowledge the family's African heritage?

2. Analyze the following quote: "Poppa thinks that marrying a white woman made him white. He's wrong." In your own words, explain what Thomas means by this.

3. Why was it so important to Thomas that his father and siblings acknowledge their African heritage? Why you feel that Piri's brother was urging him to identify with being Puerto Rican?

Reies López Tijerina: Interview after Martin Luther King's Assassination

Author
Reies López Tijerina/Elsa Knight Thompson

Date
1968

Document Type
Speeches/Addresses

Significance
An argument by Teijerina, a community activist for Chicano education, organization, and land reclamations, that the assassination of Dr. Martin Luther King Jr. fundamentally changed the way in which civil rights groups were going to organize and act in the future

Overview

The U.S. War with Mexico (1846–48) ended with the ratification of the Treaty of Guadalupe Hidalgo in 1848. This, together with the Gadsden Purchase of 1853, would set the political boundaries of America's Southwest as known to us today. When the United States and Mexico met again to exchange their ratified treaties, the delegates negotiated another agreement that the American government would recognize the legitimacy of land grants as they had been recognized under Mexican law. The United States would later renounce these terms, arguing that the U.S. delegation had overstepped its authority and therefore the new terms would not be recognized. As a result, wealthy whites began forcefully obtaining property and dislocating Mexican American residents across the region. Together with the investment of railroads and mining industries, by 1912 the region was soon transformed from a primarily rural Mexican culture to a modern American culture. In the early 1960s, Reies López Tijerina (1926–2015), through his organization La Alianza, sought to educate and inform heirs of Span-ish-land grants of their rights under the 1848 Treaty. When La Alianza attempted to regroup in 1967, several members were arrested, and a portion of the group armed themselves and took the local courthouse. The courthouse raid brought La Alianza and its pursuit of land recognition into the national conversation. Though La Alianza thought the Johnson-era War on Poverty would be a significant step forward, by 1968 it was clear that the promises from Washington were not going to be fulfilled. With the national spotlight on Tijerina, he was elected to lead the Chicano contingent of Dr. Martin Luther King Jr.'s and the Southern Christian Leadership Conference's Poor People's March on Washington. The Poor People's March prioritized political help for the domestic poor, including jobs, housing, and education, over the war in Vietnam. However, Tijerina and perhaps Dr. King had more in mind. The day after Dr. King was assassinated, Tijerina went on the radio in Berkeley, California, to address the nation in this interview conducted by Elsa Knight Thompson for radio station KPFA.

1964 photograph of Martin Luther King Jr.
(Nobel Foundation)

Document Text

Elsa Knight Thompson (Interviewer): I would like to begin, where we began when you came into my office last night . . . [when] we had the news of Martin Luther King's assassination. This morning, just as you walked into my office, some kind of a disturbance . . . was taking place, under the windows of KPFA's office. And I said, "God help us all." And I liked your reply.

Reies López Tijerina (Respondent): I said that God could not help us any longer. He has run out of patience, and we have mocked him too many times. . . . The government, I feel, is responsible, by encouraging, by not developing ways for the poor, ways for the oppressed. Only ways and means for the bankers, for the powerful, for the whites. And that is why I feel that the federal government of the United States is pushing its own people to destruction, to the end of this empire.

I: You were dealing, I believe, with Dr. Martin Luther King about the proposed march on Washington, which was to take place on the 26th of this month. Could you tell us something about what those plans were?

R: On August 26th or 28th, 1967, I approached Martin Luther King . . . and suggested to him a coalition between the brown people and the black people. Also the Indian and poor whites. He said it was high time. . . . He invited me to Atlanta, Georgia, and some twenty-five leaders of other organizations of the brown people, also white people, Indian people, and black people. It was there the coalition was formed . . . out of the various races and groups to steer and direct the coordination, the plans on the Washington march that is coming April the 22nd and will escalate up to June. . . . The steering committee and about one hundred leaders will visit various offices of the government, departments and Congress. . . . And then after that, people will start to arrive according to the plans by thousands from all over the United States. . . .

I: And you are expecting, then, that from all over the country minority people will come to Washington over a period of time?

R: Yes, yes . . . this was called by Martin Luther King, Campaign for the Poor. . . .

I: I seem to recall . . . [he said] this would be the last massive attempt to convince the government and the American people by nonviolent means. And if he, if this was not successful, that he would not try again.

R: Right. . . . His philosophy had changed. . . . For the first time the black people would ask for land. Would demand land, not just jobs, education, and housing but land. Just like the people in New Mexico are demanding land. . . .

I: When did you go to New Mexico?

R: . . . I had been there before. . . . The people that had been fighting . . . the federal government, and claiming certain rights under the Treaty of Guadalupe Hidalgo signed between the US and Mexico, February 2, 1848 . . . the people of New Mexico . . . have never surrendered to the confiscation of the land; have never surrendered to the federal government . . . [who] has conspired in a thousand ways to destroy the lives, the culture, the language, the property of this people. . . . I decided to organize and unite the people of various land grants, which are called pueblos. It is these pueblos who hold the land, not the individuals, not the heirs. . . . After the Treaty was signed, our government took full responsibility . . . to protect our lives and property. Our properties . . . original patents and titles, . . . ten years after the signing of the treaty, these documents were burned mysteriously . . . before the United States had the courtesy, according to its obligations, to ask Mexico for a copy of those titles. . . . Congress [established] a political court to adjudicate the titles . . . disapproving 33.5 million acres of the 35 million acres we were claiming in New Mexico. . . .

I: Now, you are now in the process of fighting this situation through legal channels as well as other channels? . . .

R: . . . We are going through the courts . . . and bringing in the United Nations. . . . We are also using other channels, such as occupying the land. . . . The government cannot claim [possession] because . . . we have never abandoned the land. . . . And we are not the only ones that are asking, demanding. The Indians of the Taos Pueblo, . . . the Hopi Nation, the Apaches, the Navajos. . . . So are the Seminole. . . . So this is not something rare; it is not a case of only Mexican-Americans, but all the people that occupied the land prior to the coming of the bad whites. However, we have many good whites that have bought our land in good faith; we consider them to be our neighbors, our friends, our brothers. . . .

Our government has developed into a machine, a power equal to an angry bull with whom you can no longer reason. . . . And that is why I'm afraid of the future. . . . Dr. King . . . took strictly the peaceful way. And that's how our government, and the friends of our government deal with peaceful leaders . . . [like] John F. Kennedy, Malcolm X, and Dr. King. . . . However, since we have no bullets, no money, even if we wanted to use violence, we could not. So, we will not think in terms of violence. . . .

See, the people are strong. If they discover their power, and the way the government is pushing our people, pretty soon we will have no other choice. . . . The oppressors are killing . . . the good leaders, by sniper. . . . They don't come out in the open, like Dr. King would march in the open, in the streets. Well these murderers, these killers hide. And the people might just decide to do that themselves, start hiding. Imitating the enemy.

So, it's pitiful, the situation is dark. And we ourselves are preparing ourselves to make friends with good people, with honest people, and we're trying to quit the criminals, the troublemakers, and our government is no longer the power whom we can control. . . . We ask ourselves, "why do they hate us?" . . . I think they hate us because we meddle in their business!

Glossary

Campaign for the Poor: a coalition of people and organizations that advocated and connected poor individuals and communities across the nation and marched in Washington, D.C., in 1968

Dr. Martin Luther King: a minister and civil rights activist who advocated for peaceful approaches to make social and political changes occur in American society in the 1950s and 1960s

Indian: an outdated and politically incorrect term for Native Americans

John F. Kennedy: president of the United States from 1961 to 1963 who was active in political and social change, particularly for people of color

KPFA: a public radio station broadcasting from Berkeley, California

La Alianza: a group that organized in the 1960s to protest and advocate for the land rights of New Mexicans of Hispanic descent who had lost lands as a result of legal and political actions after the Treaty of Guadalupe Hidalgo in 1848

Malcolm X: a religious leader and civil rights activist who advocated for militant approaches to make social and political changes occur in American society in the 1950s and 1960s

Southern Christian Leadership Conference: a coordinating organization that connected individual churches, organizations, and individuals to support social and political change through nonviolent forms of protest

steering committee: a small group that manages the general operations and priorities of an organization

Short-Answer Questions

1. How would you feel if you were listening to this interview the day after Dr. Martin Luther King Jr. was assassinated? What if you were a wealthy white person? What if you were a poor Mexican American?

2. Tijerina argues that the Treaty of Guadalupe Hidalgo is invalid. Given the information provided here, what is your interpretation of the status of the treaty?

3. Was the killing of Dr. Martin Luther King Jr. a dividing or uniting event in the Civil Rights Movement? In what ways?

Patricio Paiz:
"En memoria de Arturo Tijerina"

Author
Patricio Paiz

Date
1968

Document Type
Poems, Plays, Fiction

Significance
Depicts the Vietnam War from a Mexican American perspective and commemorates the death of the author's friend in the conflict

Overview

The Vietnam War, which lasted from 1954 to 1975, was a conflict between communist North Vietnam and South Vietnam. This conflict occurred under the umbrella of the Cold War, so in many ways the clash of political ideologies between the communist Soviet Union and the democratic United States was the highlight as the two superpowers used the smaller nations as their proxies in a political battle. Protests were common across the United States as leftist groups, peace activists, and students expressed their displeasure with America's involvement in the war. With the United States backing South Vietnam, it was predicted and expected that the war would not last very long, but in 1968 this view was shattered. North Vietnam launched an offensive attack known as the Tet Offensive that threatened to prolong the war indefinitely. Protests reached a new level, with more organized marches, anti-war literature, and anti-war songs.

Patricio Paiz's poem is an example of this. "En memoria de Arturo Tijerina" represents anti-war literature but not from a likely source. Traditionally, Mexican Americans had supported the U.S. government and military and willingly engaged in combat. Hispanic writers were not often at the forefront of anti-war protests; in fact, it was not until 1999 that a collection of Mexican American anti-war poems and essays was published, in an anthology entitled *Aztlán and the Viet Nam: Chicano and Chicana Experiences of the War*. Two of Paiz's poems, including this one, were selected for inclusion by editor George Mariscal. The anthology's focus was the Mexican American experience of the Vietnam War, which Paiz illustrates through his friend's death on May 10, 1968, and his own mourning.

1966 image from the Vietnam War (James K. F. Dung)

Document Text

No Mexicans or dogs,
from the Halls of Montezuma
to the shores of Tripoli.
The vineyards of Fresno, California
to the deadly sands of Africa.
From the lettuce fields of Delano, California,
to the sandy beaches of Normandy,
from the beet fields of Tejas and Colorado,
to the oil fields of Oklahoma,
the packing houses in West Tejas to
the Arctic cold of Germany,
from the aircraft carriers of the Pacific,
to Iwo Jima.

I was there—I was at the Alamo,
the Civil War, my history has
been left out.

No Mexicans or dogs.
I have fed your hungry nation,
AMERICA,
      yo me acuerdo de tí.
I was in Korea, yes,
don't forget Korea,
Forty below 0,
    I can't forget,
I won't forget,
    I remember,
        US 54404674
17,500 en Viet Nam, Basta Ya!
I remember the death march of Bataan,
in the big war,
    the Real War!
How dead can one person be?
I remember UFWOC,

the United Farmworkers of California
I remember César Chávez
and what he said, "God knows
that we are not Beasts of Burden.
We are not agricultural implements,
or rented slaves.
     WE ARE MEN!"
You have exploited me,
     you have taken advantage
of my extreme poverty.
I have processed your vegetables,
I have disposed of your garbage,
I have done so much,
     for so little.
I have been in the coal mines of Virginia
     and Kentucky, and even
     Ratón, Nuevo México.
I was there,
I have been there where no one else will go
     sheepherding in Wyoming,
     la lechuga en Arizona,
     el algodón en Mississippi,
     el betabel en Tejas,
     el campo en Hereford,
     la Causa en California,
All this, and I can't even stare
     Justicia in the face.
I am a stranger to your system
     of Justice.
I am a majority in your jails and prisons.
I am a majority
     WHY?
       In drugs,

     Why?
     is there no human decency?
I remember the Zoot Suit riots,
I remember Las Gorras Blancas de Nuevo México,
I remember Jacinto Treviño,
I remember Pancho Villa,
I remember Emiliano Zapata,
     Benito Juárez,
       I will never forget
LA CAUSA!
I am an Americano,
I was Americano before your Anglo race arrived,
I was American before America existed
I am Arturo Tijerina 5-10-68
I am César Chávez
I am Valentín de la Sierra
I am Reies López Tijerina
I am Emiliano Zapata
I am the Crusade for Justice
I am El Partido de La Raza Unida de
     Tejas, de Nuevo México
I am Chicanos Unidos Para Justicia
     de Las Vegas.
I am the Chicano Liberation Front.
Is there no other way?
Is violence the ONLY way?
César Chávez y Martin Luther King.
     No Violence.
Fasting y Brotherhood Awareness.
Amerikkka, I won't forget you.
La lechuga, el betabel,
the inhuman conditions
     that my brothers have endured.

Glossary

el algodón: cotton

Basta Ya!: Enough!

Bataan: a province in the Philippines and the site of World War II battle

el betabel: beets

Patricio Paiz: "En memoria de Arturo Tijerina"

Glossary

el campo: the field

la Causa: the cause, referring to the United Farmworkers' organizing drive

from the Halls of Montezuma / to the shores of Tripoli: lines from the "Marines' Hymn," the official theme of the U.S. Marine Corps

la lechuga: lettuce

no Mexicans or dogs: racist language commonly found on public signs in the Southwest in the first half of the twentieth century

yo me acuerdo de tí: I remember you

Short-Answer Questions

1. What is Patricio Paiz's tone in his poem? Support your response with specific stanzas from the poem.

2. Explain what Paiz means by these lines in his poem: "I am a stranger to your system / of justice. / I am a majority in your jails and prisons."

3. What events besides those related to Vietnam does Paiz specifically mention that he remembers? Why do you think he includes these details?

Staff Report: Demographic, Economic, and Social Characteristics of the Spanish Surname Population of the Five Southwestern States—U.S. Civil Rights Commission, San Antonio, TX

Author
U.S. Civil Rights Commission

Date
1968

Document Type
Essays, Reports, Manifestos

Significance
An executive report that clearly defines the demographics, economic status, and education of people with Spanish surnames living in the American Southwest in the mid-twentieth century

Overview

The U.S. Civil Rights Commission, as a federal fact-finding agency, relied heavily upon individual witnesses to inform the panel chairman and members. But the panel also needed to ensure members had enough information going into the hearings to make informed conclusions from the testimony provided. The Civil Rights Commission commissioned a staff of advisors and subject-area experts to compile information and gather documents, maps, and other examples to provide a common knowledge base among the panel members. This information base would then become part of the official record. This report contained the most basic and generalized data to orient the members of the panel to the scope of the issues they would be investigating.

Document Text

According to the U.S. Census of Population, in 1960 the Spanish surname population of the five States of the Southwest was nearly 3.5 million, or approximately 12 percent of the total inhabitants of the area. In the period 1950 to 1960, the Spanish surname population in the five states increased by more than 50 percent. Part of this increase was attributable to a more adequate identification of persons of Spanish surname but it was mostly the result of a high birth rate and continuing flow of immigrants from Mexico. In 1960 Texas and California each had approximately 1.4 million persons of Spanish surname. The Spanish surname population in 1960 accounted for nearly 30 percent of New Mexico's population, just under 15 percent of that of Texas and Arizona respectively, and 9 percent of California and Colorado's total population respectively.

Between 1950 and 1960 the most important change in growth and distribution of Spanish surname population among the five Southwestern States was the great increase in their numbers in California.

Population shifts of Spanish surname during the period between censuses were clearly from rural to urban communities and, within the rural population, generally from farm to nonfarm areas. In 1950 about 66 percent of all Spanish surnames lived in urban centers; by 1960 they accounted for 79 percent of the population living in urban areas. In California the change was from 76 percent in 1950 to 85 percent in 1960.

About 85 percent of the persons of Spanish surname in the five Southwestern States were born in the United States; more than half were native born of native parents, i.e., at least second generation American citizens. The proportion of persons of Spanish surname who were native born ranged from a low of 80 percent in California to 97 percent in Colorado.

The median age of the Spanish surname population of the Southwest in 1960 was slightly over 19 years, compared with more than 28 years for the total white population in the five states. Median age varied greatly by State. In Texas the median age for the Spanish surname population was a very low 18 years compared with 27 years for whites. In California it was 22 years contrasted with 30 years.

Males outnumber females in the total Spanish surname population in the Southwest, whereas in the United States as a whole women now outnumber men. According to the 1960 Census of Population, there were approximately 103 males for every 100 females among the Spanish surname group in the Southwest. The ratio is much higher among the farm population—about 138 males for every 100

females. Figures for 1960 also show that Spanish surname women living in rural areas who are nearing the end of their childbearing years have borne, on the average, two or more children per woman than other rural white women. The fertility rate among Spanish surname rural population of the 1950s was sufficient to double that population in each generation. In contrast the fertility rate among rural Anglos produced a potential population growth of about 26 percent in a generation.

Income

The average income level of the Spanish surname population in 1959 was higher than that of nonwhites in the five Southwestern States. Particularly in New Mexico and Arizona, where there are large concentrations of Indians, median nonwhite incomes were considerably below those of persons of Spanish surname. Nevertheless, average incomes for Spanish surname fell appreciably below that of the total white population and this pattern was general throughout the Southwest.

More than one-half (52 percent) of the rural Spanish surname families of the Southwest and not quite a third (31 percent) of those families living in urban areas had less than $3,000 income in 1959, the level of income generally associated with poverty conditions. Texas has the greatest incidence of low-income Spanish surname families: 69 percent among the rural families and 47 percent among the urban families. The smallest number of families with incomes below the poverty level occurred in California where only 17 percent of the urban and 30 percent of the rural families were in this low-income category.

Educational Attainment

On the average the educational achievement of persons of Spanish surname lags behind other ethnic groups, despite overall improvements between 1950 and 1960. In Texas the Spanish surname population in 1950 had about 3.6 years of schooling compared to 9.7 years for total whites;

by 1960 comparison was little better for the Spanish surname population but attainment was still disproportionately low (6.1 years for persons of Spanish surname contrasted with 10.8 years for total white). In Arizona persons of Spanish surname had attained a median education of less than 8 years of schooling, whereas all whites had attained a median of almost 12 years.

The early educational mortality of the Spanish surname population the Southwest is one of the highest of any group in the nation. This is particularly true for the rural population. At all ages considered, dropout rates for persons of Spanish surname in the rural population were generally much higher for the Spanish surname population than for the total United States population. In urban as well as rural areas in Texas, the percentage of persons of Spanish surname in the 16- and 17-year-old group not in school was almost twice as high as for all persons in the comparable age group throughout the United States.

Glossary

educational mortality: the point in an education when a student stops attending school

surname: the name common to all members of a family; last name

U.S. Civil Rights Commission: a panel of eight people who investigate, make recommendations, and report on allegations of discrimination to the U.S. president, Congress, and Senate

Short-Answer Questions

1. After reading the report, describe the average person with a Spanish surname living in the American Southwest at the time in question. What is their age, gender, nationality, and educational status?

2. According to the report, why are so many of the people with Spanish surnames living in poverty?

3. What other issues tend to come along with a large group of poor, undereducated young people that leaders should consider when they read a report like this?

Staff Report: Demographic, Economic, and Social Characteristics
of the Spanish Surname Population of the Five Southwestern States

Staff Report: A Study of Equality of Educational Opportunity for Mexican Americans in Nine School Districts of the San Antonio Area—U.S. Civil Rights Commission, San Antonio, TX

Author
U.S. Civil Rights Commission

Date
1968

Document Type
Essays, Reports, Manifestos

Significance
This report exhaustively illustrates systemic disparities in the public education system in the State of Texas that disproportionately affected African American and Mexican American populations

Overview

Like other reports prepared for the U.S. Civil Rights Commission, this staff report aimed to provide as much measurable information about the public education system in San Antonio, Texas, as possible. The report ran more than seventy pages and was filled with charts, tables, and graphs outlining the findings of the staff investigation. While some politicians or groups would find the report objectionable, the data it contained supported the subjective testimony of many of the witnesses called before the commission.

Document Text

This study examines the extent to which Mexican American students in nine Independent School districts of the metropolitan area of San Antonio, Texas are afforded equal educational opportunities. . . . San Antonio Independent School district occupies most of the central, developed part of the city. . . . Most of the Mexican American students are concentrated in the schools in the central and west side of the district. Anglos attend schools in the northern and eastern sections of the district. . . . Most Negro students are in a small poverty pocket in the northeastern part of the district. The Mexican American population has a low median family income; more than half live below the poverty level. Many reside in old, dilapidated and deteriorating housing. . . .

Three significant areas of education were examined. The first concerns Anglo overrepresentation on school boards and professional staff as well as ethnic isolation of Mexican American students. The study shows that Mexican American students tend to be concentrated in certain schools and Anglos in other schools and, where Mexican Americans do attend schools with substantial Anglo enrollment, they are often concentrated in separate classrooms through ability groupings and tracking practices. . . . There are few Mexican American teachers and other professional staff and . . . of these most are assigned to schools with a high concentration of Mexican American students.

The second area on which attention is focused is disparities in the educational system. It contrasts Mexican American schools with Anglo schools in terms of financial resources, teacher qualifications, and physical facilities. It demonstrates that because Mexican American districts have lower taxable property values than Anglo districts, they are unable to provide comparable educational opportunities utilizing locally raised funds. Federal and state funds, moreover, do not equalize the disparities in local financial resources. The study demonstrates that significantly more nondegree teachers are found in predominantly Mexican American school districts. Generally, Mexican Americans are educated in comparatively old, overcrowded schools, with restricted playground space, inadequate libraries and few modern conveniences, in contrast with the modern facilities in spaciousness of the schools and Anglo areas.

The third area examined is the impact of inadequate education on the Mexican American child. It documents the Mexican American's comparatively low scholastic attainment in the substantial likelihood that he will not complete high school. It shows that a disproportionate number of Mexican American students score low on achievement tests and perform poorly on IQ tests ill-designed

to measure their true ability and relate this to overrepresentation of Mexican American students in classes for low achievers and in non-college preparatory curriculum. The study also documents a significant dropout rate for Mexican Americans in Texas and in San Antonio as well as a higher percentage of retention in grade of Mexican American students. . . .

The ethnic imbalance in the schools in part reflects ethnic concentration in neighborhood residential patterns in the San Antonio areas. School attendance . . . is based on a neighborhood school policy with school zones following neighborhood lines. . . . Five of these zones are classified as open attendance areas . . . [and] are occupied by Mexican Americans and Negroes living in a mixed residential pattern, and therefore enrollments of all schools and open attendance areas are predominantly Mexican American or Negro. In spite of low percentage of Negroes in San Antonio, in none of these areas is a Negro or Mexican American child given the option of attending a school or the majority of the pupils are Anglos. . . .

Unlike the attendance in the elementary and junior high schools, senior high school attendance . . . operates under a freedom of choice basis. Choice slips must be filled out for all junior high school graduates before they enter senior high school. On these slips the student indicates his age, the high school he wishes to attend and the choice of subjects he wishes to take. The counselor fills in the questions on IQ scores, whether the pupil has fulfilled his science requirement and whether he is likely to succeed in a trade. . . .

Although the freedom of choice system theoretically offers a junior high school graduate the opportunity to attend any senior high school, there appear to be factors which limit his actual alternatives. Mexican American students almost consistently select a senior high school similar in ethnic makeup to the junior high school they have attended. . . . Thus, even where freedom of choice is purportedly permitted, ethnically balanced schools do not result. Commission staff interviews with school officials and students reveal a number of factors which operate to restrict the student's free choice of school.

School officials indicate that many Mexican American parents want to send their children to their **school previously attended by the parents. . . .** Another reason for the continued ethnic concentration through high school, according to school officials, is the prevailing pattern of ethnic concentration in neighborhoods coupled with the difficulties in obtaining transportation to other parts of town. Mexican American students who live in a Mexican American neighborhood and who go to the nearest high school—so they can walk to school instead of riding the bus—often find themselves in predominantly . . . Mexican American schools. There is no school bus transportation . . . and students going to school outside their neighborhoods must rely on public transportation. Sometimes this requires a fairly heavy expenditure of time and money. Further, one of the nine San Antonio high schools . . . is virtually inaccessible by public bus transportation.

Another important factor is the role of the counselor and the process of the school selection by the student. Some . . . school officials admit there are . . . counselors, especially in almost exclusively **Mexican American schools, who guide the Mexi**can American students toward the predominantly Mexican American vocational high schools because they believe this type of school to be most appropriate for the Mexican American student.

In August 1968, the Governor's Committee on Public School Education . . . pointed out that Texas ranked 31st among the States in terms of median level of education, and 42nd in high school graduation rates and the level of education and graduation rates of Mexican Americans with significantly lower than that of Anglos. . . . The Committee disclosed that Texas ranks eighth among the States in per capita property valuations, yet 39th in percent of those values devoted annually to public education.

Glossary

Anglos: in this document, a reference to Caucasian people

college preparatory curriculum: the types of courses and subjects that a student should be skilled in to be successful in college-level courses

dilapidated: run down as a result of long-term neglect

independent school district: a school district that operates independently from a local government, meaning it raises taxes, elects its own officials, selects subjects to be taught, and creates its own policies outside of the control of elected local governments

IQ test: a test designed to measure intellectual ability or educational level

median level of education: the average level of education in a portion or total of the population

modern conveniences: devices or utilities that make a building more pleasant or productive, yet are regarded as things expected to be found anywhere

Glossary

Negro: an outdated and politically incorrect term for people of African decent

per capita property valuations: a measure of the value of property in an area divided by the number of people living in the same area

professional staff: an employee who is not a teacher or instructor

systemic disparities: the ways that institutions and societies create systems or processes that result in the inequal treatment of people based on race, age, sex, gender, religion, or economics

Short-Answer Questions

1. After reading the report, would you argue that in the late 1960s the State of Texas valued an educated population? Why or why not?

2. Does the staff report seem to have given equal time to interviewing students/parents and staff/administrators? Please explain.

3. Given that there was no school bus, why might the Board of Education choose to build a school that could not be accessed by public transportation?

Staff Report: A Study of Equality of Educational Opportunity for
Mexican Americans in Nine School Districts of the San Antonio Area

Staff Report: Farm Workers— U.S. Civil Rights Commission, San Antonio, TX

Author
U.S. Civil Rights Commission

Date
1968

Document Type
Essays, Reports, Manifestos

Significance
An outline in clear, nonpartisan language of the realities of the situation for farm workers and their families in the Southwest in the late 1960s

Overview

Unlike other reports prepared by the staff of the U.S. Civil Rights Commission for its information base, this report focused solely on one of the major fields of employment for Mexican Americans in the Southwest. This report aimed to provide a basis for the members to judge the potential quality-of-life expectations for many residents of the Southwest.

Document Text

Each year, Texas is the origin of the largest of the three streams of migratory farm workers who travel northward to harvest the Nation's crops, mostly fruits, vegetables, sugar beets and cotton. (The other two streams originate in Florida and Southern California.) The main stream flows north and west from Texas, covering most of the North Central, Mountain and Pacific Coast States before the end of the harvest season in December.

Of the three million persons who did farm work at any time during 1967, 466,000 or 15 percent migrated. Mexican Americans provide a proportionally large part of the farm force and an even larger part of the migrant force. . . . The annual migration of over one million persons . . . reflects the fact that farm worker is one of the most poorly compensated occupations in this country. . . .

The particularly deplorable living and working conditions in South Texas account for that area's being the fountainhead of the migratory stream. . . . Whether migrants or non-migrants, farm workers rank lowest in annual income of all the Nation's occupational groups. . . . And although many farm workers do receive such benefits as housing, meals, and transportation, the value of these benefits does not compare with fringe benefits, such as paid vacations and medical insurance, commonly received by other occupational classes. . . . Housing provided farm workers is commonly substandard and transportation commonly less than safe.

Low wages are accompanied by steady unemployment and underemployment. The overall unemployment rate of agricultural workers was 6.5 percent in 1966, compared with an unemployment rate of 3.4 percent for workers in other industries. Farm workers have the shortest workyear of almost any occupation group. During 1965, only 31 percent of . . . workers in agriculture worked a full year compared to 62 percent of . . . workers in nonagricultural areas. . . .

It is not surprising, therefore, that a substantial proportion of hired farm workers is employed outside of agriculture during part of the year. During 1965, about half the migrants did nonfarm work. Eventually many people abandon farm work altogether and migrate to cities which are ill prepared to provide adequate economic opportunities for the flow of unskilled workers. . . .

Furthermore the farm worker is often beset by competition from Mexican "commuters" and illegal entrants, as well as the continuing decrease in job opportunities brought on by mechanization and the greater use of chemicals to control weed growth.

The farm worker's low wages and erratic employ-

ment are compounded by his exclusion from normal worker's benefits. Farm workers are either excluded from or inadequately covered by Federal minimum wage standards, unemployment insurance, social security benefits, Federal child labor protection, and the benefits of the National Labor Relations Act. . . . Even where there is [state] legislation, it generally is ineffective.

Exclusion of farm workers from meaningful legislation is due to well organized opposition from employers. This opposition is based on the argument that "farming is different"—different from the majority of American businesses which are subject to laws protecting workers. The farm traditionally has been portrayed to Congress as a family-run affair, at the mercy of the elements, which could be burned out one day and frozen out the next and which would be destroyed if burdened by social legislation aimed at industrial employers.

In fact, a great transformation has occurred in agriculture. Technological developments, labor saving machinery, refrigeration, improve fertilizers, crop specialization, and other advances have turned farming into an industry, resulting in the displacement of some two million farm operators and their families in an 85 percent increase in production within a decade. A farm worker in 1910 produced enough food for seven people. Today, despite an increase in per capita consumption, he produces enough for 24 people.

In 1960, less than 9 percent of all farmers owned nearly 40 percent of all farm land, [and] accounted for nearly 50 percent of farm sales. . . . It is these large, modern farms, run as profitmaking businesses, that employ the vast majority of farmworkers. . . .

Most of the farmworker's problems are indistinguishable from the problems affecting the poor generally. Some of these problems, however, are related to his particular employment status and cultural background. He is likely to be unskilled and uneducated and therefore, incapable of qualifying

---

Staff Report: Farm Workers—U.S. Civil Rights Commission, San Antonio, TX

for higher paying jobs. Often he is a Mexican or Mexican-American, "separated from the dominant, Anglo-Saxon culture of America, the inheritor of a distinctive history, divergent values, in a profound sense both of his inferiority and of his own special worth." He lacks effective economic organization and political participation and the conditions of abject poverty, poor education, poor health, squalid working and living conditions permeate every facet of his existence. . . .

A most depressing aspect of the farm labor situation is the plight of farm children. The general poverty and erratic employment patterns of their parents result in serious educational difficulties. . . . Another critical factor in the life of farm labor children is the health problems resulting from their labor. Presently, agricultural labor of children outside of school hours is exempted from the child labor provisions of the Fair Labor Standards Act. . . . Agricultural labor requiring constant bending, stooping, and lifting expends the child's energy which is needed for normal growth, and chronic fatigue lowers a child's resistance to disease. . . . It has been estimated that there are about 800,000 farm laborers under 16, comprising one fourth of the total workforce. . . .

Most important, farm workers have been continually excluded from the National Labor Relations Act of 1935 which provides machinery facilitating the orderly and peaceful organization of workers. . . . Allegations of harassment, physical violence and brutality, pro-grower conduct of state officials, arbitrary and illegal arrest, excessive bail, and neglect in bringing to trial the more than 100 cases arising from arrests of union organizers, clergymen, and sympathizers, have been made by [organizing farm] union officials. . . .

As the Migratory Labor Subcommittee has pointed out, the express exclusion of farm workers from federal labor relations legislation is "a most pernicious form of discrimination" leading to unnecessary strife and violence.

Glossary

National Labor Relations Act of 1935: American labor law that guarantees the right of non-governmental employees to unionize and the right to take collective action, such as striking or collective bargaining, and outlawed unfair labor practices that interfered with employee rights. However, the act specifically excludes government employees, managers, domestic and agricultural workers, and independent contractors from inclusion in the legal guarantees.

Short-Answer Questions

1. After reading the text, what do you think is the central reason—ignorance, greed, racism, something else—for the substandard living conditions of migratory farm workers in the United States in the late 1960s? Support your answer with the text.

2. If you were the mayor of an urban city in Texas in 1968, how could you use this report to better support the rural poor of the day and prepare for the rural poor of the future?

3. Do the living conditions of migratory farm workers reflect a failure of state governments to ensure the proper conduct of their officials or a failure of the federal government to create and enforce laws that reflect the changes in society? Why?

Father Ruiz:
Statement before the
U.S. Commission on Civil Rights

Author
Father Ralph Ruiz

Date
1968

Document Type
Speeches/Addresses; Legislative

Significance
Provides insight into the manner in which the 1960s-era federal government sought to change the sympathetic narrative about the poor offered by the media by intimidating the poor population of San Antonio

Overview

The U.S. Commission on Civil Rights was created through the Civil Rights Act of 1957 as an independent, bipartisan federal fact-finding agency. It largely functions through its State Advisory Committees, which identify and report on local issues. In 1968, CBS News aired a documentary called *Hunger in America* that portrayed with sympathy the residents of, among other locations, the depressed Chicano neighborhoods of San Antonio. After its airing, national attention was drawn to allegations of regular discrimination and violations of Mexican American civil rights in education, employment, economic security, and administration of justice. The Commission on Civil Rights then held hearings in five southwestern states—Texas, Arizona, California, Colorado, and New Mexico—in 1968. The commission elected to explore the city of San Antonio as an in-depth indicator of problems in Texas and across the nation. The forum

was the first time that experts, educators, and politicians had gathered to try to understand issues related to Mexican Americans through the discrimination experienced by residents in the American Southwest. Although many of the attendees admitted that the testimony qualitatively led to better understanding of the depths of the issues facing Mexican Americans, it provided no clear solution. The five-day event became the subject of several local and regional politicians arguing that the selection of speakers chosen to testify tainted the outcome of the fact-finding effort. Many politicians were concerned enough to provoke J. Edgar Hoover, director of the Federal Bureau of Investigation, to order an investigation into whether hunger was prevalent in the community or whether a massive attempt to defraud the federal government's social programs was underway.

Eisenhower signing the Civil Rights Act of 1957, which established a Commission on Civil Rights. (National Archives and Records Administration)

Document Text

My name is Ralph Ruiz. I am a Catholic priest of the Archdiocese of San Antonio. I am director of Inner City Apostolate on the near west side of San Antonio. In connection with the subject that I will cover in my testimony today, there is one area of particular concern to me: the rights of individual citizens to petition their national government without fear of intimidation, harassment, or retaliation. That has to be one of our most basic civil rights.

We have long known that many local government officials use repressive methods on the hungry and poor they are supposed to help. I am here talking about welfare investigations, arbitrary dismissal from the welfare rolls, unnecessary investigations to determine whether a family qualifies for food programs. The hungry and poor who need these programs are unnecessarily harassed and intimidated by these methods. We have come to expect that locally, *but we did not expect the same tactics from our federal government in Washington.*

There have been federal investigators from Washington—FBI agents—who have been to San Antonio to find out—so they say—if anyone is hungry here. But I think the real reason they were here has been to discredit the many reports which say there are hungry people in San Antonio.

Everyone knows that there are hungry people here—people in the words of the special survey by the Department of Health, Education and Welfare just completed in Texas who are suffering from: "malnutrition, anemia, retardation of the growth and development of children, and vitamin deficiencies." Some of the hungry testified a year ago before the Citizens' Board of Inquiry here in San Antonio. At that hearing, several public officials also testified that there were some 100,000 people hungry here. The CBS-TV documentary, "Hunger in America," showed the faces of the hungry because I took the CBS-TV camera crews to where the hungry were. There have been other reports as well. The 1967 application submitted by the City of San Antonio for participation in the Model Neighborhood Program talked about two San Antonios:

"In the city, 28 per cent of the families (38,444) made less than $3,000 per year, and over 6 per cent of the families had an income of less than $1,000.

"Although the economic picture appears optimistic and growth seems to be certain, it is still true that San Antonio has more area of blight than ever before.

"We have before us then two San Antonios: One, a San Antonio growing in prosperity and economic viability; the other, *a San Antonio which has grown only in the intensity of its problems.* It is the latter San Antonio to which this proposal is directed."

And the Worden School of Social Service has just issued a report showing that a majority of the poor in San Antonio have inadequate diets.

There is no question but that there are hungry people here, and it doesn't matter whether there are 100,000 or half that many or twice that many. *There should be no hungry people in San Antonio.*

But I was interrogated for some two hours several weeks ago by two FBI agents from Washington on whether there were any hungry people here. These FBI agents say they are now working for the House Appropriations Committee, which has started an investigation into hunger in America. What do FBI agents know about hunger? What purpose can they have? They can only serve one purpose—to frighten, intimidate, harass, and bother the poor and hungry who thought the government in Washington was their friend. I can take care of myself—these federal police do not frighten or intimidate me.

But what of the poor families suddenly faced with two FBI agents asking questions about whether they are hungry—how much money they make—what do they eat—why don't they eat better—why don't they really tell the truth, and then entering their homes—looking into their kitchens . . . in fact, invading their private lives and private property. We know that this has happened to at least one family here in San Antonio who were visited by the "two men with suits on." There are probably other fam-

ilies that we don't know about who have also been investigated. We also know that there have been investigators at the Robert B. Green Hospital.

The poor and hungry are frightened of these investigators. The questions concern their very livelihood, and they wonder whether these federal police will take that away; they wonder if they have done something wrong. And so, they face more fear—more apprehension—because these are "friends" from Washington. But we know they are not friends—but the opposite.

And there is an even more basic issue. These people—poor and hungry though they may be—have their own dignity and their own worth as human beings. It is not their fault that they are hungry—that they are poor—that they must depend upon a paternalistic and inadequate welfare system for their daily bread. It is very hard for these people to tell their story of deprivation and hunger—of the way they live. They have told it often here—to the Citizens' Board of Inquiry—to the CBS-TV crews and, therefore, to the nation—to me and those who work here every day. They shouldn't be forced to tell it again to federal agents whose obvious purpose is to discredit those who say there is hunger in our city.

I am concerned and shocked about this—deeply concerned and shocked. These federal investigators—whatever their stated purpose—can serve no good. They can only sow distrust and fear.

Glossary

anemia: a blood deficiency that can be caused by a lack of iron or vitamin B12 that causes weakness, tiredness, confusion, and an increased thirst

apostolate: an organization of ordinary people devoted to the teachings and outreach charity associated with the Catholic faith

archdiocese: a large administrative area of responsibility that generally contains a large number of churches and priests of the Catholic faith and is led by a cardinal

---

Father Ruiz: Statement before the U.S. Commission on Civil Rights

Glossary

bipartisan: a mutually cooperative agreement between the two dominant U.S. political parties

Chicano: a self-adopted term of pride for individuals of Mexican decent living in the United States

Citizens' Board of Inquiry: a coalition of organizations and individuals charged with investigating an issue by a political authority, generally to examine an issue without political overtones

Civil Rights Act of 1957: the first civil rights legislation since the end of post–Civil War Reconstruction in 1877, which established a Commission on Civil Rights within the executive branch, a Civil Rights Division within the Department of Justice, and aimed to strengthen protections for people of color in voting and jury rights

malnutrition: a small or unhealthy food intake that results in not getting the correct nutrition

Robert B. Green Hospital: a large hospital in San Antonio that was known for its care of the poorest members of the community

Worden School of Social Service: a college of the private Catholic university Our Lady of the Lake; the first social work school in Texas

Short-Answer Questions

1. Father Ruiz includes many specific figures and statistics in his testimony. What does this say about the audience he is trying to reach through his testimony?

2. What does Father Ruiz think about the federal agents' actions in San Antonio? How do you know? Please cite your evidence.

3. Would Father Ruiz argue that the Civil Rights Act of 1957 had gone far enough to secure the individual rights of all citizens? What leads you to this conclusion?

The Schlager Anthology of Hispanic America

Young Lords Party
13-Point Program and Platform

Author
Young Lords Party

Date
1968

Document Type
Essays, Reports, Manifestos

Significance
Espoused a radical, militant, and inclusive approach to social activism, similar to the Black Panthers' Ten Point Program

Overview

The Young Lords Party (YLP) was often referred to as the Hispanic Black Panther Party because of its radical and militant approach to social activism. The party grew from the Young Lords Organization (YLO), established by political activist José Jiménez in 1968 in Chicago, Illinois. Although the YLO disbanded by the late 1970s, it left a lasting impact.

The YLO began as a Puerto Rican street gang and evolved into an organization that advocated for minority rights and equality in education, housing, and employment. The YLO was inclusive to those outside the Puerto Rican community and welcomed African Americans, women, Latinos, and those who identified as LGBTQ. Because of its multiethnic and all-encompassing approach, the organization gained members and expanded into other cities such as New York City. It was there that the Young Lords Party (YLP), a chapter within the YLO, was established. Eventually, the YLP

disassociated from the YLO and evolved into a political activist party that developed a set of goals called the 13-Point Program.

The leadership structure of the YLO has been compared to that of the Black Panther Party because there were specific committees dedicated to health, education, and finances, and all were overseen by a leader who was also a minister. The YLO and all its chapters were visible within the community and even published a monthly newspaper that promoted various services and events. The YLO and its chapters dissolved in the late 1970s, but the impact they made created a lasting legacy. In fact, DePaul University's Center for Latino Research contacted YLO founder Jiménez and asked him to work with the center on the Lincoln Park Project, which archived existing documents centered on the organization's many meal and nutrition programs, cultural centers, free medical clinics, and organized protests.

Young Lords Party logo (Wikimedia Commons)

Document

The Young Lords Party is a Revolutionary Political Party Fighting for the Liberation of All Oppressed People

1. We want self-determination for Puerto Ricans—Liberation of the Island and inside the united states.

For 500 years, first Spain and then united states have colonized our country. Billions of dollars in profits leave our country for the united states every year. In every way we are slaves of the gringo. . . .

Que Viva Puerto Rico Libre!

2. We want self-determination for all Latinos.

Our Latin Brothers and Sisters, inside and outside the united states, are oppressed by amerikkkan business. The Chicano people built the Southwest, and we support their right to control their lives and their land. . . . The armed liberation struggles in Latin America are part of the war of Latinos against imperialism.

Que Viva La Raza!

3. We want liberation of all third world people.

Just as Latins first slaved under spain and the yanquis, Black people, Indians, and Asians slaved to build the wealth of this country. For 400 years they have fought **for freedom and dignity against racist Babylon** (decadent empire). Third World people have led the fight for freedom. All the colored and oppressed peoples of the world are one nation under oppression.

No Puerto Rican Is Free Until All People Are Free!

4. We are revolutionary nationalists and oppose racism.

The Latin, Black, Indian and Asian people inside the u.s. are colonies fighting for liberation. We know that washington, wall street and city hall will try to make our nationalism into racism; but Puerto Ricans are of all colors and we resist racism. . . .

Power To All Oppressed People!

5. We want community control of our institutions and land.

We want control of our communities by our people and programs to guarantee that all institutions serve the needs of our people. People's control of police, health services, churches, schools, housing, transportation and welfare are needed. . . .

Land Belongs To All The People!

6. We want a true education of our Creole culture and Spanish language.

We must learn our history of fighting against cultural, as well as economic genocide by the yanqui. Revolutionary culture, culture of our people, is the only true teaching.

7. We oppose capitalists and alliances with traitors.

Puerto Rican rulers, or puppets of the oppressor, do not help our people. They are paid by the system to lead our people down blind alleys. . . . We want a society where the people socialistically control their labor.

Venceremos!

8. We oppose the Amerikkkan military.

We demand immediate withdrawal of u.s. military forces and bases from Puerto Rico, Vietnam and all oppressed communities inside and outside the u.s. No Puerto Rican should serve in the u.s. army against his Brothers and Sisters. . . .

U.S. Out Of Vietnam, Free Puerto Rico!

9. We want freedom for all political prisoners.

We want all Puerto Ricans freed because they have been tried by the racist courts of the colonizers, and not by their own people and peers. We want all freedom fighters released from jail.

Free All Political Prisoners!

10. We want equality for women. Machismo must be revolutionary . . . not oppressive.

Under capitalism, our women have been oppressed by both the society and our own men. . . . Our men must support their women in their fight for economic and social equality, and must recognize that our women are equals in every way within the revolutionary ranks.

Forward, Sisters, In The Struggle!

11. We fight anti-communism with international unity.

Anyone who resists injustice is called a communist by "the man" and condemned. Our people are brainwashed by television, radio, newspapers, schools, and books to oppose people in other countries fighting for their freedom. . . . We will defend our Brothers and Sisters around the world who fight for justice against the rich rulers of this country.

Viva Che!

12. We believe armed self-defense and armed struggle are the only means to liberation.

We are opposed to violence—the violence of hungry children, illiterate adults, diseased old people, and the violence of poverty and profit. We have asked, petitioned, gone to courts, demonstrated peacefully, and voted for politicians full of empty promises. But we still ain't free. . . . When a government oppresses our people, we have the right to abolish it and create a new one.

Boricua Is Awake! All Pigs Beware!

13. We want a socialist society.

We want liberation, clothing, free food, education, health care, transportation, utilities, and employment for all. We want a society where the needs of our people come first, and where we give solidarity and aid to the peoples of the world, not oppression and racism.

Hasta La Victoria Siempre!

Glossary

Boricua: a person from Puerto Rico by birth or descent

Che: Ernesto "Che" Guevara, Argentinian revolutionary; "Viva Che!" means "Long live Che!"

Glossary

"Hasta la victoria siempre!": "Always until victory!"

"Que viva la raza!": "Long live the heritage!"

"Que viva Puerto Rico libre!": "Long live Puerto Rico the free!"

"Venceremos!": "We will win!"

yanquis: Yankees; white, non-Latino Americans

Short-Answer Questions

1. The Young Lords Party has been compared to the Black Panther Party, in part for being radical and militant. What language is used in the 13-Point Program that gives credibility to this claim?

2. The Young Lords Party was inclusive in that it promoted the rights of all minorities. Choose two of the thirteen points that specifically illustrate the all-encompassing nature of the YLO.

3. Analyze points 11, 12, and 13. What is the Young Lords Party's stance on communism and socialism? Include excerpts from the document to support your response.

East LA Walkout Demands

Author Educational Issues Coordinating Committee **Date** 1968 **Document Type** Essays, Reports, Manifestos	**Significance** An explanation of the rationale behind one of the largest student protests in U.S. history, as Chicano students, parents, and community activists protested inequality in the public education system and motivated the wider Chicano civil right movement

Overview

The Johnson-Reed Immigration Act of 1924 limited European and Asian migration into the United States, opening the door to widespread Latin American migration into the country. The Mexican Farm Worker's Act of 1942 permitted millions of Mexican laborers to work in the United States on short-term "bracero" labor contracts. Though these bracero laborers were intended to only remain within the U.S. for a few months, many stayed. Large Mexican communities arose across the American Southwest and in major industrial and service cities such as Chicago and New York. However, the east side of Los Angles was unquestionably the largest concentration of migrant Mexican families in the country.

Initially, Mexican Americans were segregated into their schools in the LA metropolitan area. Two landmark court cases—*Mendez, et al. v. Westminster School District* (1947) and *Brown v. Board of Education of Topeka*

(1954)—ruled that the segregation of students, even if school facilities are otherwise equal, was a violation of students' constitutional rights. Although schools throughout the LA metropolitan area were desegregated, Mexican Americans represented a majority in the public school system. Mexican American–dominated schools were generally run-down, staffed with under-qualified teachers, overcrowded, and featured a vocational or household training curriculum. When a small group of teachers began instructing in Mexican American and Mexican culture and history, students began questioning their education and asking the Board of Education for meaningful change. With their change requests ignored, the students, parents, teachers, and community members hastily arranged themselves as the Educational Issues Coordinating Committee (EICC) and staged a series of walkouts from community schools that included about 17,500 people and lasted for nearly a week. The EICC met with the Board of Education and read out its demands, which the board rejected, arguing they did not have the funds to execute any changes. Police arrested thirteen of the key EICC walkout organizers—who would become known as the East LA 13—and a popular protest resulted in the release of all thirteen on bail. Teachers who participated lost their jobs, but after parent and community outcries and a series of Board of Education sit-ins, the teachers were reinstated, and by 1970 all charges had been dropped.

Activists arrested for taking part in the walkouts (Los Angeles Public Library)

Document Text

Student Demands

BLOWOUTS were staged by us, Chicano students, in the East Los Angeles High Schools protesting the obvious lack of action on the part of the L.A. School Board in bringing E.L.A. schools up to par with those in other areas of the city. We, young Chicanos, not only protested but at the same time offered proposals for much needed reforms. Just what did we propose?

To begin with, we want assurance that any student or teacher who took part in the BLOWOUTS WILL NOT be reprimanded or suspended in any manner. You know the right to protest and demonstrate against injustice is guaranteed to all by the

Constitution. We want immediate steps taken to implement bilingual and bicultural education for Chicanos. WE WANT TO BRING OUR CAR-NALES HOME. Teachers, administrators, and staff should be educated; they should know our language (Spanish), and understand the history, traditions, and contributions of the Mexican culture. HOW CAN THEY EXPECT TO TEACH US IF THEY DO NOT KNOW US? We also want the school books revised to reflect the contributions of Mexicans and Mexican-Americans to the U.S. society, and to make us aware of the injustices that we, Chicanos, as a people have suffered in a "gabacho"-dominated society. Furthermore, we want any member of the school system who displays prejudice or fails to recognize, understand, and appreciate us, our culture, or our heritage removed from E.L.A. schools.

Classes should be smaller in size, say about 20 students to 1 teacher, to insure more effectiveness. We want new teachers and administrators to live in the community their first year and that parents from the community be trained as teachers' aides. We want assurances that a teacher who may disagree politically or philosophically with administrators will not be dismissed or transferred because of it. The school belongs to the community and as such should be made available for community activities under supervision of Parents' Councils.

There should be a manager in charge of janitorial work and maintenance details, and the performance of such duties should be restricted to employees hired for that purpose. IN OTHER WORDS, NO MORE STUDENTS DOING JANITORIAL WORK.

And more than this, we want RIGHTS—RIGHTS—STUDENT RIGHTS—OUR RIGHTS. We want a free speech area plus the right to have speakers of our own choice at our club meetings. Being civic-minded citizens, we want to know what the happenings are in our community, so we demand the right to have access to all types of literature and to be able to bring it on campus.

The type of dress that we wear should not be dictated to s by "gabachos," but it should be a group of Chicano parents and students who establish dress and grooming standards for Chicano students in Chicano schools.

Getting down to facilities. WE WANT THE BUILDINGS OPEN TO ALL STUDENTS AT ALL TIMES, especially the HEADS. Yeah, we want access to the heads at all times. . . . When you get right down to it, WE ONLY DEMAND WHAT OTHERS HAVE—things like lighting at all E.L.A. football fields, swimming pools. Sport events are an important part of school activity and we want FREE ADMISSION for all students. We, CHICANO STUDENTS, BLEW OUT in protest. Our proposals have been made. The big question is will the School Board take positive action. If so, WHEN?

Glossary

blowout: East Los Angeles slang term for a walkout

Chicano: a self-identifying term for people of Mexican ancestry who are born in the United States; the term became a symbol of pride in the civil rights movement of the 1960s

gabacho: literally a foreigner; in popular Mexican use, used to derogatorily describe non-Hispanic Americans or, alternatively, the United States as a nation

Short-Answer Questions

1. Given that the East LA walkouts occurred after a long series of destructive urban riots across the nation, does this statement represent an acknowledgment from the Chicano community that violence was not a useful tool in securing their civil rights? Why or why not?

2. If you were on the Los Angeles Board of Education hearing this list of demands, what alternatives do you think could have been implemented to satisfy some of the demands, even without funds?

3. If the Board of Education approved all of the EICC demands, what kinds of issues could be raised in the future?

Alurista and Rodolfo Gonzales: "El Plan Espiritual de Aztlan"

Author
Alurista and Rodolfo Gonzales

Date
1969

Document Type
Essays, Reports, Manifestos

Significance
Helped set the tone for the Chicano Movement by advocating for Chicano nationalism through an ideological framework based on indigeneity and a political program that emphasized self-determination

Overview

"El Plan Espiritual de Aztlan" is a manifesto cowritten by Rodolfo "Corky" Gonzales and the Chicano poet Alberto Urista, who is best known by his penname, Alurista. It was delivered as a speech during the First National Chicano Liberation Youth Conference held in Denver, Colorado, in March of 1969 and adopted as a foundational document of the Chicano Movement. This was a socio-cultural and civil rights movement in which activists relentlessly pursued substantial political representation, increased economic possibilities, and improved educational prospects for Mexican Americans by removing them from generational poverty, marginalization, and powerlessness. "Corky" Gonzales was the head of the Crusade for Justice, a Denver-based civil rights group that organized the youth conference, which was attended by an estimated 1,500 students from across the United States.

"El Plan" synthesized the prevailing views held by many Chicana and Chicano activists at the time, which included advocating for indigeneity and rooting Chicana/os to the land; adopting cultural nationalism to create a sense of ethnic unity; and asserting self-determination as a collective "Nation of free pueblos." The imagined Chicano nation, Aztlan, encompassed Texas and all the territory ceded by Mexico after its war with the United States from 1846 to 1848. Undoubtedly, these were radical positions that surfaced after the assimilationist tactics of the "Mexican American generation" (1940s–50s) did not produce the social acceptance and equality many had hoped for. By the mid-1960s, Chicana/o youth had grown tired of institutional reform and decided to act on their own terms. Of immediate concern was tackling systemic oppression, racism, judicial inequality, and the neglect of their communities. Inspired by the farmworker struggle in the fields and liberation movements around the world, young Chicana/os organized and protested by walking out of class, disrupting government meetings, and marching in the streets demanding change. Some of the universal demands included better schools and education, increased political and financial representation in all levels of society and government, and an end to police brutality and impunity. "El Plan" captured the call for action and offered a pathway forward.

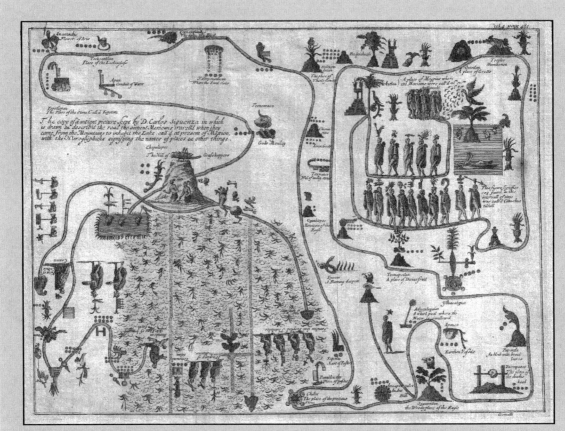

Map of the migration from Aztlán, considered a spiritual homeland in Chicano mythology (Gemelli Careri)

Document Text

PREAMBLE:

In the spirit of a new people that is conscious not only of its proud historical heritage, but also of the brutal "Gringo" invasion of our territories, We, the Chicano inhabitants and civilizers of the Northern land of Aztlan, from whence came our forefathers, reclaiming the land of their birth and consecrating the determination of our people of the sun, declare that the call of our blood is our power, our responsibility, and our inevitable destiny.

We are free and sovereign to determine those tasks which are justly called for by our house, the sweat of our brows and by our hearts. Aztlan belongs to those that plant the seeds, water the land and gather the crops, and not to foreign Europeans. We do not recognize capricious frontiers on the Bronze Continent.

Brotherhood unites us, and love of our brothers makes us a people whose time has come and who struggle against the foreign "Gabacho" who exploits our riches and destroys our culture. With our hearts in our hands and our hands in the soil, We Declare the Independence of our Mestizo Nation, a Bronze People with a Bronze Culture. Before the world, before all of North America, before our brothers in the Bronze Continent, We are a Nation of free pueblos, We are Aztlan.

March, 1969 (Adopted at Chicano Youth Conference, Denver, Colo.)

Aztlan, in the Nahuatl tongue of ancient Mexico, means "the lands to the north." Thus Aztlan refers to what is now the known as the southwestern states of this country.

THE PROGRAM:

El Plan Espiritual de Aztlan, sets the theme that Chicanos (La Raza de Bronze) must use their nationalism as the key or common denominator for mass mobilization and organization. Once we are committed to the idea and philosophy of El Plan de Aztlan, we can only conclude that social, economic, cultural and political independence is the only road to total liberation from oppression, exploitation and racism. Our struggle then must be the control of our Barrios, campos, pueblos, lands, our economy, our culture and our political life. El Plan commits all levels of Chicano society; the barrio, the campo, the ranchero, the writer, the teacher, the worker, the professional, to La Causa.

I. PUNTO PRIMERO: Nationalism

Nationalism as the key to organization transcends all religious, political, class and economic factions or boundaries. Nationalism is the common denom-

inator that all members of La Raza can agree upon.

II. PUNTO SEGUNDO: Organizational Goals

1. Unity in thought of our people concerning the barrios, the land, the poor, the middle class, the professional is committed to liberation of La Raza.

2. Economy: economic control of our lives and our communities can only come about by driving the exploiter out of our communities, our pueblos, and our lands and by controlling and developing our own talents, sweat and resources. Cultural background and values which ignore materialism and embrace humanism will lend to the act of co-operative buying and distribution of resources and production to sustain an economic base for healthy growth and development. Lands rightfully ours will be fought for and defended. Land and realty ownership will be acquired by the community for the people's welfare. Economic ties of responsibility must be secured by nationalism and the Chicano defense units.

3. Education must be relative to our people, i.e., history, culture, bilingual education, contributions. Community control of our schools, our teachers.

4. Institutions shall serve our people by providing the service necessary for a full life and their welfare on the basis of restitution, not handouts or beggar's crumbs. Restitution for past economic slavery, political exploitation, ethnic and cultural psychological destruction and denial of civil and human rights. Institutions in our community which do not serve the people have no place in the community. The institutions belong to the people.

5. Self defense of the community must rely on the combined strength of the people. The front line defense will come from the barrios, the campos, the pueblos, and the ranchitos. Their involvement as protectors of their people will be given respect and dignity. They in turn offer lives for their people. Those who place themselves on the front for their people do so out of love and carnalismo. Those

institutions which are fattened by our brothers to provide employment and political pork barrels for the gringo will do so only by acts of liberation and La Causa. For the very young there will no longer be acts of juvenile delinquency, but revolutionary acts.

6. Cultural values of our people strengthen our **identity and the moral backbone of the movement.** Our culture unites and educates the family of La Raza towards liberation with one heart and one mind. We must insure that our writers, poets, musicians and artists produce literature and art that is appealing to our people and relates to our revolutionary culture. Our cultural values of life, family, and home will serve as a powerful weapon to defeat the gringo dollar value system and encourage the process of love and brotherhood.

7. Political liberation can only come through an independent action on our part, since the two party system is the same animal with two heads that feeds from the same trough. Where we are a majority we will control; where we are a minority, we will represent a pressure group. Nationally, we will represent one party La Familia de La Raza.

III. PUNTO TERCERO: Action

1. Awareness and distribution of El Plan Espiritual de Aztlan. Presented at every meeting, demonstration, confrontation, courthouse, institution, administration, church, school, tree, building, car, and every place of human existence.

2. September 16th on the birthdate of Mexican Independence, a national walkout by all Chicanos of all colleges and schools to be sustained until the complete revision of the educational system; its policy makers, administration, its curriculum and its personnel to meet the needs of the community.

3. Self defense against the occupying forces of the oppressors at every school, every available man, woman, and child.

4. Community nationalization and organization of all Chicanos re: El Plan Espiritual de Aztlan.

5. Economic programs to drive the exploiter out of our communities and a welding of our peoples combined resources to control their own production through co-operative effort.

6. Creation of an independent local, regional and national political party.

LIBERATION

A nation, autonomously free, culturally, socially, economically and politically will make its own decisions on the usage of our lands, the taxation of our goods, the utilization of our bodies for war, the determination of justice (reward and punishment) and the profit of our sweat.

EL PLAN DE AZTLAN IS THE PLAN OF LIBERATION!

Glossary

Aztlan: Nahuatl word that means "place of the herons," the ancestral home of the Aztec (Mexica) people whose exact location is in dispute; as Chicanos constructed foundational themes, the term came to represent Texas and the Southwest—the Chicano homeland

barrio: Mexican American district, often impoverished, of a city or town

Glossary

campo: field, farmland

carnalismo: a sisterhood or brotherhood; comradeship

Chicano: often used as a synonym for Mexican American, especially one with a socio-political and cultural consciousness; although the meaning of this identity is open to debate, it has a clear origin that dates to the late nineteenth to the early twentieth centuries as a shortening of "mexicano," from the Nahuatl "Mexica" (Aztec)

gabacho: Anglo-Saxon, a white person; often used in a derisive manner

gringo: a term used to describe an English-speaking American

La Raza: literally, "The Race," but commonly recognized to mean "The People"; it celebrates the multiracial heritage of Mexican Americans, which includes Indigenous American, European, African, and Asian ancestry

pueblo: place of birth or residence, one's hometown; the people

ranchero: a person who farms or works on a ranch, particularly in the U.S. Southwest and Mexico

Short-Answer Questions

1. Aztec imagery and the Nahuatl language dominated Chicano iconography during the civil rights movement period and have been part of Mexican American aesthetics ever since. Do the indigenous themes in "El Plan" effectively expound the notion of Chicano indigeneity? Please explain.

2. The concept of Aztlan as the symbolic name for the Southwest was one of the first unifying themes to materialize from "El Plan" and has stirred controversy since. What are some pros and cons associated with the idea of Aztlan as the Chicano homeland?

3. "El Plan" is a manifesto written in the style and sensibility of its time. It is broken up into various sections outlining the overarching goals and themes of the Chicano Movement, which include calls for cultural nationalism, liberation, and collectivism. Does this type of activism still work today? Why or why not?

José Angel Gutiérrez:
"The Thirty-Ninth MAYO Walkout: A Diary"

Author
José Angel Gutiérrez

Date
1969

Document Type
Essays, Reports, Manifestos

Significance
The record of a walkout in which the student participants, with support from their community, managed to have their voices heard and reach negotiations

Overview

José Angel Gutiérrez helped organize the Mexican American Youth Organization (MAYO) because he grew up painfully aware of how society catered to the white population over Hispanics or others. Books, movies, magazine covers and articles, and newspapers all centered overwhelmingly on the white population while largely ignoring those of Hispanic heritage. This was also the case in areas such as education, employment, and medical issues.

Among those Gutiérrez helped were the students in Cristal, Texas, whose needs were blatantly disregarded. The Board of Education did not mask its discriminatory behavior; in fact, board members went out of their way to promote it. Hispanic students were kept from taking part in such things like Homecoming Court, cheerleading, sports, and educational programs. The students were frustrated and helped organize a massive walkout, vowing not to return to school until their needs were met.

Although Gutiérrez did not keep detailed records of all the walkouts he was involved with, he recorded the daily events of the student walkout in Cristal. Notably, before this walkout, the students solicited support from their families and community members before appealing to school officials and eventually escalating into a walkout. In addition, the walkout grew to include middle-school and elementary-school students in addition to high-school students. With MAYO coordinating and organizing, the students managed to have their voice heard and reach negotiations.

Gutiérrez's diary documents the students' daily struggles from December 8, 1969, to January 6, 1970, including their achievements and setbacks. The organizational expertise of both the students and the MAYO leaders is captured in the record, illustrating how this movement not only gained recognition and followers but also left a lasting legacy.

428   The Schlager Anthology of Hispanic America

Document Text

When Chicano students in Texas in the late 1960s began protesting unequal educational opportunity by walking out of school, these protests were called walkouts. . . .

In Cristal, we sought and obtained community support and leadership before urging the students to escalate their protests to a walkout. The principal leaders of the fall of 1969 walkout were the younger siblings and classmates of the seniors who had just graduated in May. The top leadership was Severita Lara, Mario Treviño, and Diana Serna, a junior and two freshmen, respectively.

The first contact . . . was between Severita and the high school principal, John B. Lair. She presented him with a list of grievances that Chicano students wanted addressed. . . . He gave her the runaround and ultimately referred her to the superintendent, John Billings, who passed the buck to the school board. . . .

Severita attempted to get a place on the school board agenda and was unsuccessful. We advised her to print up the grievances on a leaflet and pass it out at the high school. She did and was promptly suspended. . . .

The principal and his assistant . . . had suspended her without a hearing, no due process, and all persons, young and old, citizens or not, rich or poor, are entitled to due process as a constitutional right. . . .

Severita returned to the high school a heroine.

We knew that the board would not accede to the student demands. . . . As anticipated, the school board did not even pretend to listen. . . .

December 8, 1969

The air was tense. The time was eight o'clock. . . .

Outside, the students were there by the hundreds. . . .

We started opening windows for those still outside who were not able to come in or arrived late so they could see and hear. . . .

The President . . . noticed they were completely surrounded by Chicanos. They should have had chairs! . . . Their tactic of making us feel uncomfortable by standing backfired. . . . "This Board has done all it's going to do," he admonished Severita. . . .

December 9, 1969

Around 7:30 a.m. parents and students began congregating. . . . This part of our plan is based on the idea that our boycott should increase in numbers, not decrease. . . .

Empty time is the enemy of a protest. People get bored, scared, anxious, depressed, and the like. You must stay busy. . . . Marches and rallies are perfect examples. So is a newsletter and voter registration. . . .

Severita announced to the Administration trio that they were going to stay away from school until they got what they wanted. . . .

More Marches and rallies are planned for the week. The growing number of students in the walkout are beginning to cause some problems. . . . There isn't much to do.

December 14, 1969

By Sunday, Luz had already gotten parental permission from our student leaders to travel to Washington. . . .

Our community is rapidly polarizing into the Chicano side and the gringo side. . . .

Armando Treviño closed the rally. . . . The need for continued support of the student cause was stressed. He called for getting more students out of classes. . . The entire High School student body of 670 was out by Friday, now we needed to pull out the Junior High kids. . . .

I organized a car caravan to accompany them to the airport. It is a big event in Cristal. To everyone, it appears as if we made Washington listen to us. . . .

The press conference was a calm affair. The reporters were amazed that these children were hustling to Washington to see Senators, Secretaries, and others of rank. Their poise before the press was outstanding. . . .

The single act has generated more favorable publicity than meetings and rallies. The press loves it! . . .

This publicity and general good mood of the Chicano community prompted us to call a vote on pulling out the kids at the elementary grades. . . .

December 22, 1969

Last Tuesday, carloads of our students [were] being sent to Cotulla, Carrizo Springs, Uvalde, Asherton, Eagle Pass for meetings and voter registration. . . . They have gone house to house, block by block, precinct by precinct, registering everybody who was warm and breathing, but only with a Spanish surname. . . .

Voter registration among Chicanos alarms the white community. . . .

December 23, 1969

The letter offering to meet the school board and outlining our conditions for negotiation was typed and hand carried to Eddie Treviño, the only Chicano on the school board. . . .

December 24, 1969

Most of the classes were canceled or closed up early. Volunteers want to go home for their Christmas.

Our students did not attend like they did before. Christmas is in the air. . . .

December 27, 1969

Mario Treviño issued a press statement calling for a statewide boycott of schools. He told the media we **were going to spread the walkout all over Texas.** . . .

The School Board was now letting outside influence dictate their actions! Victory! . . .

January 3, 1970

Saturday's negotiations were tougher than ever. The board got tough. . . . Negotiations were rescheduled for 12:30 p.m. the following day. . . .

In order to apply more pressure to the Board, a petition was circulated that demanded of the School Board that all student demands remaining be accepted on our terms or the boycott would continue. . . .

January 5, 1970

At the evening rally, thousands of people attended. Too many wanted to voice their opinion on the final points of the agreements. . . . Just the thought of having had the walkout and the marches of defiance, to them was victory. Nobody believed we had gotten this far. . . .

The agreement was accepted and signed by our representatives. I felt bad about the agreement. The school board got too much. . . .

The walkout was almost over. . . .

January 6, 1970

The schools shook with activity this morning. . . . The students and our staff met after school to evaluate the day's happenings and to set up our new schedule for picketing at Speer's and Esquivel's. The walkout was over but not for those businesses.

Glossary

grievances: formal complaints

MAYO: Mexican American Youth Organization, a civil rights activist organization

Severita: one of the Hispanic teenagers attending school in Cristal, Texas, and one of the primary spokespeople for the protest

Short-Answer Questions

1. Why was it important for José Angel Gutiérrez to document the walkout in so much detail?

2. Why did the walkout and boycott in Cristal, Texas, gain so much support not only locally but in other cities as well?

3. Compare and contrast the interaction between the school board, teachers, and school administration with the Hispanic students at the beginning of the walkout and at the end. What do you think was a turning point in this interaction? Explain.

Crystal City Walkout Demands

Author Mexican American Youth Organization (MAYO)	**Significance** Outlines the demands of a student walkout and boycott that grew to include neighboring cities
Date 1969	
Document Type Essays, Reports, Manifestos	

Overview

On December 9, 1969, 500 Chicano students in Crystal City, Texas, began a protest in the form of a walkout and boycott. The students were upset over the discriminatory treatment they were receiving at the hands of their local educational system's administration and school board. Although the boycott only lasted a little over a month, ending on January 6, 1970, it had a monumental impact. The fact that the students in Crystal City stuck together in a boycott organized by the Mexican American Youth Organization (MAYO) helped bring awareness to the extreme discrimination the students were forced to undergo daily. In fact, as the number of students increased, eventually numbering more than 2,000, neighboring cities also began to engage in the movement. This brought about the establishment of the La Razo Unida Party, which would broaden the focus of the discrimination Mexican Americans were facing.

José Ángel Gutiérrez and Mario Compean, who helped found MAYO, created the La Razo Unida Party on January 17, 1970. The initial meeting was at Campestre Hall in Crystal City, Texas, and included over 300 attendees. The main purpose of the party was to address the lack of Mexican American representation in both local and county politics. The party existed under a larger umbrella that included other social and political movements targeting education, labor rights, and political rights, including the right to vote.

Document Text

Walkout demands were that all elections concerning the school be conducted by the student body. Concerning class representatives, the petition asked that the qualifications such as personality, leadership, and grades be abolished. These factors do not determine whether the student is capable of representing the student body. The students are capable of voting for their own representatives. The representatives are representing the students, not the faculty. All nominating must be done by the student body, and the election should be decided by a majority vote.

The present method of electing most handsome, beautiful, most popular, and most representative . . . by the faculty . . . is unfair.

National Honor Society—the grades of the students eligible must be posted on the bulletin board well in advance of selection. The teachers should not have anything to do with electing the students.

No other favorites should be authorized by school administrators or board members unless submitted to the student body in a referendum.

An advisory board of Mexican American citizens should be a part of the school administration in order to advise on the needs and problems of the Mexican American.

Teachers, administrators, and staff should be educated; they should know our language—Spanish—and understand the history, traditions, and contributions of Mexican culture. How can they expect to teach us if they do not know us? We want more Mexican American teachers for the above reason.

We want immediate steps taken to implement bilingual and bicultural education for Mexican Americans. We also want the schoolbooks revised to reflect the contributions of Mexicans and Mexican Americans to the U.S. society, and to make us aware of the injustices that we, Mexican Americans, as a people have suffered in an "Anglo"-dominant society. . . .

We want any member of the school system who displays prejudice or fails to recognize, understand, and appreciate us Mexican Americans, our culture, or our heritage removed from Crystal City's schools. Teachers shall not call students any names.

Our classes should be smaller in size, say about twenty students to one teacher, to insure more effectiveness. We want parents from the community to be trained as teachers' aides. We want assurances that a teacher who may disagree politically or philosophically with administrators will not be dismissed or transferred because of it. Teachers should encourage students to study and should make class more interesting, so that students will look forward to going to class.

There should be a manager in charge of janitorial work and maintenance details, and the performance of such duties should be restricted to employees hired for that purpose. . . . No more students doing janitorial work.

We want a free speech area plus the right to have speakers of our own.

We would like September 16 as a holiday. . . . We feel it is a great day in the history of the world because it is when Mexico had been under the Spanish rule for about 300 years. The Mexicans were liberated from the harsh rule of Spain. Our ancestors fought in this war, and we owe them tribute because we are Mexicans, too. . . .

Being civic-minded citizens, we want to know what the happenings are in our community. So, we request the right to have access to all types of literature and to be able to bring it on campus. The newspaper in our school does not carry sufficient information. It carries things like the gossip column, which is unnecessary.

The dress code should be abolished. . . .

We want Mr. Harbin to resign as Principal of Fly Jr. High.

We want a Mexican American counselor. . . .

We need more showers in the boys' and girls' dressing rooms.

Glossary

Anglo: a white, English-speaking American

civic: relating to a city or town, especially its administration

heritage: inherited traditions, monuments, objects, or culture

---

Short-Answer Questions

1. In your own words, describe three main issues the students wanted the education officials to resolve.

2. Explain why the students would have addressed the following issues specifically: "The dress code should be abolished. . . . We want Mr. Harbin to resign as principal of Fly Jr. High School. . . . We want a Mexican American counselor."

3. Although there has been a lot of attention on student protests during the Vietnam War years, there has not been much recognition about the protest in Crystal City, Texas. Why do you think this protest received so little recognition?

El Plan de Santa Barbara:
A Chicano Plan for Higher Education

Author
Chicano Coordinating Council of Higher Education

Date
1969

Document Type
Essays, Reports, Manifestos

Significance
A radical plan to address blatant discrimination against Hispanics in higher education, encompassing educational support programs, political changes, and continued research

Overview

El Plan de Santa Barbara: A Chicano Plan for Higher Education was written in 1969 by the Chicano Coordinating Council of Higher Education. The original document was 155 pages outlining in great detail the importance of Chicano studies in universities and other institutions throughout the United States. The meeting place was the University of California, Santa Barbara.

The plan specifies that opportunities for higher learning need to exist for the Hispanic community, and it suggests that these opportunities, while increasing, were few and far between. There was simply not enough being done to ensure that Hispanic students had higher learning opportunities or that students continued and

completed programs to achieve their degree. The plan asserted that there needed to be more Chicano community involvement and that political independence was necessary for Hispanic students to be successful.

The plan arose from the Chicano Coordinating Council of Higher Education's conviction that for true equality to be achieved, the Hispanic community needed access to opportunities to advance their education and achieve political independence. Having a voice in education and politics was necessary to avoid the need for assimilation to be the only course of action for coexistence in society. Chicanos did not want to lose their cultural identity, according to the council, but rather maintain it.

El Plan de Santa Barbara: A Chicano Plan for Higher Education

Document Text

Manifesto

For all people, as with individuals, the time comes when they must reckon with their history. For the Chicano the present is a time of renaissance, of renacimiento. . . .

For decades Mexican people in the United States struggled to realize the "American Dream." And some—a few—have. But the cost, the ultimate cost of assimilation, required turning away from el barrio and la colonia. . . .

As a result, the self-determination of our community is now the only acceptable mandate for social and political action; it is the essence of the Chicano commitment. . . . Chicanismo simply embodies an ancient truth: that man is never closer to his true self as when he is close to his community. . . .

For these reasons Chicano Studies represent the total conceptualization of the Chicano community's aspirations that involve higher education. To meet these ends, the university and college systems of the State of California must act in the following basic areas:

1) admission and recruitment of Chicano students, faculty, administrators and staff,

2) a curriculum program and an academic major relevant to the Chicano cultural and historical experience,

3) support and tutorial programs,

4) research programs,

5) publications programs,

6) community cultural and social action centers.

We insist that Chicano students, faculty, administrators, employees, and the community must be the central and decisive designers and administrators of those programs. . . .

Organizing and Instituting Chicano Programs On-Campus

The institutionalization of Chicano programs is the realization of Chicano power on campus. . . . The point is not to have a college with a program, but rather a Chicano program at that college. . . .

But old patterns may persist, and the anglo may move to deny and limit Chicanos, and there will be 'Mexican-Americans' to serve him. . . .

The premises for Chicano programs are: that the colleges/universities must be a major instrument in the liberation of the Chicano community: colleges/universities have a threefold responsibility: education, research, and public service to the Chicano community; only by comprehensive programs instituted and implemented by Chicanos, for Chicanos that focus on the needs and goals of the community will the larger purposes of the academic institutions and the interests of the Chicano community be served. . . .

Proposals

Proposals for centers, institutions, schools, colleges, etc., include the following: introduction, statement of justification, precedents, purposes, specific focus, components, administrative design, anticipated effect on current structure of college or university, relationship to existing programs and structures, number and criteria for staff, participating students, necessary research resources, physical plant, timetable for implementation, project budget, and regulatory changes. . . .

Recruitment and Admissions

Scope of Recruitment

Institutions of higher education must accept fundamental responsibility for recruiting Chicanos who will enroll as students or work as faculty, staff, or employees. . . .

In the final analysis, recruitment activities in institutions of higher education must contribute to the recruitment process by bringing their resources to bear on the deplorable conditions affecting Chicanos today in the elementary and secondary schools and in the junior or community colleges. . . .

Effective recruitment of Chicanos—students, faculty, staff, and employees—cannot take place unless and until there is a satisfactory relationship between recruitment programs on the one hand and hiring and admissions criteria and decision-making on the other. . . .

Support Programs

Goals of Support Programs

As a significantly larger number of Chicanos enter colleges and universities support programs are a crucial factor in determining whether the accessibility of higher education will mean a consolidating of educational gains by the Chicano movement. . . .

Support programs should be developed to encompass and achieve these goals. This focus of Chicano support programs requires the development of new structures and processes which are not currently found in traditional structures in higher education. . . .

Orientation Program

In the past, higher education has failed to encourage Chicanos; it manifests itself as a hostile environment. . . .

SUGGESTIONS: The Joint Committee on Higher Education Preliminary Outline . . . has shown that students who are eligible for higher education do not enter a college or university because of in-

sufficient financial support. . . . Financial assistance packages must be guaranteed from the student's first year to his last. . . .

Curriculum

A Chicano Studies curriculum organizes the Chicano experience, past and present, in accordance with established cultural categories. . . . Chicano Studies seek to socialize the Chicano student by providing him with the intellectual tools necessary for him to deal with the reality of his experience. . . .

A Chicano Studies curriculum should be open to students on campus. . . . The goal for Chicano Studies is to provide a coherent and socially relevant education, humanistic and pragmatic which prepares Chicanos for service to the Chicano community and enriches the total society. . . .

Political Action

Political action encompasses three elements which function in a progression: political consciousness, political mobilization and tactics. . . .

Concrete results are visible in both the increased number of Chicano students on campuses and the establishment of corresponding supportive services. The institutionalization of Chicano Studies marks the present stage of activity; the next stage will involve the strategic application of university and college resources to the community. . . .

Political Mobilization

Political mobilization is directly dependent on political consciousness. As political consciousness develops, the potential for political action increases. . . .

Campus Organizing Notes of MECHA

Introduction

MECHA is a first step to tying the student groups throughout the Southwest into a vibrant and re-

---

El Plan de Santa Barbara: A Chicano Plan for Higher Education   437

sponsive network. . . . It is the function of ME-CHA to further socialization and politicization for liberation on all campuses. . . . .

Recruitment and Education

Action is the best organizer. . . .

The best educational device is being in the Barrio as often as possible. . . .

Planning and Strategy

Actions of the group must be co-ordinated in such a way that everyone knows exact-ly what he is supposed to do. . . . A student group is more effective if it can claim the support of community and support on the campus itself from other sectors than the student population. . . .

Function of MECHA—Education

It is a fact the Chicano has not often enough written his own history, his own anthropology, his own sociology, his own literature. He must do this if he is to survive as a cultural entity in this melting pot society which seeks to dilute varied cultures into a grey upon grey pseudo-culture of technology and materialism. . . .

Glossary

chicanismo: pride in one's heritage as a Mexican American

Chicano: an American of Mexican descent or origin

institutionalization: the process by which programs are conceived, structured, enacted, and continued

MECHA: Movimiento Estudiantil Chicano de Aztlán, or Chicano Student Movement of Aztlán; a political action organization

socioeconomic: relating to or concerned with the interaction of social and economic factors

Short-Answer Questions

1. Why would the Chicano Coordinating Council of Higher Learning have specified that members of the Chicano community needed to be more involved with institutions of higher learning for Chicano students to be successful?

2. List and discuss at least three specific things the Chicano Coordinating Council of Higher Learning suggested needed to be in place to help Chicano students. What is the importance of these items?

3. It was mentioned several times that the specific needs of the Chicano people needed to be addressed. Does this include assimilation? Why or why not? Support your response with excerpts from the document.

Rodolfo "Corky" Gonzales: Arizona State University Speech

Author Rodolfo "Corky" Gonzales **Date** 1970 **Document Type** Speeches/Addresses; Essays, Reports, Manifestos	**Significance** An excellent example of the motivations and aims for the Chicano movement

Overview

The Chicano rights movement shared goals and concerns with the more prominent African American civil rights movement. However, Chicanos were equally concerned with citizenship and land rights as with discrimination, segregation, and denial of other civil rights.

Because of his successful career as a professional featherweight boxer, Rodolfo "Corky" Gonzales (1928–2005) was an immediately popular political voice in the Chicano movement when he turned to politics in the mid-1960s. His Crusade for Justice focused on the concept that the community should have control of the service institutions—such as schools, parks, communi-

ty centers, and libraries—of government as a way to guide the cultural, political, and economic rights of the community. This community, or "La Raza," became a crucial component in the growing Chicano movement. Gonzales saw the Chicano movement, based loosely on the writings of Mexican philosopher José Vasconcelos (1882–1959), as an organizing and unifying activism to unite Chicanos of all classes and educational levels to realize a Pan-American Chicano nation. In Gonzales's speech at Arizona State University, Gonzales is attempting to retain Chicano talent in Chicano communities, inspire self-reliance inside Chicano communities, and encourage a self-identification of wealthier and more educated Mexican Americans as Chicanos.

Document Text

This is probably the first time I've spoken in Arizona, at a university. It pleases me to hear that the young leadership . . . are taking an active part. They are active not only in the university but down in the community. And that is important.

Our youth's minds . . . should not be suppressed in these universities. In the past most of our youth only went to high school. . . . It's important to know that you have to not just evaporate or disappear after you get out of the college scene. College is not the launching pad out of the community. We want to see our youth come back to the community, but not on the basis of some of the lawyers that we have or some of the professional people.
. . .

You see, the reason we have problems, is because too many people do not want to get involved. . . . So, never fear that because you are involved, you're isolated from your people. Actually, you are going to be the leadership that draws your people together. It is important that our young people bring back their expertise, their professionalism, their degrees, their humanity, and their compassion, back home where it belongs, to the community.

As long as we cross that bridge and disappear, our people will be on the lowest ladder of educational attainment. . . . They'll have the highest rate of unemployment. . . . They will have the biggest social and economic problems of any other group of people, because some people said that they don't count and that they don't have to get involved. . . .

We say these are all the problems, and we say that's all right. How do these problems come to rest on our backs? How do these problems develop on a total mass of people, not on individuals? It is because the educational system teaches you that you can make it as long as you conform to society. . . . There is one fact they do not want to admit. They do not want to admit that we have a different set of

values. . . . It is that we have a cultural difference. This is why the educational system does not want to teach you that the very government that you support in wars in Vietnam and Korea and other areas, the very government you're talking about, is the same government that committed genocide against the Indian, took over his land, and controls his money. . . .

So what do we have to do with ourselves? We have to start to organize ourselves around ourselves. We have to stop going to human relations conferences to educate the gringo on how to like us. . . .

We are "La Raza Cósmica." We are the only integrated people on these two continents. We're not a minority. We're a majority, when you stretch us from here to Mexico to Peru. When we start to think on those levels, when we start to teach in the barrio how we are a colonized people, then we're able to understand how we live in this country and how this economy is based on the farm workers' struggle and the farm workers' production. Our people still use their hands in a society that is the most advanced technologically in the whole world.

When we can understand this concept, we can teach in the barrio. You are not going to teach it with radical statements, but you can teach it with grassroots, positive, simple-to-understand reasoning. . . .

We are a family and we deny it. We say, and we preach, that the biggest organizing tool that we have is nationalism. . . . That's why we're saying that's not reverse racism. That's "La Familia." First we must take care of our family. Nationalism is a tool . . . not a weapon for hatred. Nationalism is a state of being a nation, not a state of creating an outside group that hates another group. . . .

We have to realize that we have a political philosophy. We don't care for *políticos* because many of our politicians in the past that we have supported have not done anything. . . . We wanted progress. We wanted social changes, and they would not give them to us. They wanted *vendidos*, and they wanted window dressing. . . . They have to sell out or they cannot keep their positions. They have to condone the actions of the administration or they have to sacrifice their positions. . . .

No, we want to put into the heart and mind of every Mexicano that when one Mexicano is poor, we are all poor. If one is in jail, we are all in jail. If one of us has a bad education, we are all badly educated. If one of us has a problem, we all have a problem. We must understand that when they put one of our people up against the wall, that everybody needs to come up to see what's wrong. The masses will make the difference. . . .

Now we have to look at the fact that we have survived as a people because our parents survived. That is why we are here. We have survived as a people because our parents survived racism a hundred times as heavy as what we face. They survived labor ten times harder than any of us will ever work. They survived these problems and, in doing so, they had to withdraw. They withdrew and protected their families, and in some cases they put some of the young people in a cocoon. Their children later had to come to Chicano studies and colleges to find out they were Chicanos. You don't have to go into the barrio or the *campos* to tell our people they are Chicanos, but you do have to tell middle-class youth they are Chicanos.

We understand that part of it. Now we have to teach ourselves that the whole world is at our back door, our back yard. We need to go out there and decide what we're going to do with our lives. Nobody is going to decide for us.

Glossary

barrio: neighborhood; commonly an ethnic enclave of low-quality housing

campos: an agricultural field

gringo: a non-Latin American; generally a derogatory term for a non-Spanish speaking Anglo-American.

"La Familia": literally "the family," but in this context implying communities of association through a common heritage

La Raza Cósmica: a reference to a concept from the Mexican philosopher José Vasconcelos that a "fifth race" would rise in the Americas that did not observe skin color as a necessary component of belonging and would found a new civilization built on this "cosmic race"

políticos: politicians

vendidos: negotiators to obtain an object, price, or equivalent

Short-Answer Questions

1. In your interpretation of Gonzales's argument, is there a place for non-Chicanos to positively support the movement? Why or why not?

2. Describe Gonzales's argument concerning "La Familia." Is it convincing to you? Why or why not?

3. What does Gonzales see as a significant drawback to the survival mechanisms of Chicano elders? Why does he say this is a drawback?

Mexican American Marines in Vietnam

Author
U.S. Marine Corps

Date
c. 1970–72

Document Type
Cartoons, Images, Artwork

Significance
A picture of Mexican American Marines from the Vietnam War, a conflict that divided the Hispanic community but helped fuel the Chicano movement

---

Overview

The Vietnam War (1955–74) was one of the most divisive conflicts in U.S. history. Large numbers of Hispanics served in the U.S. military during the war, which became increasingly unpopular the longer it lasted. The United States first deployed troops to Vietnam in November 1955 in an effort to prevent communist North Vietnam from taking over South Vietnam. The number of soldiers increased to a peak of more than 500,000 in 1969 as the United States struggled to find a way to win the war. More than 58,000 Americans were killed in the war, with over 300,000 wounded. Estimates are that 3,070 Hispanics were killed during the conflict, or about 5.2 percent of the total killed.

More than 170,000 Hispanics served in the U.S. military during the Vietnam War. Some were drafted, while most volunteered: approximately 70 percent of Hispanics who served during the war were volunteers. Hispanics volunteered for the military out of patriotism, to gain skills, or simply to have a job. Some Hispanics joined the military, which allowed non-citizens to serve, as a way to gain citizenship. Twenty-two Hispanic members of the U.S. military won the medal of honor, the nation's highest award for bravery, during the war.

The Vietnam War was highly unpopular among Americans for a variety of reasons. Some believed the conflict was a form of colonialism, and others opposed the way the conflict was fought. Still others objected to the loss of life among U.S. service personnel, the draft, or the cost of the war. By the late 1960s, a growing number of Americans distrusted the government's management of the war.

Among Hispanic Americans, opposition to the war was tied to disapproval of colonialism and a sense that the country saw young Latinos as expendable. Many opponents of the war also argued that the nation should focus on domestic social justice issues instead of foreign wars. Hispanic opposition to the conflict peaked with the Chicano Moratorium, a group of activists that organized anti-war protests, including a 30,000-person march in Los Angeles on August 29, 1970.

Document Image

Mexican American Marines in Vietnam (USMC Archives)

Short-Answer Questions

1. Why did the United States become involved in the Vietnam War? Why did the war last so long?

2. What were the various reasons that Hispanics volunteered for the U.S. military during the Vietnam War?

3. Why was the Vietnam War so unpopular? Why did many Hispanic Americans oppose it?

Luis Valdez:
"Pensamiento Serpentino: A Chicano Approach to the Theater of Reality"

Author
Luis Valdez

Date
1973 (original), 1990

Document Type
Poems, Plays, Fiction

Significance
The poem deals with the Chicano experience in the United States and introduces pre-contact Indigenous culture as a context for social justice and a model for a spiritual vision

Overview

The poem "Pensamiento Serpentino" (Serpentine Thought) by the playwright Luis Valdez is a classic in the field of Chicano literature. Originally published in 1973 and composed in mixed English and Spanish, it stands as one of the most influential works to emerge from the genre. Conceived as an ode to Chicano indigeneity, some of its themes, such as "Hunab Ku" ("One God"; monotheism) and "In lak'ech" ("you are my other me"), transcend cultural boundaries and have become part of popular New Age consciousness. Valdez's ideas about Chicano Indianness were inspired by the Mexican scholar Domingo Martinez Paredes, a native Maya speaker and part of Mexico City's *neo-indigenismo* movement.

Valdez was at the forefront of Chicano theater when he founded El Teatro Campesino, a California theater company, in 1965 to support the United Farm Workers union headed by César Chávez. The theater emerged from the oral tradition and represented Mexican and Chicano farmworkers who suffered exploitation as agricultural workers in the United States. The dramatic style used by the Teatro was the *Acto*, a short improvisational piece whose purpose was to explain events that had real and historical basis through a populist lens. According to Valdez, the objective was to motivate the public to social action by employing parody, humor, and satire. Actos incorporated dance, music, songs, characters, and motifs from Mexican popular culture as an expression of the Chicano experience. Thus, the themes presented through the theatrical acts made it possible for Chicanos to identify as an ethnic minority in the United States. In this context, the long poem "Pensamiento Serpentino" serves to unravel indigeneity, the Spanish invasion, *mestizaje* (people of mixed race), the Mexican Revolution of 1910, the Catholic Church, and popular folklore. In sum, Valdez's work taps into the ethnic consciousness of Chicanos, challenges U.S. cultural imperialism, and articulates the notion that indigenous culture is more advanced than that of the European colonizer.

In Lak'ech, *a Mayan concept, is a theme in the poem.* (Flickrs)

Document Text

Teatro

eres el mundo
y las paredes de los
buildings más grandes
son

nothing but scenery.

The dialogue
de esta gran pantomima
de la tierra
is written in English
en German
en Francaise
in Spanish
in Italiano
en Tagalog

It is a giant improvisation
con role-playing
by men and women
y las razas del mundo
playing master and slave
rich and poor

black and white

pero underneath it all
is the truth
the Spiritual Truth
that determines all materia

la energía that creates the
universe
la fuerza con purpose
la primera cause de todo
even before the huelga
la First Cause de Creation

Dios

El Director de la Great Force
o Gran Tragedia
depending on your predelection

Los indios knew of this
long ago
hace muchos años que cantaban
en su flor y canto
de las verdades
CIENTIFICAS Y RELIGIOSAS

del mundo

Sin embargo
However

We were conquistados
and COLONIZADOS
and we (de la raza de bronce)
began to think we were EUROPEOS
and that their vision of reality
was
IT.

But REALITY es una Gran Serpiente
a great serpent
that moves and changes

and keeps crawling
out of its
dead skin

despojando su pellejo viejo
to emerge
clean and fresh
la nueva realidad nace
de la realidad vieja

And so
los oprimidos del mundo
continue to become
los liberadores

in the true progress of cosas

and the Chicano is part of the
process

el proceso cósmico that will
LIBERATE OUR CONQUISTADORES
or their descendents

así es que el gachupín y el gabacho
will be Mexicanized

but first el CHICANO must Mexicanize
himself
para no caer en cultural trampas

and that means that

not Thomas Jefferson nor Karl Marx
will LIBERATE the Chicano
not Mahatma Ghandi nor Mao Tze Tung
IF HE IS NOT LIBERATED FIRST BY
HIS PROPIO PUEBLO
BY HIS POPOL VUH
HIS CHILAM BALAM
HIS CHICHEN ITZA
KUKULCAN, GUCUMATZ, QUETZAL-
COATL.

Y qué lindo es estudiar
lo de su pueblo de uno

We must all become NEO-MAYAS
Porque los Mayas
really had it together

DIOS
Hunab Ku
El único dador de la medida
y EL MOVIMIENTO
was a mathematically moral
concept of the supreme being
EL SEÑOR DE LOS ASTROS.

RELIGION and SCIENCE were
una sola cosa
para los mayas de la antigüidad

just look at their moral concept
IN LAK'ECH: *Tú Eres Mi Otro Yo*

which they derived from
studying the sun spots.

Their communal life
was not based on intellectual
agreement
it was based on a vision
of los cosmos
porque el hombre pertenecía
a las estrellas

Así es que the Christian
concept of Love Thy Neighbor
as Thyself was engrained into
their daily behavior

they wouldn't think of
acting any other way

Because you that read this
are me
and I who write this am you
and I wish you well wherever
you are
Que Dios camine contigo.

IN LAK'ECH: Si te amo y te respeto

Luis Valdez: "Pensamiento Serpentino: A Chicano Approach to the
Theater of Reality"

a ti, me amo y me respeto yo;
si te hago daño a ti, me hago daño a mí.

That, carnales, was LEY AND ORDER
whatever I do to you
I do to myself

Even the United States
of America will someday learn
that it cannot bomb Hanoi
without inflicting violence on itself

And neither can YOU
insult a brother
do violence to a sister
Hate somebody
without that ODIO
coming back to you
somewhere
sometime
en alguna forma

Porque ésa es THE LAW
the scientific and religious
LEY of the universe.

To be CHICANO is not (NOT)
to hate the gabacho or the
gachupín or even the pobre
vendido . . .

To be CHICANO is to love yourself
your culture, your
skin, your language

And once you become CHICANO
that way
you begin to love other people
otras razas del mundo
los vietnamitas
los argentinos
los colombianos
and, yes, even los europeos
because they need us more
than we need them.

But, above all
to be CHICANO is to LOVE GOD.
For I have never read a single
poem by an Azteca, Tolteca, Maya
or Yaqui ATHEIST

Todos los indios creen en Dios.

In order to fully
EVOLVE
(evolucionar con la
serpiente)
the Chicano Movement
must
MOVE
con el MOVEMENT
of the Cosmos
with the NAHUI OLLIN
el quinto sol,
SOL DE MOVIMIENTO

It must move with the
EARTH, LA TIERRA,
It must move with the
MORNING STAR, VENUS
Quetzalcóatl, Jesucristo
it must move with GOD.

RELIGION (re-ligion)
is nothing more than the
tying back
RE-LIGARE
with the cosmic center

As Chicanos
As Neo Mayas
we must re-identify
with that center and proceed
outward with love and strength
AMOR Y FUERZA
and undying dedication to justice

Justice between man and woman
Justice between man and nature
Justice between man and god.

They all happen at once.

Jesucristo is Quetzalcoatl
The colonization is over
La Virgen de Guadalupe is Tonantzín
The suffering is over
The universe is Aztlán
The revolution is now.

European concepts of reality
ya no soplan.
Reason alone no es todo el cuento
El indio baila
He DANCES his way to truth

in a way INTELLECTUALS will
never understand

El Corazón
(YOLLO en nahuatl-*movimiento*)
feels a reality the mind
the human mind
cannot grasp.

EL ESPIRITU
the spirit
is stronger than
flesh and bone and stone
and death.

Glossary

Chichen Itza: pre-Columbian Mayan city that features a pyramid and other structures

Chilam Balam: books of Mayan wisdom, history, folklore, information, and miscellany, compiled in the seventeenth and eighteenth centuries

cultural imperialism: the imposition of a dominant nation's culture onto a nondominant nation through physical or economic colonization and the export of cultural products

indigeneity: the state, quality, or condition inherent to a people, or individual, that characterizes their position as original inhabitants to a given land or region

mestizaje: refers to the racial, cultural, and religious mixture produced from Spanish colonization that regulated caste structures to keep racialized hierarchies based on purity of blood and origin

neo-indigenismo: a cultural, spiritual, literary, and artistic movement of the middle to late twentieth century among Mexicans and Chicanos that promoted a revitalized indigenous consciousness

Popol Vuh: a sacred Mayan text

Tú Eres Mi Otro Yo: "you are my other me"; a Mayan philosophical concept

Luis Valdez: "Pensamiento Serpentino: A Chicano Approach to the Theater of Reality"

Short-Answer Questions

1. In "Pensamiento Serpentino," Valdez explores the tension between modernity and traditional Indigenous ways as he understands them. What are some of the distinctions and similarities he makes between these two worldviews and interpretations of reality?

2. The poem touches on sensitive notions of culture, spirituality, and identity, which were prevalent themes of Chicano discourse of the 1960s and 1970s. Do these ideas still resonate today as they did during the heyday of the Chicano movement? Why, or why not?

3. In many Mesoamerican Indigenous cultures, the serpent is a common symbol that is often associated with the earth and rebirth. What is the significance of Valdez titling the poem "Pensamiento Serpentino" (Serpentine Thought) in relation to the emergent Chicano politics of the time?

Sandra María Esteves:
"Blanket Weaver"

Author
Sandra María Esteves

Date
1975

Document Type
Poems, Plays, Fiction

Significance
An example of Nuyorican poetry that conveys the struggles and strength of Puerto Ricans

Overview

Sandra María Esteves is one of the founders of the Nuyorican poetry movement, which showcases artists who are Puerto Rican and living in New York City. Talented as a poet, playwright, and essayist, Estevez draws on her role as a cultural activist for her material. Beginning in the early 1970s, her poems have been chosen for anthologies centered on the experiences of the Hispanic community. Much as Martin Luther King Jr. taught that nonviolent protest through civil disobedience was more effective than violence, Esteves firmly believes that creative outlets such as writing and drawing are a superior alternative to physical acts of protest. She emphasizes individual growth and learning as the key to tolerance and peace among people from various ethnicities.

Document Text

weaver
weave us a song of many threads

weave us a red of fire and blood
that taste of sweet plum
fishing around the memories of the dead
following a scent wounded
our spines bleeding with pain

weave us a red of passion
that beats wings against a smoky cloud
and forces motion into our lungs

weave us a song
of yellow and gold and life itself
that lights a way through wild growth

Nuyorican Poets Cafe in New York (Wikimedia Commons)

burned in pain
aged with steady conviction
with bunions callouses and leathered hides

weave us into the great magnetic center
pulling your fingers into topaz canyons
a single lonely web glitters like a flash of thunder
your thumb feeling into my womb
placing sweat seeds of floral honey
into continuous universal suspension

weave us a song of red and yellow
and brown
that holds the sea and the sky in its skin
that holds the bird and mountain in its voice
that builds upon our graves
a home for injustice fear oppression abuse and disgrace
and upon these fortifications
of strength unity and direction

weave us a song to hold us
when the wind blows so cold to make our children wail
submerged in furious ice
a song pure and raw
that burns paper
and attacks the colorless venom stalking hidden
in the petal soft sweetness of the black night

weave us a rich round black that lives
in the eyes of our warrior child
and feeds our mouths with moon breezes
with rhythms interflowing
through all spaces of existence
a black that holds the movement of eternity

weave us a song for our bodies to sing

weave us a song of many threads
that will dance with the colors of our people
and cover us with the warmth of peace

Glossary

bunion: a bony bump that forms on the joint at the base of the big toe

fortifications: a defensive wall or other reinforcement built to strengthen a place against attack

oppression: prolonged cruel or unjust treatment or control

topaz: silicate mineral of aluminum and fluorine that is used as a gemstone in jewelry

Short-Answer Questions

1. What is Sandra María Esteves's purpose in reiterating the word "weave" throughout her poem? Choose two stanzas in which "weave" is used and analyze what Esteves is trying to convey to her audience.

2. Would you describe the writer's overall tone as optimistic or pessimistic? Explain your answer. Include excerpts from the poem to add credibility to your response.

3. Sandra María Esteves is known for her creativity and strong use of wordplay in her works. Choose two lines from her poem and analyze the vivid imagery she creates.

Chapter 11

"The Decade of the Hispanic" and Hispanic Politics in the 1980s

The 1980s represented a significant change for Hispanics in America, largely due to the geo-political events happening around the Western Hemisphere. Much of America's knowledge of Latino culture had been centered around the Mexican American experience in the previous century. However, with events happening in Latin American countries in the 1960s and proliferating in the 1980s, leading to the redefining of America's Hispanic population from just "Mexican" to "Latino" and ultimately, "Latino/x," the narrative began to change. The marked shift in geopolitics would also substantially shift the narrative about Latino immigration to the United States and make it a deeply contested topic coming into and out of the 1980. Immigration offered great opportunities for those coming to the United States from Latin American nations, but it also became a deeply divisive force in American society and politics.

Cuban Immigration to South Florida

The American effort to depose the Cuban government of Fidel Castro in 1961 had far-reaching consequences for Hispanics in the United States, particularly after Cas-tro aligned himself closely with the Soviet Union. The Cuban Missile Crisis of 1962 resulted in a decades-long embargo by the United States and many of her western allies that crippled the Cuban economy and led many to flee the small island nation. With Cuba only ninety miles from Florida, the United States was a natural destination for many of these migrants. They largely found their way to South Florida, particularly Miami, but they faced a problem: America's de-facto war with communism made it impossible for these immigrants to find work, as the economic and political sanctions against Cuba prevented the issuance of work visas, or "green cards." Despite these limitations, the United States was still confronted with a large number of Cuban refugees and a potential human rights disaster if it failed to act. So in 1966, Congress passed the Cuban Adjustment Act, which allowed immigrants to apply for a visa once they were in the United States for a period of time and could prove their Cuban citizenship (a difficult task for many given the lack of records in many rural parts of the country). This event marked the beginning of a demographic shift of Spanish Americans (Latinos) in the United States.

Throughout the 1970s and early 1980s, Latin America was plagued by a number of oppressive regimes and despots coupled with violent revolutions and uprisings that left much of the region without economic and social stability. Much like Cuba, nations like Nicaragua, El Salvador, and Honduras saw large numbers of their citizens journey to the United States in the hope of finding more economic and social opportunity than they would have in their home countries. Hispanic communities were no longer comprised of just Mexicans but rather of individuals from a multitude of nationalities. Despite their cultural differences, they shared a common language. This made Hispanics an increasingly powerful voice in politics, and presidents began to specifically address the concerns of those communities across the United States, particularly in the southwest.

Legislative Protection for Hispanic Americans

President Gerald Ford took the first steps in 1974 by signing an amendment to the 1965 Voting Rights Act that granted protections to those who didn't speak English as their primary language. Though the act represented a first step towards granting many Spanish-speakers an increasing opportunity to be represented in politics, they still lacked the fundamental economic and social opportunities needed to improve their status. Many businesses still refused to hire those who were not born in the United States, even if they were legally allowed to work. This lack of equity led to President Ronald Reagan signing the Immigration Reform and Control Act (IRCA) in 1986, which barred hiring practices that discriminated against an individual solely based on their place of birth. The IRCA also extended opportunities for migrant workers in the United States to gain lawful work status even if they had been here without documentation previously (a lesson he undoubtedly learned from the Delano grape workers' strike of the late 1960s, when he was governor of California). While

this law extended new opportunities and protections for Hispanic workers in the United States, it also stiffened penalties for businesses that hired undocumented workers and increased efforts to detain and repatriate those who were in the United States without proper authorization. Throughout the 1980s, many Hispanic Americans suddenly found themselves subject to the new ethnic slur of "illegal" regardless of their birthright or national origin. This discrimination in turn renewed the pressures of the Chicano movement to create a more powerful identity among the Mexican American community. It also unearthed hostilities within various Hispanic communities who now blamed the new immigrants for these issues.

The "Decade of the Hispanic"

Despite these challenges, the Hispanic population continued to boom in the United States during the 1970s, 1980s, and beyond. This increased pressure on businesses to also tailor their marketing towards the Hispanic community, something that ran counter to many of the traditional assimilation expectations that had dominated the Mexican American experience of the early twentieth century. In an article about the increasing numbers of Latino appointees during Jimmy Carter's presidency, *U.S. News and World Report* used Cuban American Maria Elena Torano's phrase "Decade of the Hispanic" to describe the ascent of Hispanic culture and its influence, and businesses likewise took notice. Coors Brewing ran a campaign in Los Angeles that coined itself the "beer for the Decade of the Hispanic" in the hopes of tapping into a market it now saw as a significant economic force. Latino music, film, and literature found itself absorbed into the American popular culture rather than lost in it. No longer was the expectation to conform to a white identity. Rather, it was acceptable for Latinos to be proud of their heritage and culture.

Further Reading

Books

Lovato, Roberto. *Unforgetting: A Memoir of Family, Migration, Gangs, and Revolution in the Americas.* New York: Harper, 2020.

Worth, Richard. *The 1970s to the 1980s (Hispanic America).* Tarrytown, NY: Marshall Cavendish Benchmark, 2009.

Articles

Del Olmo, Frank. "Latino 'Decade' Moves Into '90s." *Los Angeles Times*, December 14, 1989.

Massey, Douglas S., and Kathleen M. Schnabel. "Recent Trends in Hispanic Immigration to the United States." *International Migration Review* 17, no. 2 (1983): 212–44.

Parrado, Emilio A., and William A. Kandel. "Hispanic Population Growth and Rural Income Inequality." *Social Forces* 88, no. 3 (2010): 1421–50.

Websites

"Green Card for a Cuban Native or Citizen." USCIS website, June 16, 2020, https://www.uscis.gov/green-card/green-card-eligibility/green-card-for-a-cuban-native-or-citizen.

Torres, Arnoldo, "The Struggle of the Hispanics." *Chicago Tribune* website, August 9, 2021, https://www.chicagotribune.com/news/ct-xpm-1985-07-02-8502120853-story.html.

Cuban Adjustment Act

Author
U.S. Government

Date
1966

Document Type
Legislative

Significance
Allowed Cuban natives or citizens living in the United States to become lawful permanent residents

Overview

To combat communism abroad, the United States not only lent support for democratic struggles abroad but became more welcoming to groups and regions that were anti-communist and believed in the virtues of democracy. On the heels of the Immigration Act of 1965, which removed discrimination measures against Southern and Eastern Europeans, Asians, and other non–Western and Northern European ethnic groups, the Cuban Adjustment Act made permanent residency easier for Cubans. Drawing on the long, shared history of the United States and Cuba, President Lyndon Johnson supported Cuban exiles escaping Castro's regime. The Cuban Adjustment Act was a foreign policy measure intended to promote the tenets of U.S. democracy in the face of communist aggression.

Document Text

Be it enacted by the Senate and House of Representatives of the United States of America in Congress assembled. That, notwithstanding the provisions of section 245(c) of the Immigration and Nationality Act, the status of any alien who is a native or citizen of Cuba and who has been inspected and admitted or paroled into the United States subsequent to January 1, 1959 and has been physically present in the United States for at least two years, may be adjusted by the Attorney General, in his discretion and under such regulations as he may prescribe, to that of an alien lawfully admitted for permanent residence if the alien makes an application for such adjustment, and the alien is eligible to receive an immigrant visa and is admissible to the United

President Johnson signed the Cuban Adjustment Act.
(Yoichi Okamoto)

States for permanent residence. Upon approval of such an application for adjustment of status, the Attorney General shall create a record of the alien's admission for permanent residence as of a date thirty months prior to the filing of such an application or the date of his last arrival into the United States, whichever date is later. The provisions of this Act shall be applicable to the spouse and child of any alien described in this subsection, regardless of their citizenship and place of birth, who are residing with such alien in the United States.

SEC. 2. In the case of any alien described in section 1 of this Act who, prior to the effective date thereof, has been lawfully admitted into the United States for permanent residence, the Attorney General shall, upon application, record his admission for permanent residence as of the date the alien originally arrived in the United States as a nonimmigrant or as a parolee, or a date thirty months prior to the date of enactment of this Act, whichever date is later. SEC. 3. Section 13 of the Act entitled "An Act to amend the Immigration and Nationality Act, and for other purposes", approved October 3, 1965 (Public Law 89-236), is amended by adding at the end thereof the following new subsection:

SEC. 3. Section 13 of the Act entitled "An Act to amend the Immigration and Nationality Act, and for other purposes", approved October 3, 1965 (Public Law 89-236), is amended by adding at the end thereof the following new subsection: "(c) Nothing contained in subsection (b) of this section shall be construed to affect the validity of any application for adjustment under section 245 filed with the Attorney General prior to December 1, 1965, which would have been valid on that date; but as to all such applications the statutes or parts of statutes repealed or amended by this Act are, unless otherwise specifically provided therein, continued in force and effect."

SEC. 4, Except as otherwise specifically provided in this Act, the definitions contained in section 101 (a) and (b) of the Immigration and Nationality Act shall apply in the administration of this Act. Nothing contained in this Act shall be held to repeal, amend, alter, modify, affect, or restrict the powers, duties, functions, or authority of the Attorney General in the administration and enforcement of the Immigration and Nationality Act or any other law relating to immigration, nationality, or naturalization.

Glossary

alien: a foreigner, especially one who is not a naturalized citizen of the country where they are living

naturalization: the legal act or process by which a non-citizen of a country may acquire citizenship or nationality of the country

Short-Answer Questions

1. Why is it significant that families of non-citizens are included in the act?

2. How is the Cuban Adjustment Act related to Immigration Act of 1965? Why is that important?

3. Why was the requirement for residency lowered from two years to one? Explain.

Serna v. Portales

Author U.S. District Courts, Tenth Circuit, New Mexico	**Significance** Held that the lack of bilingual education programs and hiring of bilingual faculty was discriminatory and a violation of the Fourteenth Amendment and the Civil Rights Act of 1964
Date 1974	
Document Type Legal	

Overview

In 1972 a group of Mexican American families led by Judy Serna, a student at Lindsey Elementary School, filed suit against New Mexico's Portales Municipal Schools for discriminatory hiring practices and the denial of equal educational opportunities. Although a majority of the students in the school district were of Mexican American descent, ESL (English as a second language) students were denied bilingual education, which Serna argued was a violation of the Civil Rights Act of 1964 and the Fourteenth Amendment. Serna provided evidence that Mexican American students significantly lagged behind their peers academically due to a lack of equal educational opportunity.

The U.S. District Court of New Mexico ruled in favor of Serna in 1972 and instructed Portales Municipal Schools to hire more bilingual teachers and otherwise improve its education for bilingual students, and the Portales school district appealed to the U.S. Tenth Circuit Court of Appeals. In 1974 the U.S. Supreme Court ruled on a similar case, *Lau v. Nichols*, finding that Chinese students who did not speak English had been deprived of a meaningful bilingual education in violation of Title VI of the Civil Rights Act of 1964. Subsequently, the Tenth Circuit Court of Appeals in New Mexico that year upheld the district court's ruling in favor of Serna.

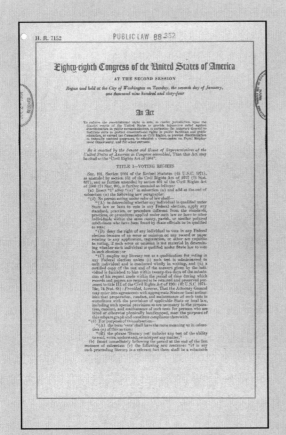

Serna *argued that denying students bilingual education was a violation of the Civil Rights Act of 1964.*
(National Archives and Records Administration)

Document Text
MEMORANDUM OPINION

MECHEM, District Judge.
Plaintiffs are minors of Spanish-surnamed heritage represented by their parents in this suit which they have brought as a class action. They seek declaratory and injunctive relief, invoking jurisdiction here under 28 U.S.C. Sections 1343, 2201 and 2203. Plaintiffs assert that defendants have discriminated against them and the members of the class they claim to represent in failing to provide learning opportunities which satisfy both their educational and social needs. They claim deprivation of due process and equal protection guaranteed by the Fourteenth Amendment of the United States Constitution and of their statutory rights under Title VI of the Civil Rights Act of 1964, specifically Section 601 (42 U.S.C. § 2000d).

... The focal point of this action pivots around the **education offered in the Lindsey School where the** Spanish-surnamed children comprise a large majority. While plaintiffs assert that educational discrimination exists throughout the Portales school system, it is alleged to be most evident at Lindsey. Plaintiffs claim discrimination is the result of an educational program within the Portales school system which is tailored to educate the middle class child from an English speaking family without regard for the educational needs of the child from an environment where Spanish is the predominant language spoken. Such a program, it is claimed, is a denial of equal educational opportunity to the Spanish-surnamed children.

Plaintiffs do not claim that the program in the Lindsey School is inferior to that offered in any other school within the district. In fact plaintiffs contend that the educational program at Lindsey is substantially the equivalent of that offered at the Brown, James and Steiner schools. It is the similarity of these programs which is the crux of plaintiffs' claim of inequality of educational opportunity.

Although the programs offered at Lindsey are similar in many regards with programs offered at Brown, James and Steiner, plaintiffs are not correct in their assertion that the education offered at Lindsey is the same as that offered in the other schools. In the current school year, six Spanish-American teachers are employed at Lindsey. The school is continuing a bilingual-bicultural program for first graders which was instituted in the 1971-1972 school year and also provides a limited program in English as a second language which reaches approximately 40 students in the second through sixth grades. Neither of these programs or any other bilingual-bicultural program is offered in the other Portales elementary schools nor are any Spanish-surnamed teachers employed in those three schools.

Defendant school district asserts that the programs which have been established at Lindsey and the increase in the number of teachers with a Spanish surname indicate its awareness of the needs of the Spanish-surnamed children and constitutes sufficient affirmative action to remedy whatever deficiencies may have existed. The evidence presented, however, indicates that the achievement of children at Lindsey is consistently lower than that of the children attending the other three elementary schools. . . .

Evidence relating to I.Q. test scores of children in the Portales school system was admitted at the trial with the recognition that such scores are not conclusive evidence of student achievement or failure. What becomes apparent from an examination of these scores, however, is that the performance of the children at every level at Lindsey School is not what it should be when compared with the performance of students at the other schools. Coupled with the testimony of educational experts regarding the negative impact upon Spanish-surnamed children when they are placed in a school atmosphere which does not adequately reflect the educational needs of this minority, as is found to be the situation in the Portales schools, the conclusion becomes inevitable that these Spanish-surnamed children do not in fact have equal educational opportunity and that a violation of their constitutional right to equal protection exists.

The administrators of the Portales school district are aware of these conditions, have taken some steps to alleviate the problem, and have made positive improvements. These corrections, however, are not adequate. Under these circumstances, it is incumbent upon the school district to reassess and enlarge its program directed to the specialized needs of its Spanish-surnamed students at Lindsey and also to establish and operate in adequate manner programs at the other elementary schools where no bilingual-bicultural program now exists. . . .

Of particular importance is the recruitment and hiring of more qualified Spanish-speaking teachers and teacher aides at each of the district schools as positions and personnel become available. The presence of qualified teachers who can speak Spanish should be a significant factor toward enabling the Spanish-surnamed students to effectively participate in the educational process.

Defendant school district also contends that it is seriously restricted by its operating budget in expanding its bilingual-bicultural programs. Evidence at the trial established that there are sources of funds available to implement and maintain such programs. Federal funds are available for bilingual-bicultural programs in the elementary and secondary schools under Titles I and VII of the Elementary and Secondary Education Act of 1965 (Title I, 20 U.S.C. § 241a et seq.; Title VII, 20 U.S.C. § 880b et seq.). The State of New Mexico's Bilingual Instruction Act, 11 N.M.S.A. § 77-21-1 et seq., similarly has made funding available for the "special education needs" of students with a limited English-speaking ability caused by living in an environment where the dominant language is not English. These are some of the available sources of funding for a bilingual-bicultural program. Defendant school district is directed to investigate and utilize wherever possible the sources of available funds to provide equality of educational opportunity for its Spanish-surnamed students.

It is also claimed that an obstacle to expanding bilingual-bicultural programs in the Portales school system is the absence of qualified teachers. Defendant school district has made an effort to recruit and has recruited Spanish-speaking teachers. It points to the fact that it has received few applications from such teachers and that the teacher turnover in the Portales Municipal Schools is relatively low. However great the effort, this is not an acceptable justification for not providing specialized programs where the deprivation of them violates a constitutional right and where funding is available. It is incumbent upon the school district to increase its recruiting efforts and, if those recruiting efforts

Serna v. Portales

are unsuccessful, to obtain sufficient certification of Spanish-speaking teachers to allow them to teach in the district. . . .

Plaintiffs did not meet their burden of proof in establishing discrimination by the Portales school district in its employment practices regarding nonteaching personnel. The evidence did prove, however, that the defendant school district is not providing an educational program which affords equality of educational opportunity for all of its students. . . .

Glossary

deprivation: denial of something considered to be a necessity

due process: a reference to "due process of law," a right guaranteed by the Fourteenth Amendment

equal protection: a reference to "equal protection of the laws," a right guaranteed by the Fourteenth Amendment

surname: a hereditary name common to all members of a family

Short-Answer Questions

1. How would you describe the tone in the court's ruling, especially in its opinion of the Portales school district?

2. Explain how the Portales school district violated the Fourteenth Amendment, specifically its guarantees for due process of law and equal protection of the laws, in terms of providing resources for Mexican Americans.

3. Do you see a relationship between *Serna v. Portales* and *Brown v. Board of Education of Topeka*? Explain.

Gerald Ford:
Address to the Republican National Hispanic Assembly

Author	Significance
Gerald Ford	Incorporated Hispanic American interests and issues within the Republican platform in an effort to draw Hispanic Americans to the Republican Party
Date	
1975	
Document Type	
Speeches/Addresses; Presidential/Executive	

Overview

Noting the growth of the Hispanic American community during the mid-twentieth century, the Republican Party focused on attracting Hispanic Americans to the party. Many Hispanic Americans felt politically and culturally isolated by the Chicano Movement, a Mexican American activist movement that focused largely on labor rights and educational reform, during the 1960s and gravitated toward the Republican Party. During the 1960s and into the 1970s, Hispanic Americans started being elected to political positions despite the discrimination that was prevalent. In this address, President Gerald Ford recognized the political gains that Hispanic Americans had made and noted his party's support for these changes. Ford asserted that the Republican Party needed to continue to support Hispanic Americans, which was important both for their advancement and for the expansion of Republican power. The Hispanic American vote was vital to Ford's campaign because it was a large voting base that the Republican Party had failed to attract in previous years.

Document Text

I'm happy to welcome you to the White House this morning. I've looked forward for some time to this meeting with the Republican National Hispanic Assembly. I am glad you're here. I am well aware of one of your most urgent priorities—increasing the number of Hispanic Americans in leadership positions in this Administration. I share this objective with you. Fernando De Baca, one of my principal assistants who specializes in Hispanic affairs, has been a most effective advocate in this regard. Doug Bennett in our Personnel office has kept me posted on efforts to improve the recruiting of Hispanic Americans. In addition to Fred, Hispanic Americans in key posts in this Administration include Fernando Oaxaca, Associate Director of OMB, Bert Gallegos, Administrator of the Community Services Administration, and

President Gerald Ford (David Hume Kennerly)

Ricardo Nunez, who will be Director of HEW's Cuban Refugee Program.

Hispanic Americans deserve a strong voice in this Administration and in the conduct of national affairs. Altogether, 58 presently serve in policy-making posts. You also need more advocates and representatives in the Congress, like my good friend Manuel Lujan of New Mexico, who I am glad to see here. In this connection, the Voting Rights Act which I signed into law last summer can be a very effective instrument for progress in this area. I strongly support its special provisions for breaking down language barriers and guaranteeing full voting rights for Hispanic Americans. Make sure the legislation is utilized for your maximum advantage, not just because you represent an important segment of the Republican Party, but because you represent an important segment of our national population. Our common goal is to make life better for the Hispanic community in America—by improving the standard of living of all, expanding the quality of education, which includes stressing the value of bi-lingual education programs; by encouraging greater participation in the Minority Business Enterprise Program; and by whipping the problems of unemployment and inflation which concern us all.

As Republicans, you know that we face a very important challenge in the next eleven months. Whether or not we withstand that challenge and achieve victory depends, in large part, on your efforts to win support for the party within the Hispanic community. It depends, too, on this Administration's record of help and encouragement for Hispanics. We will do our part. I know you will do your part, too. Since I'm here to listen more than to talk this morning, I'm anxious to hear any concerns or suggestions you may wish to present at this time.

Glossary

HEW: U.S. Department of Health, Education, and Welfare

Minority Business Enterprise Program: designed to increase minority involvement in federal contract programs

OMB: U.S. Office of Management and Budget

utilized: made practical and effective use of

Short-Answer Questions

1. What do you think are the motivations behind Ford's and the Republican Party's strategies to attract Hispanic American voters?

2. Ford lists the name of several Hispanic Americans that are in positions of power. Why do you think he does that?

3. Evaluate the language and tone Ford uses in his address. What effect do you think this had on Hispanic Americans during the 1970s in the wake of the Chicano Movement?

Plyler v. Doe

Author United States Supreme Court	**Significance** Ruled that states could not ban undocumented children from public schools
Date 1982	
Document Type Legal	

Overview

In 1975, the state of Texas passed a law prohibiting the use of state funds to educate undocumented immigrants, and Tyler Independent School District's superintendent James Plyler subsequently required that undocumented children be charged tuition for attending public schools. Lawyers on behalf of Mexican children in the Tyler Independent School District (as John Doe, et al.) filed a class-action suit that same year claiming that the law was unconstitutional, and in 1982 the Supreme Court ruled that the Texas law violated the Fourteenth Amendment, specifically the Equal Protection Clause, which applies to all persons regardless of citizenship or immigration status. While supporters of the Texas statute argued that the presence of undocumented children in public schools would diminish the quality of education and denying them enrollment would help curb illegal immigration, the Court upheld that there was no merit to either theory and no legal or constitutional basis for the Texas law.

Document Text

Syllabus

Held: A Texas statute which withholds from local school districts any state funds for the education of children who were not "legally admitted" into the United States, and which authorizes local school districts to deny enrollment to such children, violates the Equal Protection Clause of the Fourteenth Amendment. Pp. 210–230.

(a) The illegal aliens who are plaintiffs in these cases challenging the statute may claim the benefit of the Equal Protection Clause, which provides that no State shall "deny to any person within its jurisdiction the equal protection of the laws." Whatever his status under the immigration laws, an alien is a

468   The Schlager Anthology of Hispanic America

Courthouse in Tyler, Texas (Library of Congress)

"person" in any ordinary sense of that term. This Court's prior cases recognizing that illegal aliens are "persons" protected by the Due Process Clauses of the Fifth and Fourteenth Amendments, which Clauses do not include the phrase "within its jurisdiction," cannot be distinguished on the asserted ground that persons who have entered the country illegally are not "within the jurisdiction" of a State even if they are present within its boundaries and subject to its laws. Nor do the logic and history of the Fourteenth Amendment support such a construction. Instead, use of the phrase "within its jurisdiction" confirms the understanding that the Fourteenth Amendment's protection extends to anyone, citizen or stranger, who is subject to the laws of a State, and reaches into every corner of a State's territory. Pp. 210–216.

(b) The discrimination contained in the Texas statute cannot be considered rational unless it furthers some substantial goal of the State. Although undocumented resident aliens cannot be treated as a "suspect class," and although education is not a "fundamental right," so as to require the State to justify the statutory classification by showing that it serves a compelling governmental interest, nevertheless the Texas statute imposes a lifetime hardship on a discrete class of children not accountable for their disabling status. These children can neither affect their parents' conduct nor their own undocumented status. The deprivation of public education is not like the deprivation of some other governmental benefit. Public education has a pivotal role in maintaining the fabric of our society and in sustaining our political and cultural heritage; the deprivation of education takes an inestimable toll on the social, economic, intellectual, and psychological well-being of the individual, and poses an obstacle to individual achievement. In determining the rationality of the Texas statute, its costs to the Nation and to the innocent children may properly be considered. Pp. 216–224.

(c) The undocumented status of these children *vel non* does not establish a sufficient rational basis for denying them benefits that the State affords other residents. It is true that, when faced with **an equal protection challenge respecting a State's** differential treatment of aliens, the courts must be attentive to congressional policy concerning aliens. But in the area of special constitutional sensitivity presented by these cases, and in the absence of any contrary indication fairly discernible in the legislative record, no national policy is perceived that might justify the State in denying these children an elementary education. Pp. 224–226.

(d) Texas' statutory classification cannot be sustained as furthering its interest in the "preservation of the state's limited resources for the education of its lawful residents." While the State might have an interest in mitigating potentially harsh economic effects from an influx of illegal immigrants, the Texas statute does not offer an effective method of dealing with the problem. Even assuming that the net impact of illegal aliens on the economy is negative, charging tuition to undocumented children constitutes an ineffectual attempt to stem the tide of illegal immigration, at least when compared with the alternative of prohibiting employment of illegal aliens. Nor is there any merit to the suggestion that undocumented children are appropriately singled out for exclusion because of the special burdens they impose on the State's ability to provide high-quality public education. The record does not **show that exclusion of undocumented children is** likely to improve the overall quality of education in the State. Neither is there any merit to the claim that undocumented children are appropriately singled out because their unlawful presence within the United States renders them less likely than other children to remain within the State's boundaries and to put their education to productive social or political use within the State. Pp. 227–230.

No. 80–1538, 628 F. 2d 448, and No. 80-1934, affirmed.

BRENNAN, J., delivered the opinion of the Court, in which MARSHALL, BLACKMUN, POWELL, and STEVENS, JJ., joined. MARSHALL, J., *post*, p. 230, BLACKMUN, J., *post*, p. 231, and POWELL, J., *post*, p. 236, filed concurring opinions. BURGER, C. J., filed a dissenting opinion, in which WHITE, REHNQUIST, and O'CONNOR, JJ., joined, *post*, p. 242.

Glossary

alien: undocumented immigrant

discernible: able to recognize

inestimable: too great to calculate

Short-Answer Questions

1. The Supreme Court notes that education is not a "fundamental right" but still argues on behalf of the defendant. Explain what evidence the court uses in its ruling and why it is significant.

2. What evidence does Plyler use to support his case, and how does that speak to issues concerning immigration in general?

3. Do you think the fact that the defendants are children had any influence on the court's decision? Explain.

Plyler v. Doe

Virginia Escalante, Nancy Rivera, and Victor Valle: "Inside the World of Latinas"

Author
Virginia Escalante, Nancy Rivera, and Victor Valle

Date
1983

Document Type
Essays, Reports, Manifestos

Significance
Told the stories of Latinas in Southern California's Latino community

Overview

During the summer of 1983, the *Los Angeles Times* published a series on the Latino community of Southern California. Created by Latino writers, photographers, and editors, this series told the complex story of the people and of the art, politics, religion, labor, and education related to the community. In addition, many articles explored the culture and tensions felt within the family unit. Although much of the series focused on telling the triumphs and successes, the creators did not shy away from highlighting the struggles faced within the Latino community in the early 1980s. The *Los Angeles Times* won the coveted Pulitzer Prize for Public Service following the publication of the series.

Included in the series was an article written by *Times* staff writers Virginia Escalante, Nancy Rivera, and Victory Valle. "Inside the World of Latinas" focused on the lived experience of five women: Julia Luna Mount, Nancy Gutierrez, Cristina Ramirez, Catalina (Katie) Castillo Fierro, and Maria Elena Gaitan. Each woman interviewed had very different life stories, which are briefly explored in the article. Also explored throughout the interviews are the interactions among the women's various relationships: work, personal, and familial. In addition, the women interviewed express the fears plaguing them in the early 1980s. The article allows the reader to examine how different women viewed themselves and their communities during a polarizing time.

Document Text

For many Latinas, there is a double burden of racism and sexism. . . .

Julia Luna Mount, 61, mother of four, grandmother of 10, now is protesting the end of the world. . . .

I want to emphasize the fact that as minorities, as Mexicanos, we lack housing, medical attentiont, good schools, jobs. We lack for everything that you can think of. For us, it's always been an economic struggle, but right now it's a struggle for survival. . . .

Nuclear energy is a very difficult subject to get into with people in our area. Mexicanos are less informed for many reasons. . . .

I can still see that we're going to have to someday go to the polls and do away with something that's killing us. But we're not going to win unless people are educated. . . .

The whole process of this nuclear menace should become a women's problem. War affects us more than anything else because we're the ones who lose our future husbands, husbands and children.

If women controlled the world, we would not have wars because we are the givers of life.

One of the few Latinas in corporate management, [Nancy] Gutierrez made it without a college degree; higher education was reserved for the men in the family.

But to enter the business world now, she emphasizes, a degree is vital.

Hispanic women need a support system to nurture those two variables. And a lot of them don't have that.

I had two very strong role models in my grandmother and my mother. But I happen to be a Hispanic from New Mexico—third, fourth, fifth generation—versus a lot of the Latinas that are here in California who are not. They're first generation.

They have no support system . . .

I think that, No. 1, we have a tendency sometimes to maybe not go as far as our potential would take us because we have very strong family ties . . . We're, first of all, a very family-oriented people, a very loyal people to that commitment. We also fight the issues of sexism within our own race, within our own heritage . . . Those are extra pressures that the Hispanic woman has to face.

There's something else. We have to have an ability to be multi-personalities, because we have to come in and assimilate into the culture of the corporation, into the culture of the peer group, which is predominantly non-minority. . . .

Cristina Ramirez is a 29-year-old organizer for the International Ladies Garment Workers Union in Los Angeles. . . .

Today, as a union organizer in the garment industry, she sees firsthand the new roles that Latinas take on as they enter the work force. For Latinas who come to this country to escape economic and political oppression, the garment industry often gives them their first job, but in a world of work dominated by men. . . .

Latinas, observes Ramirez, must remember they have the same rights as men.

Catalina (Katie) Castillo Fierro, 59, the mother of five, is a housewife. . . .

We learned a lot (in Mexico). We learned other customs, other ways of thinking, how to work in the yard and in the home.

When we came back (to California in 1941), we didn't know how to speak a single word of English. . . .

I have relatives that have changed their names. Well, it's their choice, but I think that I am proud of what I am, where I come from and of knowing two languages.

But the more you know, the more advantaged you are. This is what I tell my children . . .

Maria Elena Gaitan, 33, is flourishing as a poet, writer, actress and musician.

She co-authored "La Condicion Femenina" . . . and is working on a second drama, "The Rape of Teresita Dominguez." . . . She marched and lobbied for change in immigration, farm worker and public education policies.

Gaitan has remained active ever since. She has been a candidate for the Los Angeles school board and, at the Hispanic Urban Center, trained parents to be advocates for public education. Her involvement with education [follows] on a family tradition. . . .

After I left high school and went to Cal Arts, I was in that enclave of music, but it was incongruous with the tremendous social movements that were happening among Chicanos as a result of the civil rights movement.
My mother was teaching at Lincoln High School at the heart of where the blowouts (student walkouts) happened. And here I was, in some institutions that were still segregated, like the Pasadena Symphony where I wasn't prepared for the racism and elitism of the classical music

environment. Many of the adults and the rich kids wouldn't even speak to me. It made me angry, and for me, it became a matter of choosing. . . . I was on the verge of joining the Musicians Union. . . .

As the movimiento began developing, I was simply in it. I was in the marchas; I would fast (for the farm workers). I saw the Chicano movement at its height and at its fullest, with all its victories, its opportunism, its male supremacy and its rip-offs . . .

I was in the farm workers movement because the idea of my people being campesinos and being exploited was the most enraging of all . . .

Sometimes I think, "Well, I'm a victim of racism. How do I fight back and not die?" One way is through the arts.

Two casualties of racism, she observes, are self-image and self-expression.

Racism affects self-image because if everything that you see does not reflect your type, your beauty, what you are, it means that somewhere along the line, someone is deciding that you are not beautiful, capable or worthy. If we hear this long enough, it succeeds in convincing us. That's what fads are all about. You put something out and bait people with it . . . It's an aspect of self-hatred that's real evident to me. . . . The way that racism affects self-expression, quite simply, is that it doesn't allow us to learn reading and writing skills the way we should. . . .

That's why the collective ability of Chicanos, the ability of kids of color to read and write, is minimized.

It's quite natural that some of us can't read and write because of how we went into the classroom—many of us speaking Spanish first—and how violently the public school place took away our ability to communicate by forbidding us Spanish. . . .

Because Chicanas are among the most exploited workers in the country, it's more essential for them to be in touch with what goes on in the whole world. That way, they will understand what their position in this society is and fight for their equality.

They will understand there is a history of struggle. They don't have to reinvent it. A Chicana doesn't have to do anything but be active where she is because she affects those around her, her family, her workplace, the politics that go on here.

She has power because she's a fundamental part of the productive society. When Chicanas realize this, hey, honey, I've got news for you. They'll be real angry about how unequally they've been treated and exploited.

Glossary

assimilate: to be absorbed into a culture or population

campesinos: peasant farmers

Chicano: an American of Mexican descent

marchas: walks, marches

movimiento: a movement

Short-Answer Questions

1. What are some of the most significant concerns of the women interviewed for this piece? What does this tell us about the Latina community in the early 1980s?

2. Summarize what Maria Elena Gaitan sees as the "two casualties of racism." How does she see this as affecting her community?

3. In a detailed response, analyze these women's interactions with work and politics. How do they view these relationships?

David Reyes: "In Pursuit of the Latino American Dream"

Author
David Reyes

Date
1983

Document Type
Essays, Reports, Manifestos

Significance
Described how the Latino community in Southern California defined and pursued the American dream in the 1980s

Overview

During the summer of 1983, the *Los Angeles Times* published a series on Southern California's Latino community. The series was created by Latino writers, editors, and photographers who worked to tell the story of the history, art, politics, family unit, religion, labor, education, success, and struggles of the Latino community. Following its publication, the series won the Pulitzer Prize for Public Service.

Included in the series was an article written by David Reyes titled "In Pursuit of the Latino America Dream." In his article, Reyes explores what the Latino American dream is through the stories of Frederick P. Aguirre and Barbara Ledesma Brown, both middle-class residents of Orange County, California. The examination focuses on middle-class Latinos and how the American dream is viewed through that community's eyes. The article not only employs statistics but examines the interactions and experiences of this community. Ultimately, Reyes paints a small picture of what it looks like to live in what he describes as "two worlds."

Document Text

In contrast to most Latinos elsewhere, the "new Hispanic" in Orange County is adapting well to the suburban life style, far from the crowded substandard housing, spray-painted graffiti and neighborhood youth gangs that plague the barrios, sociologists and demographers say.

These experts say that Orange County is a citadel for successful Latinos, who tend to be better educated, earn more money and be politically more sophisticated than Latinos elsewhere in the nation.

Leobardo Estrada, a UCLA demographer, offers this observation:

"Look at the forces at work in Orange County . . . (To) survive in an affluent area where most

Orange County, CA, in the 1980s (Flickr)

of the people are white and upwardly mobile . . . you've got to be sharp, impressive and bright."

In many ways, Orange County Latinos offer a glimpse of the promise of the Latinos' absorption into middle America. Most still speak Spanish and retain a cultural identity to Mexico. Yet they are proud Americans and have adapted well in an English-speaking world.

Already, Latinos in Orange County boast a higher percentage of high-salaried wage earners than do their counterparts in the state's other populous counties. Of the estimated 300,000 Latinos in Orange County, 14.2% earn at least $35,000 a year, according to 1980 Census figures. In contrast, only 8.8% of the Latinos in Los Angeles County earn that much. Orange County's Latino population grew from 160,168 in 1970 to 285,000 in 1980, an increase of nearly 78%, according to Census figures. The heaviest growth has occurred in the county's northern and central sections, where a substantial Latino influence has been felt in terms of language and culture, especially in the schools.

Orange County Latinos are so diverse, however, that they defy labels. Politically, most tend to be Democrats, although Republicans seem to be gaining ground.

The Latinos' sense of cultural identity ranges from "I am assimilated"—a group more comfortable driving BMW cars and wearing dark-blue pin-striped "power suits," and whose only Spanish is heard at the county's best Mexican restaurants ordering food—to those who name their children after Mayan and Aztec gods and insist on the Spanish language in the home. . . .

Most Orange County Chicanos interviewed said they prefer living here than in Los Angeles County, where big-city acceptance of different racial groups is routine and where politics are less conservative, because they enjoy Orange County's relatively smaller population, its beaches, its cleaner neighborhoods and its environment, which are viewed as conducive to raising families. . . .

Critics such as UC Irvine Spanish Prof. Alejandro Morales insist that Chicanos should question the American Dream and try going contra la corriente (against the flow). As have the Italians in New York and other immigrant groups, Latinos may find assimilation will cost them "their culture, their language and their religion," Morales said.

"They should be emphasizing their differences, so they can apply a very unique vision of the world," Morales said. "But the American uses a different value system (to get ahead) . . . And once you accept the middle-class dream, the house in suburbia, the jazzy car, a pool, and become a member of the club, well I think that's bad." . . .

The middle-class Latinos represent the tip of a Latinization process that is moving slowly southward along the Santa Ana Freeway from such Los Angeles County cities as Norwalk, Santa Fe Springs and Whittier into the Orange County communities of Buena Park and Anaheim. In Santa Ana, where almost half of the city's population is Latino, growth is rippling outward.

In Orange County, the Latino population was 286,339 at the time of the 1980 Census. That included 232,472 people of Mexican origin, 5,534 of Puerto Rican origin, 4,820 of Cuban origin and 43,313 listed as Central American, South American and of "other" Spanish origin.

Orange County cities with the largest percentages of Latinos in 1980 were Santa Ana, with about 45% of the total population of 203,000; La Habra, 22% of its 45,200 residents; Stanton, 21% of 21,200, and Placentia, 20% of 35,000. . . .

Most of the Latino growth has been centered in Santa Ana, the county's urban heart. . . .

Many county and city officials said during interviews that they did not understand "where all the Mexicans suddenly came from."

But according to UCLA's Estrada, the Latino population explosion occurred hand in hand with the county's economic boom. He explained:

"They needed people to build those glittering buildings you see by the freeways down there, then landscape them and work in the cafeterias. Officials in Orange County pretended that the Mexicans hired by contractors as carpenters, cleanup crews and for other jobs would disappear after the construction was finished. In fact, the more buildings they built, the more illegals they needed.

"They don't understand that they've hired thousands of illegals coming in, mostly Mexican and some who were skilled labor."

Santa Ana's rapid Latino influx has not made for a smooth transition, city officials concede. Many admit candidly that Latinos as a group represent a political disenfranchised community. In Santa Ana there is only one Latino councilman, and despite a school district that is 84% minority, Santa Ana has an all-white school board.

Some whites cling to the hope that their Latino neighbors will simply go away, said former Santa Ana Mayor Gordon Bricken.

"It is astonishing that anybody still harbors any kind of belief in a great white hope here in Santa Ana," Bricken said. "A lot of people believe that in our city. What this has done, I think, has caused a lot of people to operate on a set of principles not really matched by what's here."

He noted that many Latinos have already broken through social, racial and cultural barriers. They include insurance man Ray Villa, Santa Ana's first Chicano councilman from 1968 to 1972; county Postmaster Hector Godinez, who with Santa Ana attorney Rudy Montejano, sits on the Rancho Santiago Community College board of trustees; Superior Court Judge Jame O. Perez, the first Chicano to become a judge in Orange County, and Manuel Esqueda, a retired bank manager.

These make up a visible "old guard" network and serve as role models for the next generation of Latinos, many say.

Glossary

assimilation: the process in which an immigrant group begins to resemble the society they have immigrated to

barrios: Spanish-speaking quarters of a town or city

Chicano: someone who is native of, or descends from Mexico, and lives in the United States

citadel: fortress

Short-Answer Questions

1. Analyze the argument that Reyes is making in this article.

2. Summarize the concept of assimilation in the story of Latinos in Orange County.

3. Briefly explain how Latinos, in this piece, have broken racial, social, and cultural barriers. What does this tell us about the America of 1983?

Frank Sotomayor:
"Latinos: A Diverse Group Tied by Ethnicity"

Author
Frank Sotomayor

Date
1983

Document Type
Essays, Reports, Manifestos

Significance
Explored the diversity found within the Latino community of Southern California

Overview

The *Los Angeles Times* published an important series in the summer of 1983 that showcased the stories of Southern California's Latino community. The series' creators were Latino writers, editors, and photographers who wanted to help readers understand the growing community. The series focused on the history, art, politics, religion, labor, and education of the Latino community in Southern California. In addition, the creators wanted to showcase statistics and the personal stories of members of the community in the early 1980s. Published in seventeen parts, the series illustrated the successes and struggles that the Latino community experienced. The primary connecting thread throughout the articles was the question, What does the "Latino American dream" look like? Following its publication, the series won the Pulitzer Prize for Public Service.

On July 25, 1985, the piece "Latinos: A Diverse Group Tied by Ethnicity" was published as part of the series. Written by Frank Sotomayor, a co-editor and writer at the *Times*, the piece examines the diversity found in the Latino community of primarily Los Angeles County, estimated at two million people in the 1980s. In his article, Sotomayor argues that a "collective identity" can be found in this diverse community. Although connected by ethnicity and other factors, he stresses, it is important to note that the Latino community is not monolithic.

Document Text

Daniel and Maria Elena Castro were in the forefront of the 1960s Chicano political and social movement.

They felt so strongly about the Mexican/Chicano culture that they named their son Quetzalcoatl after the Aztec god and their daughter Tonantzin after a Mayan mother of the gods.

To their chagrin, they discovered two years ago that Quetzalcoatl, then 5, was losing the Spanish language and Chicano culture after entering a Pasadena private school, where he was the only Latino in class.

They met with Chicano parents facing similar dilemmas and decided to set up Resolana, a Saturday morning school where their children would be taught Spanish and *la cultura*.

"We all had the intent to raise our children as Chicanos," said Castro, 38. . . .

The Resolana parents reflect one element of the Latino community of 2 million people in Los Angeles County, a population of vast economic, social and cultural diversity.

More than 1.6 million of the county's Latinos are of Mexican origin, according to the 1980 Census, ranging from descendants of settlers who came to California when it was part of Mexico to newly arrived immigrants. A growing wave of Central American refugees is adding to the diversification of the Latino population, which also includes Puerto Ricans, Cubans and South Americans.

Despite economic and political differences among—and within—the groups, Latinos share important cultural traits and most share the Spanish language and Roman Catholic religion. They want to be part of the national economic and social life without having to give up their ethnic identity or culture.

"Few groups have had as consistent a history of collective identity, of pronounced preferences for ethnic group labels and of resistance to assimilationist forces," said social researcher Carlos H. Arce.

"Latinos retain a lot of our culture and identity, and we want to pass that along to our children," said Felix Gutierrez, a USC journalism professor and fifth-generation Angeleno. . . .

But those Chicanos who move away from heavily Latino residential areas often must battle the tides of assimilation to retain their ethnic identity.

The Resolana parents made a conscious decision to pass on their Spanish-language fluency and Chicano culture in a systematic manner. This attitude is in sharp contrast to the way Daniel Castro was raised.

His parents, who had suffered discrimination because they were Mexican, decided in the late 1940s that the best way for their children to advance in the Anglo-dominated society was to speak only English.

That approach was typical of the "survival strategy" that many Mexican-American families adopted to cope with discrimination.

"But Mexican-Americans found out that they could be assimilated and it didn't make any difference. They still suffered discrimination," said Castro, a Pasadena businessman who has a doctorate in sociology from UC Santa Barbara.

"People tried to change their name, their religion, their culture, but they couldn't change their skins," Castro said. "Once you come to a realization that I am what I am, then it's easier to live with yourself."

The Castros and some of the other Resolana families live in predominantly Anglo, middle-class neighborhoods. Resolana gives their children the contact with other Chicanos and the bilingual training that they would otherwise miss.

Yolanda Gonzalez, a teacher at a Lincoln Heights elementary school, conducts the Saturday morning classes. "The Japanese, the Armenians and other ethnic groups have their special schools," she said, "but this is the only Chicano family school that I know of." She hopes other Latino parents will follow the model of Resolana. . . .

Most of the Resolana parents are college graduates and are in business, law, education or government service. . . . Like the Latino community as a whole, most are Roman Catholics, but some are Protestants; most are Democrats, but a few are Republicans. . . .

At the other end of the Latino spectrum are the refugees streaming into Pico-Union after feeling the revolutions, violence and poverty of Central America. . . .

The exact size of the Central American population is unknown, primarily because most came without immigration papers and since the 1980 Census was taken.

. . . Polita Huff had made the most conscious effort to pass on the Spanish language to her children.

Huff learned Spanish from her mother, who was born in the Mexican state of Sonora. Her father is of Irish ancestry. Her husband is Anglo and does not speak Spanish.

"I spoke to our two children strictly in Spanish until they were about 3," she said. "I wanted to pass on that cultural uniqueness—the Spanish language—to them."

The language and culture were not lost in two generations of Latino-Anglo marriages in the case of Huff. The same is not always true; it is an individual or family choice, of course. . . .

In addition to family ties, a whole network of Spanish-language publications, radio, television, films and other media provide a foundation for the Latino culture. For example, 10 local radio stations do at least some of their programming in Spanish, and there are dozens of Latino arts groups and hundreds of social and cultural organizations.

This helps provide unifying forces for Latinos. But cultural similarity does not translate into unity in politics or across economic classes.

Friction sometimes occurs among Chicanos, Mexicanos and Central Americans competing for the same jobs. . . .

In the field of politics, observers point that Latinos do show unity on some issues, such as the importance of education. They believe that the lack of agreement on other political matters is to be expected in a heterogeneous community.

With the growing importance of Latin America in U.S. foreign policy, Father Loren Riebe of St. Thomas the Apostle Catholic Church believes the Central Americans will help "bridge the incredible gap—culturally and politically—between the United States and Latin America." . . .

Daniel Castro said he feels a kinship with new immigrants from Mexico and Central America but does not expect much interaction with them because "we just don't have the same interests."

Glossary

assimilation: to absorb into a culture or population

Chicano: person of Mexican descent born in the United States

refugee: a person who has been forced to leave their country to escape war, persecution, or natural disaster

Short-Answer Questions

1. Summarize how the Latino community has tried to continue teaching their culture to succeeding generations.

2. Analyze how interviews and personal stories illustrate the diversity within Los Angeles County's Latino community.

3. Briefly explain what Sotomayor means by factors that create a "collective identity" in this article.

Ronald Reagan: Address to the Nation on United States Policy in Central America

Author Ronald Reagan	**Significance** Speech given by President Reagan that outlined his administration's policy concerning communism in Central America
Date 1984	
Document Type Speeches/Addresses; Presidential/Executive	

Overview

During World War II (1939–45), the United States and the Soviet Union were allied in the fight against their common enemies. Following the end of the war in 1945, the wartime alliance began to fall apart, and America and its allies began to fear the spread of communism. The Cold War was born out of the tensions between the United States and the Soviet Union. Throughout the 1950s, 1960s, and 1970s, the United States began to focus on how to stop the spread of communism—a policy known as containment.

Stopping the spread of communism and reducing the level of nuclear weapons became the focus of American diplomacy. Ronald Reagan (1911–2004) became the fortieth president of the United States and served from 1981 to 1989. Throughout his presidency, Reagan dealt with how to form foreign policy during the Cold War, which included the goal of "peace through strength." On May 9, 1984, President Ronald Reagan addressed the nation from the White House's Oval Office and outlined a plan for foreign policy in Central America. His speech focused on several countries in Central America that could be a threat to American interests. Reagan laid out an unambiguous message that the United States did "not start wars" and would "never be the aggressor" against the Soviet Union but that it would defend its allies from Soviet aggression. The president made clear to the American people that they were not in imminent danger of nuclear war. Still, he argued that the Soviet Union was using other tactics in Central America that would pose a threat. In his speech, Reagan discussed the way forward concerning these threats to freedom and economics in the Western Hemisphere. Finally, Reagan described the legislation and other measures necessary to prevent communism from spreading further.

Ronald Reagan (Wikimedia Commons)

Document Text

My fellow Americans:

. . . I asked for this time to tell you of some basic decisions which are yours to make. I believe it's my constitutional responsibility to place these matters before you. They have to do with your national security, and that security is the single most important function of the Federal Government. In that context, it's my duty to anticipate problems, warn of dangers, and act so as to keep harm away from our shores.

Our diplomatic objectives will not be attained by good will and noble aspirations alone. In the last 15 years, the growth of Soviet military power has meant a radical change in the nature of the world we live in. Now, this does not mean, as some would have us believe, that we're in imminent danger of nuclear war. We're not. As long as we maintain the strategic balance and make it more stable by reducing the level of weapons on both sides, then we can count on the basic prudence of the Soviet leaders to avoid that kind of challenge to us.

They are presently challenging us with a different kind of weapon: subversion and the use of surrogate forces, Cubans, for example. We've seen it intensifying during the last 10 years, as the Soviet Union and its surrogates move to establish control over Vietnam, Laos, Cambodia, Angola, Ethiopia, South Yemen, Afghanistan, and recently, closer to home, in Nicaragua and now El Salvador. It's the fate of this region, Central America, that I want to talk to you about tonight.

The issue is our effort to promote democracy and economic well-being in the face of Cuban and Nicaraguan aggression, aided and abetted by the Soviet Union. It is definitely not about plans to send American troops into combat in Central America. . . .

The defense policy of the United States is based on a simple premise: We do not start wars. We will never be the aggressor. We maintain our strength in order to deter and defend against aggression, to preserve freedom and peace. We help our friends defend themselves.

Central America is a region of great importance to the United States. . . . It's at our doorstep, and it's become the stage for a bold attempt by the Soviet Union, Cuba, and Nicaragua to install communism by force throughout the hemisphere.

When half of our shipping tonnage and imported oil passes through Caribbean shipping lanes, and nearly half of all our foreign trade passes through the Panama Canal and Caribbean waters, America's economy and well-being are at stake. . . .

What we see in El Salvador is an attempt to destabilize the entire region and eventually move chaos and anarchy toward the American border.

As the National Bipartisan Commission on Central America, chaired by Henry Kissinger, agreed, if we do nothing, if we continue to provide too little help, our choice will be a Communist Central America with additional Communist military bases on the mainland of this hemisphere and Communist subversion spreading southward and northward. . . .

If we come to our senses too late, when our vital interests are even more directly threatened, and after a lack of American support causes our friends to lose the ability to defend themselves, then the risks to our security and our way of life will be infinitely greater. But there is a way to avoid these risks, recommended by the National Bipartisan Commission on Central America. It requires long-term American support for democratic development, economic and security assistance, and strong-willed diplomacy.

There have been a number of high-level, bilateral meetings with the Nicaraguan Government, where we presented specific proposals for peace. . . .

We can and must help Central America. It's in our national interest to do so, and morally, it's the only right thing to do. But helping means doing enough—enough to protect our security and enough to protect the lives of our neighbors so that they may live in peace and democracy without the threat of Communist aggression and subversion. This has been the policy of our administration for more than 3 years.

But making this choice requires a commitment from all of us—our administration, the American people, and the Congress. So far, we have not yet made that commitment. . . .

The people of Central America want democracy and freedom. They want and hope for a better

future. Costa Rica is a well-established and healthy democracy. . . .

Communist subversion is not an irreversible tide. . . . And where democracy flourishes, human rights and peace are more secure. The tide of the future can be a freedom tide. All it takes is the will and resources to get the job done.

In April 1983 I addressed a Joint Session of the Congress and asked for bipartisan cooperation on behalf of our policies to protect liberty and democracy in Central America. . . . I appointed 12 distinguished Americans from both political parties to the National Bipartisan Commission on Central America.

The Bipartisan Commission rendered an important service to all Americans—all of us from pole to pole in this Western Hemisphere. Last January the Commission presented positive recommendations to support democratic development. . . . The recommendations reinforced the spirit of our administration's policies that help to our neighbors should be primarily economic and humanitarian, but must also include sufficient military aid. . . .

The simple questions are: Will we support freedom in this hemisphere or not? Will we defend our vital interests in this hemisphere or not? Will we stop the spread of communism in this hemisphere or not? Will we act while there is still time?

There are those in this country who would yield to the temptation to do nothing. They are the new isolationists, very much like the isolationists of the late 1930's who knew what was happening in Europe, but chose not to face the terrible challenge history had given them. They preferred a policy of wishful thinking, that if they only gave up one more country, allowed just one more international transgression, then surely sooner or later the aggressor's appetite would be satisfied. Well, they didn't stop the aggressors; they emboldened them. They didn't prevent war; they assured it.

Legislation is now before the Congress that will carry out the recommendations of the National Bipartisan Commission. . . .

It's up to all of us—the administration, you as citizens, and your representatives in the Congress. The people of Central America can succeed if we provide the assistance I have proposed. We Americans should be proud of what we're trying to do in Central America, and proud of what, together with our friends, we can do in Central America to support democracy, human rights, and economic growth while preserving peace so close to home. Let us show the world that we want no hostile Communist colonies here in the Americas—South, Central, or North.

Glossary

Central America: region where North and South America meet; includes the countries of Belize, Costa Rica, El Salvador, Guatemala, Honduras, Nicaragua, and Panama

communism: economic and political system of the Soviet Union; an economic system in which a single party owns the means of production, or one in which all goods are held in common

Soviet Union: the Union of Soviet Socialist Republics (U.S.S.R.), a communist country that was founded in 1922 and dissolved in 1991, and the center of the Soviet Bloc, a group of communist allies during the Cold War

surrogate forces: forces acting in the interest of another entity

Short-Answer Questions

1. Summarize the overall focus of President Reagan's speech. What is the purpose of a speech like this one?

2. Evaluate who the intended audience is for this speech. What clues does this document give about that?

3. Analyze this speech's significance and what it tells us about America during the Cold War.

Tato Laviera: "AmeRícan"

Author	Significance
Tato Laviera	Nuyorican poem that showcases the intersecting themes of identity, family, and history
Date	
1985	
Document Type	
Poems, Plays, Fiction	

Overview

Poet Jesús Abraham "Tato" Laviera was a significant figure in the Nuyorican movement, a cultural movement of people who are of Puerto Rican origin or descent who reside in New York City. Laviera was born in 1951 in Puerto Rico. His family moved to New York City in 1960, and he was educated at Cornell University and Brooklyn College. From an early age, he wrote poetry that addressed themes of history, immigration, and identity. His poetry was written in Spanglish, a mixture of English and Spanish. The fact that Laviera wrote in a mix of English and Spanish, with rich historical metaphors, made his work unique at the time. In addition, Laviera emphasized the musicality of his poetry, which was influenced by the rhythm and voice of many cultures. Most of his life was dedicated to working with human rights organizations.

One overarching theme found throughout Laviera's poetry is identity. His famous poem AmeRícan touches on this idea of identity and what it means to be in the generation between two identities. Published in 1985, AmeRícan is a quintessential example of Nuyorican poetry. Nuyorican poetry explores the immigrant experience through a strong political background. Poetry lies at the heart of the Nuyorican genre and continues to be a vital part of the movement today.

Puerto Rican immigrants going to New York (Library of Congress)

Document Text

we gave birth to a new generation,
AmeRícan, broader than lost gold
never touched, hidden inside the
puerto rican mountains.

we gave birth to a new generation
AmeRícan, it includes everything
imaginable you-name-it-we-got-it
society.

we gave birth to a new generation,
AmeRícan salutes all folklores,
european, indian, black, spanish
and anything else compatible:

AmeRícan, singing to composer pedro
flores' palm trees up high in
the universal sky!

AmeRícan, sweet soft spanish danzas
gypsies moving lyrics la
española cascabelling
presence always singing at our
side!

AmeRícan, beating jíbaro modern trouba
dours crying guitars romantic
continental bolero love songs!

AmeRícan, across forth and across back
back across and forth back
forth across and back and forth

our trips are walking bridges!
it all dissolved into itself, an
attempt was truly made, the
attempt was truly absorbed,
digested, we spit out the
poison, we spit out in malice,
we stand, affirmative in action,
to reproduce a broader answer
to the marginality that gobbled
us up abruptly!

AmeRícan, walking plena-rhythms in new
york, strutting beautifully alert,
alive many turning eyes won
dering, admiring!

AmeRícan, defining myself my own way
any way many many ways Am
e Rícan, with the big R and the
accent on the í!

AmeRícan, like the soul gliding talk of
gospel boogie music!

AmeRícan, speaking new words in spanglish tenements, fast tongue
moving street corner "que
corta" talk being invented at

the insistence of a smile!

AmeRícan, abounding inside so many
ethnic english people, and out
of humanity, we blend and mix
all that is good!

AmeRícan, integrating in new york and
defining our own destino, our
own way of life,

AmeRícan, defining the new america,
humane america, admired
america, loved america, harmo-
nious america, the world in
peace, our energies collectively
invested to find other civili-
zations, to touch God, further
and further,
to dwell in the spirit of divinity!

AmeRícan, yes, for now, for i love this, my
second land, and i dream to
take the accent from the
altercation, and be proud to
call myself american, in the u.s.
sense of the word, AmeRícan,
America!

Glossary

bolero: a genre of love song popular throughout the Spanish-speaking world

danzas: musical genre that originated in southern Puerto Rico

destino: Spanish for destiny

jíbaro: word that refers to traditional Puerto Rican farmers who live in the mountains and have a musical style

Pedro Flores: Puerto Rican composer of popular ballads and boleros

plena-rhythms: an Afro–Puerto Rican musical genre

Glossary

que corta: Spanish for "that cuts" or "who cuts"

Spanglish: a hybrid language of Spanish and English

Short-Answer Questions

1. Briefly summarize the message of "AmeRícan" by evaluating the language and historical references Laviera includes.

2. Analyze how the poem's rhythm and format influence how it is meant to be read and how it falls into the Nuyorican genre.

3. In a detailed response, analyze how you think "AmeRícan" tells the story of the Nuyorican experience and the identities claimed by the author.

Reyes Cárdenas: "If We Praise the Aztecs"

Author	**Significance**
Reyes Cárdenas	Articulates the uncertain future that Mexican Americans faced regarding identity and national belonging in the aftermath of the Chicano movement
Date	
1986	
Document Type	
Poems, Plays, Fiction	

Overview

In his poem "If We Praise the Aztecs," Reyes Cárdenas expresses the dilemma faced by many Mexican American activists in the years following the decline of the Chicano Movement. Being of that generation himself, his insight allows him to capture the mixed feelings felt by many Chicanas and Chicanos who had championed various causes during the turbulent period of the 1960s and 1970s. These causes included social, cultural, and political actions that were defined ideologically by their militant and revolutionary undercurrents. By the time Cárdenas published "If We Praise the Aztecs" in his 1986 book of poems *I Was Never a Militant Chicano*, that radical activist period was in the past. Nonetheless, both the title of the poem and his book, like much of his work, are purposely iron-ic considering that writing Chicano poetry is itself a revolutionary act. Cárdenas's clever wording aside, it is difficult to ignore the contradictions presented here. The poem warns Mexican Americans of the perils of romanticizing the indigenous past, fetishizing revolutionary heroes, and subscribing to the "white way" (American ideas of capitalism and politics). Alternatively, Cárdenas reminds his audience that there is another way to exist, one that cannot be delayed. Overall, the poem synthesizes the apprehension that many Chicana/os felt during the Reagan Era of the1980s, a period that was emblematic of conspicuous consumption and personal success contrasted against a backdrop of economic inequality and the distress of disadvantaged communities.

Document Text

If we praise the Aztecs
or Zapata
we praise something
too far removed.
If we embrace Guevara
we must realize
that revolution
works only on rare occasions.
If we succumb
to the Great White Way

we learn the hard way.
If we try "the middle of the road"
we crossed the
dividing line.
If we live for the future
we betray the present.
There's only one way
to go about it
so why put it off
any longer?

Glossary

Aztecs: Mesoamerican culture that flourished from the 14th through the 16th centuries

Guevara: Ernesto "Che" Guevara, a Marxist revolutionary, an important figure in the Cuban Revolution, a guerilla leader in South America, and a countercultural symbol of rebellion

succumb: to give in; to yield

Zapata: Emiliano Zapata Salazar, a Mexican revolutionary, especially important in the Mexican Revolution of 1910–20

Short-Answer Questions

1. Reyes Cárdenas wrote "If We Praise the Aztecs" in response to cultural changes occurring at a certain time in United States. What point do you think he is trying to make in his critical approach toward Chicano politics and icons in relation to that moment?

2. Due to the political climate of the 1960s and 1970s, Chicano activists were often branded as radical extremists for simply demanding social justice. What are some points in the poem that depict this public feeling, and how does Cárdenas treat them?

3. "If We Praise the Aztecs" was published in a book that Cárdenas titled *I Was Never a Militant Chicano*. Keeping in mind the contradictions embedded in his work, what message do you think Cárdenas projected to the Mexican American community?

Frank del Olmo:
"Latino 'Decade' Moves into '90s"

Author
Frank del Olmo

Date
1989

Document Type
Essays, Reports, Manifestos

Significance
Examined the complicated idea of the "decade" of the Latino

Overview

The concept of "the decade of the Hispanic," became popular around Los Angeles, California, in the 1980s. But in his 1989 commentary piece "Latino 'Decade' Moves into '90s" for the *Los Angeles Times*, editor Frank del Olmo emphasizes that the concept of a "decade of the Hispanic" was manufactured. He argues that progress for Latinos does not belong to one particular period and began prior to its coinage in 1978, in a *U.S. News & World Report* article about Latinos working in President Jimmy Carter's administration. The commentary begins by examining the use of the phrase within print media and culture and notes that it has become a part of a larger conversation. Del Olmo first identifies the concept as a local (Los Angeles area) marketing tool rather than a celebration of the achievements of Latinos in the his-

torical record. Then, in a broader context, he highlights the significant achievements of the Latino community throughout the 1970s and 1980s. For del Olmo, the concept of a "decade of the Hispanic" is not something of consequence because achievement cannot be relegated to a single decade as it is an ever-evolving advent of change and progress. His argument is explored through art, politics, education, and sports.

Frank del Olmo (1948–2004) was a successful editor, columnist, and reporter for the *Los Angeles Times*. He began his work with the *Times* as an intern in 1970 and continued working for the newspaper until his death. During his career, he received several awards, including a Pulitzer Prize for Public Service. During the time of this publication, he served as the *LA Times*'s editorial page editor.

Document Text

Does anybody remember that the 1980s were supposed to be "the Decade of the Hispanic"? Probably. Should anybody care? I think not.

For the term "Decade of the Hispanic" was contrived and artificial. And, in fact, the progress for Latinos it was supposed to symbolize began long before the 1980s. More importantly, it will continue into the 1990s.

The phrase "Decade of the Hispanic" was first used in an article about Latino appointees working in the Carter Administration published by U.S. News & World Report in 1978. Many Latinos working in Washington, D.C., at the time were quoted by the news magazine, but the final word went to a Cuban-American named Maria Elena Torano.

"The blacks had the decade of the '60s; women had the '70s. The '80s will be the decade for Hispanics," she said.

U.S. News used Torano's phrase to end the 1,500-word report, and even ran a picture of her, using "The '80s will be the decade for Hispanics" as the caption underneath. Times librarians found 173 additional print-media citations of that phrase in the ensuing 11 years.

As near as I can remember, the phrase was first widely used in the Los Angeles area as part of an advertising campaign in the early '80s. Then, as now, the Coors Brewing Co. saw the Latino community as a growing market for its beer. So it plastered billboards all around town of a smiling Latino holding a beer and toasting the world as he proclaimed Coors "the beer for the Decade of the Hispanic."

Because of those billboards, I have always associated the phrase more with marketing than I have with the arts, politics, business and the other fields in which Latinos became more visible and prominent during the 1980s. Because of that increased visibility, the glib, easy conclusion to reach about the '80s is that they were, indeed The Decade for Latinos.

But if you look a little more closely, you'll find that all the advances and triumphs of the '80s were presaged in the '70s. Just look at the progress made in California and the Southwest.

For example, the most evident impact Latinos had in the '80s was in the arts. East Los Angeles' Los Lobos became one of the country's most popular rock groups, and Tucson's Linda Ronstadt returned to her Latino roots with a hit album of classic Mexican songs. Latino-themed films like "Stand and Deliver," "La Bamba" and "The Milagro Beanfield War" were produced, and some became major hits. Latino actors played major roles in popular TV series like "L.A. Law" and "Miami Vice."

But I would argue that the precursor to all this artistic ferment was the 1978 opening of Luis Valdez's hit play, "Zoot Suit," in Los Angeles and in 1979 on Broadway. And many of the Latino artists whose artworks were displayed at the Los Angeles County Museum of Art in 1989 were painting murals in the city's barrios in the 1970s too.

Equally dramatic changes occurred in the world of politics, but even there the groundwork was laid in the 1970s. Throughout California, the number of Latinos holding public office rose from 231 in 1973 to 460 in 1984 and 580 today, according to the National Assn. of Latino Elected Officials.

That number is expected to increase even more as Latino activists take advantage of recent court decisions against the at-large voting system that many political analysts claim works against Latino candidates in local elections. But all this progress stems from changes made in the Voting Rights Act in 1975, which extended protection to other minorities in addition to African-Americans. That act provided the leverage for groups like the Mexican American Legal Defense and Educational Fund to challenge discriminatory voting laws and the Southwest Voter Registration and Education Project to conduct hundreds of get-out-the-vote drives from South Texas to Northern California. . . .

Because of the ups and downs of the political world, some community activists argue that the most lasting kinds of political change take place at the less visible grass-roots level. They point to the emergence of groups that focus on issues of local concern to the average Latino worker and taxpayer. Even here, trends begun in the 1970s gained momentum in the '80s. . . .

But, ironically, the biggest political opportunity Latinos got in the 1980s did not involve U.S. citizens. When Congress enacted the landmark Immigration Reform and Control Act of 1986 to stem the flow of illegal immigrants to this country, it offered illegal aliens already living here the chance to legalize their status. More than half of the 3 million people who took advantage of that so-called "amnesty" program are Latinos, and under the 1986 law they can become citizens, and voters, in the 1990s. If they take advantage of the opportunity, the coming decade could see even greater political progress for Latinos than the 1980s.

One area where Latinos still lagged behind during the 1980s was in business. Of course, Vons' President Bill Davila became one of the best-known business executives in Los Angeles in the '80s thanks to the television commercials he does for his supermarket chain. But in other corporations, Latinos are barely working their way into executive suites. Still, that does not mean businessmen are ignoring the Latino community—just trying to figure it out. The 1980s were the decade when dozens of major corporations became aware just how fast the Latino market is growing and joined early pioneers in trying to plug into it. The most noteworthy result of this trend was the founding of a second Spanish television network, Telemundo, to compete with the long-established Univision.

In education, the record was decidedly mixed for Latinos in the '80s. . . .

Sports fan that I am, a review of the '80s cannot pass without recalling how much fun "Fernandomania" was when it seized the city in 1980. A portly left-handed pitcher from Etchohuaquila, Mexico, made the Dodgers more popular than ever with local fans—and helped the team's veteran Spanish-language broadcaster Jaime Jarrin become almost as well known as—well—Fernando Valenzuela.

Glossary

Carter Administration: presidency of the thirty-ninth U.S. president, Jimmy Carter, from 1977 to 1981

contrived: something that is created rather that happening naturally or spontaneously

Maria Elena Torano: Cuban-American public policy expert and, in the 1980s, founder of the National Association of Spanish Broadcasters

National Assn. of Latin Elected Officials: a nonpartisan organization established in 1976 to help Latino elected officials effectively serve their communities

Glossary

Voting Rights Act of 1975: extended the Voting Rights Act of 1965 and addressed voting discrimination against members of "language minority groups"

zoot suit: men's suit with high-waisted, wide-legged, peg-leg pants and oversize shoulder pads, popular among Chicanos in the first half of the twentieth century

Short-Answer Questions

1. What does Frank del Olmo argue that the phrase "the Decade of the Hispanic" refers to? Briefly explain examples of his assertion.

2. Summarize what del Olmo sees as advances and triumphs that should be the markers of success in the 1970s and 1980s. How does that narrative differ from what he saw in print media and advertising?

3. Evaluate the significance of politics in del Olmo's argument. What was the importance of grass-roots movements? How did successes in politics differ from those in the business world?

"The Decade of the Hispanic: An Economic Retrospective"

Author National Council of La Raza **Date** 1990 **Document Type** Essays, Reports, Manifestos	**Significance** Identified economic trends in the 1980s that characterized Hispanics' economic situation, revealing discriminatory practices toward Hispanics

Overview

The National Council of La Raza (NCLR), later renamed UnidosUS, was established in 1968 with the mission of reducing poverty, discrimination, and creating new opportunities for Hispanic Americans. The NCLR, a nonprofit, nonpartisan organization, applied research, policy analysis, and advocacy measures to provide much-needed assistance in developing programs and resources to serve low-income and disadvantaged Hispanic communities. In this report examining conditions of the 1980s, the NCLR focused on housing, education, employment, immigration, and civil rights enforcement and found numerous disparities and inequalities between Hispanic and white communities, including how reporting was conducted. The 1980s witnessed an increase in the growth of the Hispanic population generally and in the workforce. Efforts to improve the economy largely bypassed the Hispanic community, who were significantly excluded from economic assistance and employment. Poverty increased as family size grew, and regardless of type of employment or how many in a household worked, discriminatory measures kept wages low and benefits withheld from Hispanic families despite their positive impact on employment numbers.

Document Text

Immigration alone does not explain the prevalence of economic disadvantage among Hispanics. Although foreign-born Hispanics have slightly higher poverty rates and lower median incomes than U.S.-born Hispanics, the most significant **economic differential lies between Hispanics and Whites.** According to the 1980 Census, the most recent reliable information source: About two-thirds of all Hispanics were born in the United States. Following the 1970s—a decade of substantial Hispanic immigration—1980 Census data on foreign-born Hispanics produced only a slight depression in measures of Hispanics' overall economic status in that year. In 1980, the overall Mexican American poverty rate was 21.4%, compared to 19.2% among U.S.-born Mexican Americans only. 1980 Census data show a substantial economic differential between U.S.-born Hispanics and Whites. According to these data, the U.S.-born Hispanic family poverty rate of 19.2% was 140% higher than the 8.0% poverty rate among White families. In the 1980 Census, the overall Mexican American family poverty rate was 21.4%. Within **this overall rate, the foreign-born Mexican American** poverty rate was 24%, while that of U.S.-born Mexican Americans was 19.2%. In other words, if the foreign-born had not been counted in the overall 1980 Mexican American poverty rate, the overall rate would have been 10% lower. Looking at 1987, even if excluding the foreign-born would lower the overall Mexican American family poverty rate by a full 30%—three times its impact in 1980—the native-born Mexican American family poverty rate would decrease only from 25.8% to 18.1%, remaining significantly higher than the 1987 rate of 8.2% among White families.

Glossary

census: an official count or survey of a population, typically recording various details of individuals

differential: of, showing, or depending on a difference; differing or varying according to circumstances or relevant factors

---

Short-Answer Questions

1. Looking at the data, what does the economic disparity between Hispanics and whites reveal? Explain.

2. In the reporting, U.S.-born Mexican Americans are tabulated with foreign-born Mexican Americans to produce the total poverty rate among Mexican Americans. Why might this be problematic?

3. How might errors in reporting affect economic assistance to different groups within the Hispanic population, in this case foreign-born and U.S.-born? Explain.

Chapter 12

Latinos in Modern Politics

The "Decade of the Hispanic" carried into the 1990s with a surge of Hispanic political participation, not just in local politics but on the national level as well. While the Hispanic voice had been amplified thanks to the support of presidents like Gerald Ford and Jimmy Carter and aspiring political leaders like Robert Kennedy in the 1970s, by the 1990s the number of political leaders who were of Hispanic descent began to increase. This was in large part due to a massive dispersion of Hispanic communities across the country.

The Hispanic Population Boom and Growing Political Influence

Once considered a group of individuals concentrated in the Southwest, by the end of the 1990s Hispanics represented the largest minority in the United States by many demographic estimates. In 681 counties, the Hispanic population boomed by nearly 90% throughout the decade with the largest concentration in the Pacific Northwest, Chicago, and in the Carolinas and Mid-Atlantic. Perhaps the state most heavily impacted by the change was Florida where nearly half of its counties experienced significant growth in their Hispanic population by 2000.

The result of this massive migration of Hispanic voters was that nationwide, Hispanic voters began to be heard for the first time by both parties. Hispanic voters could not necessarily be counted on to vote Democrat or Republican, but rather, based on how they specifically viewed the party and candidate representing their interests at the time of the election. This political independence made them an invaluable asset in the numbers game of national politics. Hispanic concerns began driving political decisions across the country.

The Hispanic Swing Vote

The Hispanic vote was targeted by both Democrats and Republicans, but it was the latter that had more success during the 1980s as economic success and social growth was far more of a unifying factor than the Democrat approach of a singular Hispanic identity. This identity was difficult to unify since the experiences of those of Mexican, Puerto Rican, Cuban, and in the countless other countries of Latin America differed greatly. It made the Hispanic voter a swing vote that depended on several different factors, particularly the messaging of the politician.

One of the key issues that defined the Hispanic swing vote was that of illegal immigration and the immigrant experience as a whole. Prior to the 1970s, most Latino organizations were against illegal immigration. This was in large part due to the demographic of the Hispanic voter. They were of Mexican heritage, meaning their families had either come to the United States legally on work visas or had perhaps simply been assimilated into the United States with the annexation of the Southwest following the Mexican–American War. In the 1980s, this was largely no different as many Hispanic voters sided with President Ronald Reagan despite his more aggressive tactics to combatting drugs and illegal immigration.

Proposition 187

In 1994, the political climate undertook a significant change as Proposition 187 in California sought to deny illegal immigrants and their children access to public services including healthcare and education. This aggressive approach served to unify the Hispanic voters into a solid bloc in the 1990s, a bloc that would turn the state of California solidly Democrat from that point on. The move was seen by many Latinos as a target against them because many had been accused of being illegal even if they had been born and raised in the United States. Proposition 187 reshaped the Latino influence on politics, largely in favor of the Democratic Party, but it reshaped the voice and message of the Republican Party as well.

The DREAM Act

In the wake of the Proposition 187 fiasco, politicians running for national office began to realize the need to focus on reforming the immigrant experience if they were going to win the Latino vote. In his 2012 speech from the Rose Garden, President Barack Obama announced the DREAM Act (Development, Relief, and Education for Alien Minors Act) which would allow minors who entered the United States with their parents the opportunity for educational opportunities, and ultimately citizenship, regardless of their immigration status. Obama tapped into the Hispanic voters' communal experience in his speech by telling the American people to imagine facing the sudden threat of "deportation to a country that you know nothing about, with a language that you may not even speak."

Latinos and the Republican Party

For the Latino voter, the DREAM Act symbolized their goal in America and the potential result if their voice was not heard. This was furthered by Obama's nomination of Sonia Sotomayor to the Supreme Court, the first Hispanic to serve on the court. The Republican Party consequently saw this effect and in the 2016 election, it attempted run two Hispanic candidates for election: Marco Rubio and Ted Cruz. Rubio, despite his experience as the son of two Cuban immigrants, was soundly defeated in the primaries as the Latino voice was drowned out by a new, louder voice emerging from the Republican Party: the far right which was represented by Donald Trump.

In a 2016 rally in Phoenix, Trump focused heavily on the issue of immigration, tying immigrants to the problems plaguing American cities like drugs, crime, and violence. Without a strong candidate running against him, Latinos did not show up (as they had done in 2000 and 2004) to the polls and Trump won the election, leaving the Hispanic population once again feeling politically and racially targeted. This belief was reinforced by the verbal assault on New York's Congresswoman Alexandria Ocasio-Cortez in Washington, D.C. by two Republican congressmen and Trump's 2018 State of the Union speech that linked immigrants to gangs like MS-13 in El Salvador. By the end of Trump's term in office, the Latinos once again found themselves to be an important voting bloc that would shape the 2020 election and national politics moving forward.

Further Reading

Books

Jacobson, Robin Dale. *The New Nativism: Proposition 187 and the Debate over Immigration.* Minneapolis: University of Minnesota Press, 2008.

Ono, Kent A., and John M. Sloop. *Shifting Borders: Rhetoric, Immigration, and California's Proposition 187.* Philadelphia, PA: Temple University Press, 2002.

Articles

Barreto, Matt A., Luis R. Fraga, Sylvia Manzano, Valerie Martinez-Ebers, and Gary M. Segura. "'Should They Dance with the One Who Brung 'em?' Latinos and the 2008 Presidential Election." *PS: Political Science and Politics* 41, no. 4 (2008): 753–60.

Peralta, J. Salvador, and George R. Larkin. "Counting Those Who Count: The Impact of Latino Population Growth on Redistricting in Southern States." *PS: Political Science and Politics* 44, no. 3 (2011): 552–61.

Reny, Tyler. "Demographic Change, Latino Countermobilization, and the Politics of Immigration in US Senate Campaigns." *Political Research Quarterly* 70, no. 4 (2017): 735–48.

Websites

Fry, Richard. "IV. Hispanic Dispersion in the 1990s." Pew Research Center's Hispanic Trends Project, Pew Research Center, December 30, 2019, https://www.pewresearch.org/hispanic/2008/10/22/iv-hispanic-dispersion-in-the-1990s/.

Nadeem, Reem. "Most Latinos Say Democrats Care about Them and Work Hard for Their Vote, Far Fewer Say so of GOP." Pew Research Center Race & Ethnicity. Pew Research Center, November 10, 2022, https://www.pewresearch.org/race-ethnicity/2022/09/29/most-latinos-say-democrats-care-about-them-and-work-hard-for-their-vote-far-fewer-say-so-of-gop/.

"Profile of the Unauthorized Population - US." Migrationpolicy.org, October 1, 2022, https://www.migrationpolicy.org/data/unauthorized-immigrant-population/state/US.

Linda Chávez:
"Toward a New Politics of Hispanic Assimilation"

Author
Linda Chávez

Date
1991

Document Type
Essays, Reports, Manifestos

Significance
Explores the role of assimilation for the Hispanic community

Overview

In her first book, *Out of the Barrio: Toward a New Politics of Hispanic Assimilation*, Linda Chávez explores Hispanic progress through the lens of education, affirmative action, and immigration policy. When it was published in 1991, the book proved controversial for its author's assessment of the Hispanic population as not a permanent underclass but an upwardly mobile group and her assertion that bilingual education, affirmative action, and other public policies were not helping but hindering Hispanic progress.

In the final chapter, "Toward a New Politics of Hispanic Assimilation," Chávez examines the concept of assimilation through four broad categories: language and culture, political participation, education, and entitlements. She compares Hispanic immigrants and their descendants' processes of assimilation with that of other immigrant groups, including German, Greek, and Italian. She argues that "assimilation represents the opportunity to succeed in America," and she holds "ethnic leaders" and "elites who create and influence public policy" responsible for resisting assimilation and thus advancement. Throughout the essay, Chávez uses data and historical examples of assimilation within other immigrant groups to explore the process for Hispanic Americans.

Chávez is chair of the Center for Equal Opportunity, a conservative think tank that promotes equal opportunity and nondiscrimination in America. Earlier in her career, Chávez worked in the presidential administrations of Ronald Reagan, George H.W. Bush, and George W. Bush, the latter as the first Latina nominated to a cabinet position when President Bush nominated her as secretary of labor.

Linda Chávez (Gage Skidmore)

Document Text

Assimilation has become a dirty word in American politics. It invokes images of people, cultures, and traditions forged into a colorless alloy in an indifferent melting pot. But, in fact, assimilation, as it has taken place in the United States, is a far more gentle process, by which people from outside the community gradually became part of the community itself. Descendants of the German, Irish, Italian, Polish, Greek, and other immigrants who came to the United States bear little resemblance to the descendants of the countrymen their forebears left behind. America changed its immigrant groups—and was changed by them. Some groups were accepted more reluctantly than others—the Chinese, for example—and some with great struggle. Blacks, whose ancestors were forced to come here, have only lately won their legal right to full participation in this society; and even then civil rights gains have not been sufficiently translated into economic gains. Until quite recently, however, there was no question but that each group desired admittance to the mainstream. No more. Now ethnic leaders demand that their groups remain separate, that their native culture and language be preserved intact, and that whatever accommodation takes place be on the part of the receiving society.

Hispanic leaders have been among the most demanding, insisting that Hispanic children be taught in Spanish; that Hispanic adults be allowed to cast ballots in their native language and that they have the right to vote in districts in which Hispanics make up the majority of voters; that their ethnicity entitle them to a certain percentage of jobs and college admissions; that immigrants from Latin America be granted many of these same benefits, even if they are in the country illegally. . . . For all of these people, assimilation represents the opportunity to succeed in America. Whatever the sacrifices it entails—and there are some—most believe that the payoff is worth it. Yet the elites who create and influence public policy seem convinced that the process must be stopped or, where this has already occurred, reversed.

From 1820 to 1924 the United States successfully incorporated a population more ethnically diverse and varied than any other in the world. We could not have done so if today's politics of ethnicity had been the prevailing ethos. . . . The millions of Latin immigrants who are joining the already large native-born Hispanic population will severely strain our capacity to absorb them, unless we can revive a consensus for assimilation. But the new politics of Hispanic assimilation need not include the worst features of the Americanization era.

. . . We should not be tempted to shut our doors because we fear the newcomers are too different from us ever to become truly "American." Nonetheless, Hispanics will be obliged to make some adjustments if they are to accomplish what other ethnic groups have.

LANGUAGE AND CULTURE

Most Hispanics accept the fact that the United States is an English-speaking country; they even embrace the idea. A Houston Chronicle poll in 1990 found that 87 percent of all Hispanics believed that it was their "duty to learn English" and that a majority believed English should be adopted as an official language. . . . But Hispanics, especially more recent arrivals, also feel it is important to preserve their own language. . . . There is nothing inconsistent in these findings, nor are the sentiments expressed unique to Hispanics. . . . The debate is not about whether Hispanics, or any other group, have the right to retain their native language but about whose responsibility it is to ensure that they do so.

The government should not be obliged to preserve any group's distinctive language or culture. . . .

If Hispanic parents want their children to be able to speak Spanish and know about their distinctive culture, they must take the responsibility to teach their children these things. . . . The best way for Hispanics to learn about their native culture is in their own communities. Chinese, Jewish, Greek, and other ethnic communities have long established after-school and weekend programs to teach language and culture to children from these groups. Nothing stops Hispanic organizations from doing the same things. . . .

Hispanics should be interested not just in maintaining their own, distinctive culture but in helping Latin immigrants adjust to their American environment and culture as well. Too few Hispanic organizations promote English or civics classes,

although the number has increased dramatically since the federal government began dispensing funds for such programs under the provisions of the Immigration Reform and Control Act, which gives amnesty to illegal aliens on the condition that they take English and civics classes. . . .

POLITICAL PARTICIPATION

The real barriers to Hispanic political power are apathy and alienage. Too few native-born Hispanics register and vote; too few Hispanic immigrants become citizens. . . . Ethnic politics is an old and honored tradition in the United States. . . .

Politics has traditionally been a great equalizer. One person's vote was as good as another's, regardless of whether the one was rich and the other poor. . . . The emphasis is always on rights, never on obligations. Hispanic voter organizations devote most of their efforts toward making the process easier—election law reform, postcard registration, election materials in Spanish—to little avail; voter turnout is still lower among Hispanics than among blacks or whites. . . . Ethnic politics was for many groups a stepping-stone into the mainstream. . . .

EDUCATION

Education has been chiefly responsible for the remarkable advancements most immigrant groups have made in this society. . . . If Hispanics hope to repeat the successful experience of generations of previous immigrant groups, they must continue to increase their educational attainment, and they are not doing so fast enough. . . . Despite more than two decades of affirmative action programs and federal student aid, college graduation rates among native-born Hispanics, not to mention immigrants, remain significantly below those among non-Hispanics. . . . Only a substantial commitment to the education of their children on the part of this generation of Hispanic parents will increase the speed with which Hispanics improve their social and economic status.

Glossary

alienage: experience of being isolated from a group or activity

Americanization: government practice that was designed to prepare foreign-born residents for full participation in citizenship

apathy: lack of concern

assimilation: the process in which a minority group takes on the characteristics the dominant culture

ethos: the character, sentiment, or moral nature of a person or society

Short-Answer Questions

1. How does Chávez propose that Hispanics in the United States retain their language and other aspects of their culture, if they wish to do so?

2. Chávez explains that for some, assimilation offers "the opportunity to succeed in America." Analyze what she means by this statement and what historical precedents she gives for this.

3. Briefly summarize Chávez's argument in this essay.

Proposition 187

Author
Dick Mountjoy, Ronald Prince, and Barbara Kiley

Date
1994

Document Type
Legislative

Significance
Sought to bar unauthorized immigrants from most public services, including health care and education

Overview

Proposition 187 was a California ballot initiative that sought to prohibit illegal immigrants from accessing public services such as health care and education. In 1994, the initiative was put forth by the "Save Our State" Committee, an organization opposed to illegal immigration, and authored by committee chair Ronald Prince, co-chair Barbara Kiley, and California assemblyperson Dick Mountjoy. Proponents of the bill argued on behalf of California taxpayers, citing that taxpayers paid billions of dollars in assistance to illegal immigrants, largely for health care and education. California had experienced an increase in immigration during the early 1990s, and polling showed broad support for immigration reform, including

Proposition 187. California Democrats and student organizations spoke out publicly against the initiative, seeing it as an attack on the Hispanic population and an expression of bigotry against Latinx and Asian immigrants. However, the initiative passed by a wide margin in November 1994, with almost a quarter of Latinx population voting in favor of the initiative. The large percentage of Latinx votes in favor of the initiative highlighted a realignment of Hispanic political affiliations as many Hispanic voters changed voter registration from Democrat to Republican. It also pinpointed how Hispanic Americans sought to distance themselves from Hispanic noncitizens in an effort to assert their Americanness.

Protesters marching against Proposition 187 (Wikimedia Commons)

Document Text

Proposition 187: Text of Proposed Law

This initiative measure is submitted to the people in accordance with the provisions of Article II, Section 8 of the Constitution. This initiative measure adds sections to various codes; therefore, new provisions proposed to be added are printed in italic type to indicate that they are new.

PROPOSED LAW

SECTION 1. Findings and Declaration.

The People of California find and declare as follows: That they have suffered and are suffering economic hardship caused by the presence of illegal aliens in this state. . . . Therefore, the People of California declare their intention to provide for cooperation between their agencies of state and local government with the federal government, and to establish a system of required notification by and between such agencies to prevent illegal aliens in the United States from receiving benefits or public services in the State of California.

SECTION 2. Manufacture, Distribution or Sale of False Citizenship or Resident Alien Documents: Crime and Punishment.

Section 113 is added to the Penal Code, to read:

113. Any person who manufactures, distributes or sells false documents to conceal the true citizen-

ship or resident alien status of another person is guilty of a felony, and shall be punished by imprisonment in the state prison for five years or by a fine of seventy-five thousand dollars ($75,000).

SECTION 3. Use of False Citizenship or Resident Alien Documents: Crime and Punishment.

Section 114 is added to the Penal Code, to read:

114. Any person who uses false documents to conceal his or her true citizenship or resident alien status is guilty of a felony, and shall be punished by imprisonment in the state prison for five years or by a fine of twenty-five thousand dollars ($25,000).

SECTION 4. Law Enforcement Cooperation with INS.

Section 834b is added to the Penal Code, to read:

834b. (a) Every law enforcement agency in California shall fully cooperate with the United States Immigration and Naturalization Service regarding any person who is arrested if he or she is suspected of being present in the United States in violation of federal immigration laws. . . .

SECTION 5. Exclusion of Illegal Aliens from Public Social Services.

Section 10001.5 is added to the Welfare and Institutions Code, to read:

10001.5. (a) In order to carry out the intention of the People of California that only citizens of the United States and aliens lawfully admitted to the United States may receive the benefits of public social services and to ensure that all persons employed in the providing of those services shall diligently protect public funds from misuse, the provisions of this section are adopted. . . .

SECTION 6. Exclusion of Illegal Aliens from Publicly Funded Health Care.

Chapter 1.3 (commencing with Section 130) is added to Part 1 of Division 1 of the Health and Safety Code, to read:

CHAPTER 1.3. PUBLICLY-FUNDED HEALTH CARE SERVICES.

130. (a) In order to carry out the intention of the People of California that, excepting emergency medical care as required by federal law, only citizens of the United States and aliens lawfully admitted to the United States may receive the benefits of publicly-funded health care, and to ensure that all persons employed in the providing of those services shall diligently protect public funds from misuse, the provisions of this section are adopted. . . .

SECTION 7. Exclusion of Illegal Aliens from Public Elementary and Secondary Schools.

Section 48215 is added to the Education Code, to read:

48215. (a) No public elementary or secondary school shall admit, or permit the attendance of, any child who is not a citizen of the United States, an alien lawfully admitted as a permanent resident, or a person who is otherwise authorized under federal law to be present in the United States.

(b) Commencing January 1, 1995, each school district shall verify the legal status of each child enrolling in the school district for the first time in order to ensure the enrollment or attendance only of citizens, aliens lawfully admitted as permanent residents, or persons who are otherwise authorized to be present in the United States. . . .

SECTION 8. Exclusion of Illegal Aliens from Public Postsecondary Educational Institutions.

Section 66010.8 is added to the Education Code, to read:

66010.8. (a) No public institution of postsecondary education shall admit, enroll, or permit the

510   The Schlager Anthology of Hispanic America

attendance of any person who is not a citizen of the United States, an alien lawfully admitted as a permanent resident in the United States, or a person who is otherwise authorized under federal law to be present in the United States. . . .

SECTION 9. Attorney General Cooperation with the INS.

Section 53069.65 is added to the Government Code, to read:

53069.65. Whenever the state or a city, or a county, or any other legally authorized local governmental entity with jurisdictional boundaries reports the presence of a person who is suspected of being present in the United States in violation of federal immigration laws to the Attorney General of Cali-

fornia, that report shall be transmitted to the United States Immigration and Naturalization Service. . . .

SECTION 10. Amendment and Severability.

The statutory provisions contained in this measure may not be amended by the Legislature except to further its purposes by statute passed in each house by roll call vote entered in the journal, two-thirds of the membership concurring, or by a statute that becomes effective only when approved by the voters. In the event that any portion of this act or the application thereof to any person or circumstance is held invalid, that invalidity shall not affect any other provision or application of the act, which can be given effect without the invalid provision or application, and to that end the provisions of this act are severable.

Glossary

illegal alien: a foreign person who is living in a country without having official permission to live there

severability: a provision in a piece of legislation that allows the remainder of the legislation's terms to remain effective, even if one or more of its other terms or provisions are found to be unenforceable or illegal

Short-Answer Questions

1. Analyze the penalties for agencies, governments, and locales that violate immigration laws under Proposition 187.

2. Under Proposition 187, what do you think is the purpose of singling out education?

3. Proposition 187's main issue was rooted in illegal border crossings and poor border enforcement. Proponents of the measure argued that not enough was being done to prevent illegal border crossings, while critics argued the measure did not actually strengthen border enforcement. How do you think these measures have impacted arguments surrounding immigration?

Lionel Sosa:
The Americano Dream:
How Latinos Can Achieve Success in
Business and in Life

Author Lionel Sosa	**Significance** Highlights the obstacles, such as their own culture, that Latinx Americans face and must overcome to be successful
Date 1998	
Document Type Essays, Reports, Manifestos	

Overview

Lionel Sosa (b. 1939) worked as a marketing consultant and was named one of the twenty-five most influential Hispanics in America by *Time* magazine in 2005. Drawing on his own experiences as well as those of other successful Latinos, his book *The Americano Dream* illustrates the obstacles that Latinos face and must overcome. One of those obstacles is their heritage. In this passage from the first chapter, Sosa highlights the influences of family and religion that guide the decisions made by Latinx peoples in the United States. These cultural norms, while in some ways beneficial, also deter many Latinx people in the United States from becoming successful as breaking from tradition is necessary to climb the economic ladder. Earlier generations used tools of colonialism, such as religion, to maintain strong family ties; however, those same tools were used to keep those generations subservient. Sosa called on the new generation of Latinos to shake off this colonial mentality.

Document Text

Two major forces hold us Latinos back in business: the values taught by our own families and the values taught by our church.

"But wait!" you'll say. "Family and church are precisely the forces in our lives that are the strongest." True, but you must realize that the "truths" that priests and parents have inculcated in our psyche may not be the absolute truth.

I've been to countless Masses in both Anglo and Latino communities (I still go every Sunday), and the message I hear in each setting is radically different, yet it emanates from fundamentally the same church, the same

512   The Schlager Anthology of Hispanic America

Catholicism. One says there is hope, the other says subservience is a virtue. Latinos, especially in Mexico, Central America, and the northern cone of South America, where the *indio* was enslaved by Spanish conquerors, have historically been taught to be subservient. Our "*si, señor*," and "*mándeme*" are akin to the black slave's "yassuh, massa," the conditioned response when his name was called. After all, a slave is a slave, whether black or brown.

"Whatever will be, will be," Latinos are told. "It is God's will—*lo que quiera Dios*." Latinos believe this. It is drilled into us by our parents, who learned it from their own parents the Indian slaves of the *conquistadores*, and by our priests, who learned it from their own priests. Indeed, it is as though Latinos follow a kind of heavenly marketing plan:

• Goal: *Lo que Dios quiera*—whatever God wants

• Strategy: *Como Dios quiera*—however God wants it

• Measurement of success: *Así lo quiere Dios*—and that's the way God wants it

This kind of teaching worked very well—for the Spaniards. It kept the *indio* right where they wanted him, as a slave, and all in the name of goodness and God.

Glossary

vinculcated: taught

subservient: prepared to obey others unquestioningly

Short-Answer Questions

1. What is the significance of linking the enslavement of Latin American peoples under Spanish rule to the enslavement of African peoples? Explain.

2. Sosa says, "You must realize that the 'truths' that priests and parents have inculcated in our psyche may not be the absolute truth." Explain what he means by that.

3. How does Sosa incorporate the "colonial mindset" into his message for Latinx peoples? Why does he do this?

DREAM Act

Author United States Senate	**Significance** Designed to protect undocumented children from deportation and create a pathway to citizenship
Date 2001	
Document Type Legislative	

Overview

The United States routinely denies equal economic or social opportunity to people in the country without documented legal status or citizenship, including the children of undocumented immigrants. First introduced in the Senate in 2001 by Senator Dick Durban (D-Ill.) and Senator Orrin Hatch (R-Utah) as S. 1291 and reintroduced in Congress several times since then, the Development, Relief, and Education for Alien Minors (DREAM) Act was related to earlier immigration reform measures designed to protect undocumented youth from deportation or denial of access to U.S. resources. The DREAM Act proposes a conditional pathway to citizenship for undocumented youth who have completed high school in the United States and wish to attend a U.S. postsecondary institution or serve in the military. After a six-year conditional period that would require higher education or military service along with other requirements, eligible residents would qualify for permanent resident status and then be able to apply for citizenship.

Various iterations of the bill have been introduced in both the Senate and the House, but as of 2023 the DREAM Act has failed to pass in either chamber of Congress.

Democratic senators supporting the DREAM Act (Wikimedia Commons)

Document Text

A BILL to amend the Illegal Immigration Reform and Immigrant Responsibility Act of 1996 to permit States to determine State residency for higher education purposes and to authorize the cancellation of removal and adjustment of status of certain alien college-bound students who are long-term United States residents.

Be it enacted by the Senate and House of Representatives of the United States of America in Congress assembled,

SECTION 1. SHORT TITLE.

This Act may be cited as the "Development, Relief, and Education for Alien Minors Act" or "DREAM Act". . . .

SEC. 3. CANCELLATION OF REMOVAL AND ADJUSTMENT OF STATUS OF CERTAIN LONG-TERM RESIDENT STUDENTS.

(a) Special Rule for Children in Qualified Institutions of Higher Education.—

(1) In general.—Notwithstanding any other provision of law and subject to paragraph (2), the Attorney General may cancel removal of, and adjust to the status of an alien lawfully admitted for permanent residence, subject to the conditional basis described in section 4, an alien who is inadmissible or deportable from the United States, if the alien demonstrates that—

(A) the alien has applied for relief under this subsection not later than two years after the date of enactment of this Act;

(B) the alien has not, at the time of application, attained the age of 21;

(C) the alien, at the time of application, is attending an institution of higher education in the United States (as defined in section 101 of the Higher Education Act of 1965 (20 U.S.C. 1001));

(D) the alien was physically present in the United States on the date of the enactment of this Act and has been physically present in the United States for a continuous period of not less than five years immediately preceding the date of enactment of this Act;

(E) the alien has been a person of good moral character during such period; and

(F) the alien is not inadmissible under section 212(a)(2) or 212(a)(3) or deportable under section 237(a)(2) or 237(a)(4).

(2) Procedures.—The Attorney General shall provide a procedure by regulation allowing eligible individuals to apply affirmatively for the relief available under this paragraph without being placed in removal proceedings.

(b) Termination of Continuous Period.—For purposes of this section, any period of continuous residence or continuous physical presence in the United States of an alien who applies for cancellation of removal under this section shall not terminate when the alien is served a notice to appear under section 239(a) of the Immigration and Nationality Act.

(c) Treatment of Certain Breaks in Presence.—An alien shall be considered to have failed to maintain continuous physical presence in the United States under subsection (a) if the alien has departed from the United States for any period in excess of 90 days or for any periods in the aggregate exceeding 180 days.

(d) Statutory Construction.—Nothing in this section may be construed to apply a numerical limitation on the number of aliens who may be eligible for cancellation of removal or adjustment of status under this section.

(e) Regulations.—

(1) Proposed regulations.—Not later than 90 days after the date of the enactment of this Act, the Attorney General shall publish proposed regulations implementing this section.

(2) Interim, final regulations.—Not later than 180 days after the date of the enactment of this Act, the Attorney General shall publish final regulations implementing this section. Such regulations shall be effective immediately on an interim basis, but are subject to change and revision after public notice and opportunity for a period for public comment.

Glossary

aggregate: total

inadmissible: not accepted as valid

statutory: required, permitted, or enacted by a statute (law)

Short-Answer Questions

1. What is the purpose of the DREAM Act? Who qualifies under the DREAM Act, and why is that important?

2. What conditions must undocumented immigrants meet to qualify under the DREAM Act?

3. The United States has a long history of accepting or educating certain groups into becoming "good Americans." How does the language of the DREAM Act reflect this?

Sonia Sotomayor:
"A Latina Judge's Voice"

Author
Sonia Sotomayor

Date
2001

Document Type
Speeches/Addresses

Significance
An examination, by the third female and first Hispanic Supreme Court justice, of the importance of broad representation for women and minorities in law and government

Overview

This lecture was delivered by Sonia Sotomayor at the University of California, Berkeley, School of Law in 2001. At the time, Sotomayor was an appeals court judge. Later, she was appointed to the Supreme Court by President Barack Obama in 2009, becoming the first person of Hispanic descent appointed to the Supreme Court. Born in New York and the daughter of Puerto Rican parents, Justice Sotomayor grew up understanding the hypocrisy of America's "melting pot" ideology: the U.S. claims to take pride in its ethnic diversity but ignores the problems underrepresented groups face, especially in law and government positions. Calling out the low number of women and people of color who occupy these positions, Sotomayor further asserts that so few representatives speaking for such a broad swath of society cannot necessarily represent all members of these underrepresented groups. For Sotomayor, her experiences as a Latina influence how she approaches issues and topics, which is valuable to overseeing cases.

U.S. Supreme Court justice Sonia Sotomayor
(Collection of the Supreme Court of the United States)

Document Text

Who am I? I am a "Newyorkrican." For those of you on the West Coast who do not know what that term means: I am a born and bred New Yorker of Puerto Rican–born parents who came to the states during World War II. . . .

America has a deeply confused image of itself that is in perpetual tension. We are a nation that takes pride in our ethnic diversity, recognizing its importance in shaping our society and in adding richness to its existence. Yet, we simultaneously insist that we can and must function and live in a race and color-blind way that ignores these very differences that in other contexts we laud. That tension between "the melting pot and the salad bowl"—a recently popular metaphor used to describe New York's diversity—is being hotly debated today in national discussions about affirmative action. Many of us struggle with this tension and attempt to maintain and promote our cultural and ethnic identities in a society that is often ambivalent about how to deal with its differences. In this time of great debate we must remember that it is not political struggles that create a Latino or Latina identity. I became a Latina by the way I love and the way I live my life. My family showed me by their example how wonderful and vibrant life is and how wonderful and magical it is to have a Latina soul. They taught me to love being a Puertorriqueña and to love America and value its lesson that great things could be achieved if one works hard for it. But achieving success here is no easy accomplishment for Latinos or Latinas, and although that struggle did not and does not create a Latina identity, it does inspire how I live my life.

I was born in the year 1954. That year was the fateful year in which *Brown v. Board of Education* was decided. When I was eight, in 1961, the first Latino, the wonderful Judge Reynaldo Garza, was appointed to the federal bench, an event we are celebrating at this conference. When I finished law school in 1979, there were no women judges on the Supreme Court or on the highest court of my home state, New York. There was then only one Afro-American Supreme Court Justice and then and now no Latino or Latina justices on our highest court. Now in the last twenty plus years of my professional life, I have seen a quantum leap in the representation of women and Latinos in the legal profession and particularly in the judiciary. In addition to the appointment of the first female United States Attorney General, Janet Reno, we have seen the appointment of two female justices to the Supreme Court and two female justices to the New York Court of Appeals, the highest court of my home state. One of those judges is the Chief Judge and the other is a Puerto Riqueña, like I am. As of today, women sit on the highest courts of almost all of the states and of the territories, including Puerto Rico. One Supreme Court, that of Minnesota, had a majority of women justices for a period of time. . . .

That same point can be made with respect to people of color. No one person, judge or nominee will speak in a female or people of color voice. I need not remind you that Justice Clarence Thomas represents a part but not the whole of African-American thought on many subjects. Yet, because I accept the proposition that, as Judge Resnik describes it, "to judge is an exercise of power," and because, as another former law school classmate, Professor Martha Minnow of Harvard Law School, states, "there is no objective stance but only a series of perspectives—no neutrality, no escape from choice in judging," I further accept that our experiences as women and people of color affect our decisions. The aspiration to impartiality is just that—it's an aspiration because it denies the fact that we are by our experiences making different choices than others. Not all women or people of color in all or some circumstances, or indeed in any particular case or circumstance, but enough people of color in enough cases will make a difference in the process of judging. The Minnesota Supreme Court has given an example of this. As reported by Judge Patricia Wald formerly of the D.C. Circuit Court, three women on the Minnesota Court with two men dissenting agreed to grant a protective order against a father's visitation rights when the father abused his child. The *Judicature Journal* has at least two excellent studies on how women on the courts of appeal and state supreme courts have tended to vote more often than their male counterpart to uphold women's claims in sex discrimination cases and criminal defendants' claims in search and seizure cases. As recognized by legal scholars, whatever the reason, not one woman or person of color in any one position, but as a group we will have an effect on the development of the law and on judging. . . .

Each day on the bench I learn something new about the judicial process and about being a professional Latina woman in a world that sometimes looks at me with suspicion. I am reminded each day that I render decisions that affect people concretely and that I owe them constant and complete vigilance in checking my assumptions, presumptions and perspectives and ensuring that to the extent that my limited abilities and capabilities permit me, that I reevaluate them and change as circumstances and cases before me require. I can and do aspire to be greater than the sum total of my experiences but I accept my limitations. I willingly accept that we who judge must not deny the differences resulting from experience and heritage but attempt, as the Supreme Court suggests, continuously to judge when those opinions, sympathies and prejudices are appropriate. . . .

Glossary

affirmative action: a set of procedures designed to eliminate unlawful discrimination among applicants, remedy the results of such prior discrimination, and prevent such discrimination in the future

quantum leap: a huge, often sudden, increase or advance in something

Short-Answer Questions

1. What are the results of having too few people from underrepresented groups serving in government and legal positions, according to Sonia Sotomayor?

2. How does Justice Sotomayor believe her experiences as a Latina work to her advantage or disadvantage? Explain.

3. Explain Justice Sotomayor's characterization of America as "deeply confused" in terms of the "melting pot and the salad bowl" metaphor.

Samuel P. Huntington:
"The Hispanic Challenge"

Author
Samuel P. Huntington

Date
2004

Document Type
Essays, Reports, Manifestos

Significance
Asserts that Hispanic immigration patterns in the United States threaten American unity

Overview

Hispanic immigration into the United States, primarily from Mexico, has created in immigrant communities a duality—as the African American philosopher W. E. B. Du Bois once put it, a sense of "double consciousness." Mexican Americans have long been forced to grapple with their identities as both Mexican and American. Many Mexican Americans over the years have formed communities in which they can maintain their Mexican identity while also challenging anti-immigration legislation that threatens their communities and their families. The 1990s saw a wave of immigration from Mexico and, as a result, anti-immigration legislation, such as California's Proposition 187, to curtail the rights of immigrants. By resisting assimilation into American culture, according to Samuel P. Huntington in his *Foreign Policy* essay, Mexican Americans have used their networks to challenge existing U.S. power structures. This has been especially true in U.S. southern border states, which are the largest areas of settlement for Mexican immigrants. In his essay, Huntington addresses Hispanic immigration to the United States, declares that Latino immigrants "have not assimilated into mainstream U.S. culture," and expresses his fear that continued Hispanic immigration "threatens to divide the United States."

2004 photograph of Samuel P. Huntington (Wikimedia Commons)

Document Text

The persistent inflow of Hispanic immigrants threatens to divide the United States into two peoples, two cultures, and two languages. Unlike past immigrant groups, Mexicans and other Latinos have not assimilated into mainstream U.S. culture, forming instead their own political and linguistic enclaves—from Los Angeles to Miami—and rejecting the Anglo-Protestant values that built the American dream. The United States ignores this challenge at its peril. . . .

Blood Is Thicker Than Borders

Massive Hispanic immigration affects the United States in two significant ways: Important portions of the country become predominantly Hispanic in language and culture, and the nation as a whole becomes bilingual and bicultural. The most important area where Hispanization is proceeding rapidly is, of course, the Southwest. As historian [David] Kennedy argues, Mexican Americans in the Southwest will soon have "sufficient coherence and critical mass in a defined region so that, if they choose, they can preserve their distinctive culture indefinitely. They could also eventually undertake to do what no previous immigrant group could have dreamed of doing: challenge the existing cultural, political, legal, commercial, and educational systems to change fundamentally not only the language but also the very institutions in which they do business."

Anecdotal evidence of such challenges abounds. In 1994, Mexican Americans vigorously demonstrated against California's Proposition 187—which limited welfare benefits to children of illegal immigrants—by marching through the streets of Los Angeles waving scores of Mexican flags and carrying U.S. flags upside down. In 1998, at a Mexico–United States soccer match in Los Angeles, Mexican Americans booed the U.S. national anthem and assaulted U.S. players. Such dramatic rejections of the United States and assertions of Mexican identity are not limited to an extremist minority in the Mexican American community. Many Mexican immigrants and their offspring simply do not appear to identify primarily with the United States.

Empirical evidence confirms such appearances. A 1992 study of children of immigrants in Southern California and South Florida posed the following question: "How do you identify, that is, what do you call yourself?" None of the children born in Mexico answered "American," compared with 1.9 percent to 9.3 percent of those born elsewhere in Latin America or the Caribbean. The largest percentage of Mexican-born children (41.2 percent) identified themselves as "Hispanic," and the second largest (36.2 percent) chose "Mexican." Among Mexican American children born in the United States, less than 4 percent responded "American," compared to 28.5 percent to 50 percent of those born in the United States with parents from elsewhere in Latin America. Whether born in Mexico or in the United States, Mexican children overwhelmingly did not choose "American" as their primary identification.

Demographically, socially, and culturally, the *re-conquista* (re-conquest) of the Southwest United States by Mexican immigrants is well underway. A meaningful move to reunite these territories with Mexico seems unlikely, but Prof. Charles Truxillo of the University of New Mexico predicts that by 2080 the southwestern states of the United States and the northern states of Mexico will form La República del Norte (The Republic of the North). Various writers have referred to the southwestern United States plus northern Mexico as "MexAmerica" or "Amexica" or "Mexifornia." "We are all Mexicans in this valley," a former county commissioner of El Paso, Texas, declared in 2001.

This trend could consolidate the Mexican-dominant areas of the United States into an autonomous, culturally and linguistically distinct, and economically self-reliant bloc within the United States. "We may be building toward the one thing that will choke the melting pot," warns former National Intelligence Council Vice Chairman Graham Fuller, "an ethnic area and grouping so concentrated that it will not wish, or need, to undergo assimilation into the mainstream of American multi-ethnic English-speaking life."

A prototype of such a region already exists—in Miami.

Miami is the most Hispanic large city in the 50 U.S. states. Over the course of 30 years, Spanish speakers—overwhelmingly Cuban—established their dominance in virtually every aspect of the city's life, fundamentally changing its ethnic composition, culture, politics, and language. The Hispanization of Miami is without precedent in the history of U.S. cities. . . .

Irreconcilable Differences

The persistence of Mexican immigration into the United States reduces the incentives for cultural assimilation. Mexican Americans no longer think of themselves as members of a small minority who must accommodate the dominant group and adopt its culture. As their numbers increase, they become more committed to their own ethnic identity and culture. . . .

Continuation of this large immigration (without improved assimilation) could divide the United States into a country of two languages and two cultures. . . . Americans should not let that change happen unless they are convinced that this new nation would be a better one.

Such a transformation would not only revolutionize the United States, but it would also have serious consequences for Hispanics, who will be in the United States but not of it. [Lionel] Sosa ends his book, *The Americano Dream*, with encouragement for aspiring Hispanic entrepreneurs. "The Americano dream?" he asks. "It exists, it is realistic, and it is there for all of us to share." Sosa is wrong. There is no Americano dream. There is only the American dream created by an Anglo-Protestant society. Mexican Americans will share in that dream and in that society only if they dream in English.

Glossary

anecdotal: based on or consisting of reports or observations of usually unscientific observers

empirical: based on, concerned with, or verifiable by observation or experience rather than theory or pure logic

Short-Answer Questions

1. What evidence does the author give that Mexican Americans have resisted assimilation into U.S. culture?

2. What might be some of the results or consequences if Hispanic communities do not assimilate fully into mainstream American culture, according to the author?

3. The author writes that as the number of Mexican Americans increases, "they become more committed to their own ethnic identity and culture." Does the author seem to admire or lament this commitment? Please explain.

Herman Badillo:
"From Kennedy Democrat to Giuliani Republican"

Author
Herman Badillo

Date
2006

Document Type
Essays, Reports, Manifestos

Significance
Highlights Badillo's turn from the tenets of the Democratic Party toward those of the Republican Party, defined as self-reliance, lower taxes, and toughness on crime

Overview

Herman Badillo (1929–2014) was the first Puerto Rican elected to several posts in the New York City area, including serving in the U.S. House of Representatives. A strong Democratic supporter for much of his early political career, Badillo became disenchanted with the New York Democratic Party, chiding the party as being too originalist in its message and not adapting with the problems of the 1970s through early 2000s. He also noted that the New York Democratic Party was plagued with corruption and failed to tackle certain problems that were harming the city, such as crime, poverty, and theft, and instead was focused on getting votes. Badillo's eventual alignment with the Republican Party, particularly with former New York mayor Rudy Giuliani, represented a shift in political affiliations among Latinx communities toward more conservative policies, such as those affiliated with the Republican Party. Badillo outlines his philosophical shift in this chapter, "From Kennedy Democrat to Giuliani Republican," of his book *One Nation, One Standard: An Ex-Liberal on How Hispanics Can Succeed Just Like Other Immigrant Groups*.

Herman Badillo (Library of Congress)

Document Text

Under Rudy, crime was reduced. The crime rate went way down, and the city was far more secure. . . . Some innocent people did get killed because the police made errors. . . .

Racial profiling was not the evil it was made out to be. . . . The ratio of blacks and Hispanics among those being stopped and frisked was not out of line with the ratio of blacks and Hispanics committing crimes.

Working closely with Giuliani showed me what I believed all along: Competent leadership, vision, and accountability could all lead to a renaissance on the Hudson. Decades of liberal misrule under multiple Democrats and the left-wing Republican-turned-Democrat John Lindsay had brought the city to its knees. Within a few months of Giuliani's inauguration, however, crime and disorder were declining while personal security and a citywide sense of optimism were on the way up. . . .

After this campaign I very publicly switched my registration to Republican. . . . The New York State Democratic Party has remained in the past and cannot make things better, because its members don't understand what is wrong. Over the years, I found myself disagreeing more and more with city and state Democratic policies and positions. For decades, Democratic leaders had advocated the same old solutions with no accountability and came up with the same old failures. In contrast, the Republican Party demonstrated a willingness to realistically address the vital issues we faced. Hard experience convinced me that Democratic leaders are never going to change.

I felt increasingly that the Democratic Party took large portions of its constituency for granted. Too many die-hard Dems, locally as well as nationally, continued to cling to the tired slogans of generations past as if they were a political life raft. Workfare was anathema to Democrats, but not to me.

Glossary

anathema: something or someone that one intensely dislikes

competent: capable

the Hudson: the Hudson River, which flows from upstate New York through New York City and forms the border between Manhattan and New Jersey

Short-Answer Questions

1. Badillo says that "competent leadership, vision, and accountability could all lead to a renaissance on the Hudson." What does he mean by that? Explain.

2. Why does Badillo argue that Democrats are rooted in the past and "cannot make things better"?

3. Badillo states, "Workfare was anathema to Democrats, but not to me." How does this reflect his own personal and political journey? Does it also reflect the political journey of other Latinx people? Explain.

Leslie Sanchez: "The Emerging Latino Republican Majority"

Author Leslie Sanchez	**Significance** Predicted shifts in Hispanic voting toward the Republican Party
Date 2007	
Document Type Essays, Reports, Manifestos	

Overview

In her 2007 book *Los Republicanos: Why Hispanics and Republicans Need Each Other*, Leslie Sanchez predicts shifts in Hispanic voting that could impact the future of American politics. *Los Republicanos* uses a historical lens to examine possible future voting tendencies. The ten-chapter book aims to debunk the "cultural and political myths," as the author describes them, surrounding "Hispanics and Republicans alike." Leslie Sanchez has served in political and government positions and as a political pundit throughout her career. In addition, she has worked as the deputy press secretary for the Republican National Committee (RNC) and with the George W. Bush White House Initiative on Hispanic Education.

In chapter four, "The Emerging Latino Republican Majority," Sanchez examines three major groups, which she calls "the youngbloods," "the faith seekers," and "the southern newbies," who she believes will contribute to Republican success with Hispanic voters. She uses her own firsthand knowledge as well as demographic statistics to support her commentary. Her primary assertion is that Latinos are "conservative in their views," which creates a natural connection with Republican platforms.

Document Text

A lot of elderly folks within the Hispanic community view the civil rights movement as their overarching issue. I think for my generation, the new focus is economic empowerment, creating wealth within our respective communities, and finding educational opportunities. . . .

The weakness of focusing on the civil rights messages of the past is that they are then viewed as being divisive. I know that the National Council of La Raza and other civil rights groups that represent the Hispanic community have been criticized in the past for not doing enough to connect the barrio with Wall Street. . . .

Political parties profile voters based on their lifestyles, to see whom they are most likely to vote for. They look far beyond party registration to other minutiae—magazine subscriptions, purchases, church memberships, and countless other small details of a voters life—to see if their constituents are more likely to vote for them or for their opponent. . . .

Right now, the partisans look at Hispanics and say they must be Democrats. But when you profile us as a group, without looking at our surnames, you would get a very different impression.

Cast aside your preconceptions, and take a look how we live and what we believe, instead of our heritage. We attend church at higher rates, we form more businesses and at a faster rate than the general population. We marry at a high rate. . . . We support tax cuts, we are pro-life, we oppose same-sex marriage. . . . These descriptions could all apply just as easily to Republicans as they do to Hispanics. . . .

These basic conservative sensibilities are not limited to Mexicans (who make up 60 percent of the Hispanics in the United States) but extend to Hispanics from other national backgrounds as well.

The Republican National Committee agreed to release previously undisclosed findings from our surveys of Hispanics leading up to the 2000 election. We found that:

- Three to one, Hispanic voters said that government should be based on "person al responsibility" rather than "group guarantees" or "bureaucratic paternalism."

- Hispanics view welfare, four to one, as a "safety net" rather than a permanent source of income. Also four to one, and unlike liberals of all races, they believe that the American dream is real for them—that "opportunity related to the work ethic will make them successful."

- Eighty percent of Hispanic male voters and 75 percent of Hispanic female voters report being part of the labor force, a sign of a strong cultural work ethic, and a flat contradiction of the myth that Hispanic illegal aliens come to the United States to go on welfare.

- Among the Hispanic voters we surveyed, about 53 percent are both married and own their own homes. This fits the demographic of Republicans in most racial groups.

To be sure, much of the Hispanic leadership is way out of touch with this cultural conservatism, often reaching to the farthest left extreme of the American political spectrum. . . .

Ask Hispanic voters what they think about immigration, and you'll hear mixed attitudes. . . .

Education consistently ranks at the top of Hispanic voters' concerns, no matter who is doing the polling. . . .

Clearly, Latinos are conservative in their views. This fact, combined with three emerging trends of Latino economic success, political mobilization through our churches, and our geographical expansion to new parts of the country, will contribute to a new paradigm that will shape the Hispanic vote in future elections. This new Latino political paradigm will bring more and more Hispanics to the GOP, resolving the obvious tension between Latinos' beliefs and an incompatible Democratic platform.

The Youngbloods

. . . Are these the "un-Latinos" who break the Hispanic cultural norms? You could say that. . . . They are the up-and-coming class of Latino professionals that form the Association of Latino Professionals in Finance and Accounting (ALPFA). . . .

ALPFA is actually a part of a much larger phenomenon that I call the "Hispanic Youngbloods." These young (under 40), well-educated and business-minded Latinos are growing in numbers, as are the groups that serve them. . . .

What is unique about these Hispanic Youngbloods is their attempt to create a cross-section of business and culture for both professional comraderie and cultural relevance. . . .

Leadership groups like ALFPA will shape the national political dialogue in ways that did not exist before. . . .

The Hispanic Youngblood phenomenon, moving from urban centers on the East Coast to include Latino professionals in the West, offers a mirror image to the 1960s Chicano civil rights movements, whose influence began in California and moved eastward. . . .

As their numbers and influence swell, the Hispanic Youngbloods will have a dramatic impact on politics as community leaders.

Faith Seekers

Not only do we have the polls to show how conservative Latinos are, but we also have real signs that a conservative awakening is happening in our f aith communities. . . .

Generally, much is made about the impact of the evangelical turnout in elections. . . .

Another leader in this area is the Rev. Luis Cortés, Jr., chairman and CEO of *Nueva Esperanza* in Philadelphia. . . . Cortés attributes the Latino evangelical success to aggressive outreach and establishment of the connection at home. . . .

Southern Newbies

We have seen the conservatism of Latino opinion, and the fact that Latinos are becoming more active in their churches. We have also seen the level of economic success Latinos have achieved as a group in a relatively short time, and the way our increasingly active faith communities are beginning to make us take stock in what values we vote for.

Another factor in transforming the Latino vote into a Republican majority will be our expanding footprint within the United States. Just 15 years ago, no one would have expected Hispanic communities to take root in such states as Tennessee, Georgia, Arkansas and South Carolina, but today they have. . . .

Today, 75 percent of Latinos live in just five states—California, Texas, New York, Illinois and Florida. Together, these account for 180 Electoral College votes. But only five states with proportionally large Hispanic populations are usually in play: Arizona, Nevada, Colorado, Florida and New Mexico, accounting for 56 electoral college votes.

These states are clearly important in any close election, and so obviously the Latino vote is critical there. But look beyond 2008 at the political impact of our growth in nontraditional areas. . . .

Glossary

GOP: "Grand Old Party," a nickname for the Republican Party

partisans: adherents to a single party or cause

Short-Answer Questions

1. Briefly explain what Sanchez calls the "new Latino political paradigm" and how she views this will bring more Hispanics to the GOP.

2. Describe the three emerging groups Sanchez depicts.

3. In a detailed response, analyze what Sanchez's overall argument is in this piece.

Lorna Dee Cervantes: "Coffee"

Author	Significance
Lorna Dee Cervantes	Depicted the infamous killing of more than forty Indigenous Mexicans at the hands of a paramilitary organization and its connections to multinational corporations that procure resources from Latin America
Date	
2007	
Document Type	
Poems, Plays, Fiction	

Overview

Members of the paramilitary group Máscara Roja ("Red Masks"), aligned with the Institutional Revolutionary Party (PRI) that was in power at the time, brutally murdered more than forty Indigenous Tzotzil people, including twenty-one women and fifteen children, from the villages of Acteal, Los Chorros, Pechquil, and Yabtelum in the Mexican state of Chiapas on December 22, 1997. The victims, members of a Roman Catholic pacifist group named Las Abejas ("The Bees") that sympathized with Zapatista rebels challenging the PRI, were assembled in a chapel in Acteal to pray for safe deliverance after having been forced from their homes by the Máscara Roja, who demanded they either join the group or be killed.

The investigation that followed revealed that although local government and police officers did not participate in the violence, they did nothing to prevent its occurrence and even tampered with evidence that might have helped bring the perpetrators responsible for the carnage to justice. There continues to be a great deal of anger surrounding the massacre at Acteal, with accusations that many people who were not participants were unfairly punished while some of those who were involved were not held accountable.

In her vivid and evocative poem, "Coffee," Chicana poet Lorna Dee Cervantes recounts the terrible slaughter in Chiapas and the cover-up that followed. She also provides a condemnation of major consumer brands based in the United States, whose exploitative neocolonial practices in Latin America helped catalyze the sort of political destabilization that led to the 1997 murders. Cervantes makes clear that the unwavering drive for corporate profits that motivates global capitalism has long contributed to the centuries-old abuse and extermination of Indigenous people. She closes her poem by pondering possible means of challenging the corporations and the disruption they have brought to Latin America.

Lorna Dee Cervantes
(Poleth Rivas / Secretaría de Cultura CDMX)

Document Text

I.
In Guatemala the black buzzard
has replaced the quetzal
as the national bird. The shadow
of a man glides across the countryside,
over the deforested plantations; a death
cross burnishes history into myth
as it scours the medicinal land into coffee;
burial mounds that could be sites
of unexcavated knowledge hold only
blasted feathers and the molding bones
of freedom. Golden epaulets glint
in the fluorescent offices, crystal
skulls shine in the eyes of the man
with the machete, within the site
of an AK-47. Under the rubble
of the ruling class, a human heart
beats in the palm, the tumba of ritual mercy
drums in the thunder clap, a hurricane wind
sounds the concha. In Quetzaltenango, foreign
interests plot the future of Mayan hands
and Incan gold. While on Wall Street,
the black sludge of a people trickles through
cappuccino machines like hissing snakes.

II.
Acteal. December 22, 1997. Bloodied
mud sucks the plastic sandals of a child,
velas gutter through the saged prayers
in the church blasted through with
twenty-two splintered holes the size
of a baby's tender fists. Melon heads pop
and the hacking drum of a machete
meeting bone counts down the hours
of matanza. . . .
. . . 140 federales
stand smoking in the twilight, at their feet,
the trampled harvest of peasants gleams
through the saturated leaves. Homero
Tovilla Cristiani picks up the phone: "I have
notified General Jorge Gamboa Solis. Everything
is under control. There is no massacre in Acteal".
He places the receiver again off the cradle
on the well-ordered desk. Meanwhile, a young
Tzotzil bloodies her knuckles scratching a hole
in a hole in the adobied wall of a cave feathered
with Jaguar
fur where 14 women and children wait,
shivering in the dark. An infant picks up the call.
The first woman in the line gazes into the coked-
up eyes
of her assassin projecting his automatic weapon
into the ear of the whimpering baby at her breast.
500 years of history gets written into her eyes, as
a Tzotzil
mother wedges her sleeping newborn into the hole.
She spits in the reddening dirt, and covers
her luz like a cat. Forty five pairs of shoes
get lost in Acteal. Matted hair clings
to the coffee plants, each green leaf,
another listening ear; each red seed,
another eye, dislodged from its skull. I hear
nothing happened in Acteal. And if it did
no one knows who they are. The PRI
press machine stands on the ridge

of Destiny, staring Truth in the eye
as men lie to the cameras. Twenty yards
away, the survivors are speaking
the names of the men paid 600 dollars
American. . . .
I hear forty-five graves being dug today.
The women form a chain of hearts.
They have dried the earth baked with their tears.
Each one carries a red mud brick
from the killing floor where the people
were hacked into pieces the size of a bat.
Here, the "Bat People," Tzotziles, will
build a house for their dead, and pray. . . .

VI.
"No more genocide in my name. . . ."
A young girl in trenzas sings outside
The Mexican Consulate in Denver.
"Go back where you came from!"
shouts a car of gringos speeding
down memory lane, and are nearly drowned out
by the ritual drums and the Native chants.
First World faces sing out above the placards
like severed heads or scalps. "No more Genocide
. . ."
. . . in Guatemala, Colombia, El Salvador, Chile,
Sand Creek, Wounded Knee. . . . Not with arms.
Not with training. Not with money. No more
of my tax dollars to but the man who drives
the Humvee that transports the soldier who shoots
the bullet that blinds the toddler, that enters the
heart
of Guadalupe Lopez Méndez who dies in Ocosingo
asserting her civil rights. No more Genocide
in my name. We shall not overcome. We shall fight
this way forever. . . .
La plumage de justicia hangs from the broken
arrows of palabras breaking the media block
of Truth and Consequences of Free Trade Agreements.
Horrific to read, to imagine, to know to tell . . .

but the only end to bullets for profit in knowledge
. . .
knowledge that will not appear wedged between
commercials for Taster's Choice and
Nobody Doesn't Like Sara Lee like the living body
of an indigenous child found two days after a massacre
in a bullet-ridden cave. Is this any way to fight
a drug war? Coffee, sugar, chocolate,
cattle. . . . "N . . . E . . . S . . . T . . . L . . . E . . . S . . .
Néstles makes the very best . . . MUR . . . DER!"
310 kilos of cocaine are found in Mazatan,
the municipality where the governor, Julio Cesar
Ruiz Ferro, has two large mansions, a ranch
with a hundred hectare banana plantation and
is building a luxury hotel with 100 suits, under-
ground
parking, boat dock, restaurant, bar and disco.
Revenue from taxing an impoverished indigenous
population was good this year. Meanwhile,
the Mexican Red Cross sends contaminated
and expired drugs to the thousands of refugees
dying of exposure, pneumonia, and other infec-
tions
in the frigid mountains. "Néstles makes the very
best . . .
MUR . . . DER!" 15 billion served, ground flesh
for the masses. I will grind Zapatista coffee
with the tongues of witness. I will wear
the huipil and honor the mothers. I will write
the dark into dawn. I will sit in the offices,
sit down the lying dog press, picket
the congress into action. I will not bank
with assassins. I will buy crafts, not Kraft,
Néstles, Proctor & Gamble, McDonald's, Sara Lee.
. . .
I will fight this way forever. . . .
"A culture isn't vanquished until the hearts
of its mothers are lying on the ground."
I will fight this way forever: I will say.
I will fight this way forever: I will pay.
I will fight this way forever: I will pray.
Amen. Y Con Safos.

Lorna Dee Cervantes: "Coffee"

Glossary

epaulets: ornaments worn on the shoulders of a uniform

federales: the national police force of Mexico

General Jorge Gamboa Solis: governor of Chiapas at the time of the 1997 massacre

Guadalupe Lopez Méndez who dies in Ocosingo: 38-year-old Tzeltal Indian killed by a police unit that opened fire on anti-government protestors in Chiapas in 1998

Homero Tovilla Cristiani: government secretary of Chiapas at the time of the 1997 massacre

huipil: a rectangular, one-piece garment worn by Indigenous women in Central America

La plumage de justicia: the feather of justice, of truth

luz: bright light

metanza: massacre, killing

palabras: speech, words

quetzal: brightly colored bird found in Central America

Quetzaltenango: municipality in Guatemala that produces coffee
saged: cleansed or purified; burning sage is a traditional cleansing or purifying ritual

Sand Creek: the site of a notorious 1864 massacre in Colorado where members of the state militia killed over 200 Cheyenne and Arapaho Indians

trenzas: hair braids

tumba: a traditional Central American drum

Tzotzil: Mayan people indigenous to Chiapas, Mexico

velas: candles or vigils

Wounded Knee: Lakota Sioux settlement that became the scene of a battle when U.S. Army troops arrived to disarm members participating in the Ghost Dance movement, leading to over 300 Lakota deaths

Y Con Safos: And With Respect

Short-Answer Questions

1. What kind of language and metaphors does Cervantes employ in her poem to describe the events of the massacre? How might it be more effective in conveying what occurred compared to a straightforward account?

2. How does Cervantes identify large corporations as bearing some responsibility for violent events such as the one she describes in her poem? What larger historical context does she use?

3. What sort of strategies does Cervantes outline in her poem for holding corporations accountable for their actions? What are some of the potential challenges one might encounter while using these strategies in an attempt to bring about change?

Lorna Dee Cervantes: "Coffee"

Bill Richardson:
Democratic National Convention Speech

Author
Bill Richardson

Date
2008

Document Type
Speeches/Addresses

Significance
At the 2008 Democratic National Convention, offered praise for soon-to-be presidential candidate Barack Obama's skill at predicting some of the Bush administration's foreign policy blunders

Overview

Governor Bill Richardson of New Mexico delivered an address on the final day of the Democratic National Convention (DNC) held in in August 2008, which culminated in Senator Barack Obama of Illinois accepting the Democratic Party's nomination to run for president of the United States. Richardson himself had sought the be the nominee before dropping out early in 2008 when he failed to do well in the initial round of primary and caucus contests.

The son of a Mexican-born mother and a half-Mexican father, Richardson came to be one of the most visible Hispanic politicians by the start of the twenty-first century. After earning degrees from Tufts University, Richardson moved to Santa Fe, New Mexico, and in 1982 was elected to Congress as the representative of the highly diverse third district. Richardson spent the next fourteen years in Congress, where he served in such roles as chairman of the Congressional Hispanic Caucus in the Nineth-eighth Congress and a deputy majority whip. He developed a close working relationship with President Bill Clinton, helping to steer the passage of the North American Free Trade Agreement (NAFTA) in 1993 and negotiating the release of American hostages held in Iraq and North Korea. Richardson's diplomatic efforts, which included a brief tenure as the U.S. Ambassador to the United Nations, resulted in his being nominated three times for the Nobel Peace Prize. He served as the secretary of energy from 1998 to 2001 and then returned to New Mexico, where he was elected governor in 2002 and served a second term following his reelection in 2006.

Richardson drew upon his diverse background in foreign relations in his speech at the DNC. In his speech, he praises Obama for his early criticism of the American invasion of Iraq in 2003 and his commitment to improving dealings between the United States and Mexico and Latin America.

Richardson at the Democratic National Convention in 2008 (Wikimedia Commons)

Document Text

Fellow citizens—I am not known as a quiet man. But I hope you will allow me, for a moment, to bring quiet to this great hall.

Because at a time when young men and women are dying for our country overseas, America faces a question worthy of silent reflection. And the American people are watching to see how we answer it. What is the best measure of a person's capacity to protect this country? There are often moments of great importance that go unnoticed in the unruly course of history.

And six years ago, there was a moment of great clarity and foresight. And if the world had known to listen, perhaps today there would be less heartache and sorrow. In October 2002, on a small stage before a small crowd, Barack Obama gave a speech that was barely noticed at the time.

In the midst of great fervor—brought about by an administration that questioned the patriotism of anyone who disagreed with it—Barack Obama called the coming war what it was: "a war based not on reason but on passion, not on principle but on politics." He was right!

Barack's words were prescient and brave. "I know that an invasion of Iraq without a clear rationale and without strong international support will only fan the flames of the Middle East and strengthen the recruitment arm of Al-Qaeda." He was right!

He said: "A successful war against Iraq would require a U.S. occupation of undetermined length, at undetermined cost, with undetermined consequences." He was right!

Instead, Barack Obama urged President Bush—who's never in the mood to be urged in a direction other than his own folly—to finish the fight with bin Laden and Al-Qaeda. He was right!

Six years ago, in this simple but forceful speech, Barack Obama did more than just challenge President Bush. He offered a detailed vision for foreign policy—including the vigorous enforcement of the nuclear nonproliferation treaty, condemnation of human rights abuses even among our allies and a commitment to reconciliation between Pakistan and India. He was right!

At the same time, there was another voice. After 9/11, John McCain turned his sights toward Iraq—a country that had nothing to do with 9/11—and called for a full-scale invasion. Barack Obama foresaw chaos. John McCain said we'd be welcomed as liberators, and that Iraq would pay for its own rebuilding. John McCain was wrong. Barack Obama was right!

Barack Obama was among the first to call for a timetable for responsible withdrawal. But John McCain, to this day, condemns the idea. The Iraqis are calling for a withdrawal timetable, but John McCain would keep us in Iraq for 100 years. John McCain is wrong. Barack Obama is right.

And Barack Obama saw the foolishness of embracing Pakistan's Musharraf. John McCain thought we should support the dictator and let him take care of the Pakistani terrorists. Musharaff is now gone, and the terrorists are stronger than ever. John McCain was wrong. Barack Obama was right.

With America fighting two wars, the 9/11 terrorists still at large, Iran pursuing nuclear weapons and Russia in Georgia, America needs a president who gets it right the first time. That president will be Barack Obama. With a vision of foreign policy that has ranged far beyond Iraq, Barack Obama has found a kindred spirit in another leader of great strength and wisdom—Joe Biden.

Barack Obama and Joe Biden believe we must fight the terrorists—not where we imagine them to be, but where we know them to be, like Afghanistan and Pakistan. We must lead a global effort to secure loose nuclear materials—not where we imagine them to be, but where we know them to be, in Russia, and the countries of the former Soviet Union.

It's time we had a president committed to fighting poverty in the Third World and ending the genocide in Darfur; who leads international efforts to stop global warming, strengthens our friendship with Mexico and Latin America, and stands behind Israel with full-time diplomacy to achieve peace in the Middle East; a president who ends the global scourge of AIDS in our time and sets an example of moral leadership by following our Constitution, shutting down Guantanamo and ending torture.

We must do all of this, not because we imagine these are American ideals, but because we know they are.

And ladies and gentlemen, Barack Obama and Joe Biden believe it's time to finish the job and get bin Laden. We don't need another four years of more of the same. It's time for the change America needs. This is the judgment and vision of Barack Obama. This is the preparation he has to be president of the United States. And this is the man we need to return our country into the goodwill of other nations and the grace of history.

Thank you, and God bless our country.

Glossary

Al-Qaeda: terrorist organization responsible for the attacks of September 11, 2001

bin Laden: Osama bin Laden, Saudi national who founded and led Al-Qaeda

Darfur: region in western Sudan in Africa that became the site of armed conflict in 2003

Guantanamo: location of American naval installation in Cuba where the United States detained and brutally interrogated suspected terrorists

John McCain: Arizona senator who ran as the Republican presidential nominee in 2008

Musharraf: Pervez Musharraf, president of Pakistan from 2001 to 2008

prescient: prophetic, visionary

Short-Answer Questions

1. What are the general criticisms Obama had for the Bush administration's foreign policy decisions that Richardson identifies in his speech? What changes does he insist Obama will make if elected president?

2. How does Richardson connect the Bush administration's foreign policy record to the Republican presidential candidate, Senator John McCain?

3. In what ways does Richardson refer to 9/11 in his speech? What does he identify as the primary responsibilities of a president in a post-9/11 world?

Bill Richardson: Democratic National Convention Speech

Sonia Sotomayor:
Supreme Court Nomination Speech

Author
Sonia Sotomayor

Date
2009

Document Type
Speeches/Addresses

Significance
Marked the nomination, in 2009, of the first Hispanic and third woman appointed to the Supreme Court

Overview

In 2009, President Barack Obama nominated Sonia Sotomayor to the Supreme Court, the first Hispanic woman and only third woman to be appointed to the court. The daughter of working-class Puerto Rican immigrants, Sotomayor grew up in public housing in New York. Having experienced firsthand the difficulties women and the Hispanic population faced in climbing the social, political, and judicial ladder, Sotomayor speaks in favor of being a force for change by combining her experiences with the foundation of U.S. law to create a more equal society.

Document Text

Thank you, Mr. President, for the most humbling honor of my life. You have nominated me to serve on the country's highest court, and I am deeply moved.

I could not, in the few minutes I have today, mention the names of the many friends and family who have guided and supported me throughout my life, and who have been instrumental in helping me realize my dreams.

I see many of those faces in this room. Each of you, whom I love deeply, will know that my heart today is bursting with gratitude for all you have done for me.

The President has said to you that I will bring

Sotomayor with Barack Obama and Joe Biden (Pete Souza)

my family. In the audience is my brother Juan Sotomayor—he's a physician in Syracuse, New York; my sister-in-law, Tracy; my niece Kiley—she looks like me.

My twin nephews, Conner and Corey.

I stand on the shoulders of countless people, yet there is one extraordinary person who is my life aspiration. That person is my mother, Celina Sotomayor.

My mother has devoted her life to my brother and me. And as the President mentioned, she often worked two jobs to help support us after dad died. I have often said that I am all I am because of her, and I am only half the woman she is.

Sitting next to her is Omar Lopez, my mom's husband and a man whom I have grown to adore. I thank you for all that you have given me and continue to give me. I love you.

I chose to be a lawyer and ultimately a judge because I find endless challenges in the complexities of the law. I firmly believe in the rule of law as the foundation for all of our basic rights.

For as long as I can remember, I have been inspired by the achievement of our founding fathers. They set forth principles that have endured for more than two centuries. Those principles are as meaningful and relevant in each generation as the generation before.

It would be a profound privilege for me to play a role in applying those principles to the questions and controversies we face today.

Although I grew up in very modest and challenging circumstances, I consider my life to be immeasurably rich. I was raised in a Bronx public housing project, but studied at two of the nation's finest universities.

I did work as an assistant district attorney, prosecuting violent crimes that devastate our communities. But then I joined a private law firm and worked with international corporations doing business in the United States.

I have had the privilege of serving as a federal District Court trial judge, and am now serving as a federal Appellate Circuit Court judge.

This wealth of experiences, personal and professional, has helped me appreciate the variety of perspectives that present themselves in every case that I hear. It has helped me to understand, respect and respond to the concerns and arguments of all litigants who appear before me as well as to the views of my colleagues on the bench.

I strive never to forget the real world consequences of my decisions on individuals, businesses and government.

It is a daunting feeling to be here. Eleven years ago, during my confirmation process for appointment to the Second Circuit, I was given a private tour of the White House. It was an overwhelming experience for a kid from the South Bronx.

Yet never in my wildest childhood imaginings did I ever envision that moment, let alone did I ever dream that I would live this moment.

Mr. President, I greatly appreciate the honor you are giving me, and I look forward to working with the Senate in the confirmation process. I hope that as the Senate and American people learn more about me, they will see that I am an ordinary person who has been blessed with extraordinary opportunities and experiences. Today is one of those experiences.

Thank you again, sir.

Glossary

aspiration: a hope or ambition of achieving something

daunting: seeming difficult to deal with in anticipation; intimidating

Short-Answer Questions

1. How does Justice Sotomayor integrate her experiences into the principles of the Founding Fathers?

2. Explain how Justice Sotomayor views the rule of law.

3. Why does Justice Sotomayor believe that her life experiences are important to her Supreme Court appointment?

Barack Obama: Speech at the National Council of La Raza

Author	Significance
Barack Obama	Highlighted the importance of immigration reform for the Hispanic community and the decline of Hispanic allegiance to the Democratic Party
Date	
2011	
Document Type	
Presidential/Executive; Speeches/Addresses	

Overview

In the 2008 presidential election, Barack Obama won a large percentage of the Latino vote, mostly running on a platform that prioritized immigration reform. During his reelection campaign, however, President Obama realized that he had largely failed to deliver on that promise, and as a result his popularity among Hispanic voters dipped in the years leading up to his reelection bid. In his speech to the National Council of La Raza, the United States' leading Hispanic civil rights group, documented in a White House press release immediately afterward, President Obama sought to address the problems still facing Latinos while also touting his administration's accomplishments. He addressed the flaws in the immigration system and the failure of Congress to pass the DREAM Act, which had led many Latino voters to become disillusioned with the Obama administration and more broadly with the Democratic Party, blaming him and the party for failing to end the deportations of undocumented immigrants.

Document Text

We've cut taxes for middle class workers, small businesses, and low-income families. We've won credit card reform and financial reform, protections for consumers and folks who use payday lenders or send remittances home from being exploited or ripped off. We've worked to secure health care for 4 million children, including the children of legal immigrants, and we are implementing health reform for all who have been abused by insurance companies, and all who fear going broke if they get sick—big victories for a Latino community that suffers from lack of health insurance more than any other. . . .

We know the recent recession has hit Latino families especially hard. We must continue our work on job creation to make sure every-

Barack Obama: Speech at the National Council of La Raza 545

Official White House portrait of Barack Obama (Pete Souza)

one who wants a job can find one; to make sure paychecks actually cover the bills; to make sure families don't have to choose between buying groceries and buying medicine; between sending their kids to college and being able to retire. My number one priority, every day, is to figure out how we can get businesses to hire and create jobs with decent wages. And in the short-term, there are some things we should do right away. I want to extend the tax relief we put in place for middle-class families, so that folks have more money in their paychecks. I want to cut red tape that keeps entrepreneurs from turning new ideas into thriving businesses. I want to sign trade deals so our businesses can sell more goods made in America to the rest of the world. And the hundreds of thousands of construction workers who lost their jobs when the housing bubble burst—I want to put them back to work building our roads and bridges and airports. There is work to be done. There are workers ready to do it. Bipartisan proposals for all of this would already be law if Congress would just send them to my desk. And I'd appreciate it if you'd all help me convince them to do it. Let's get it done. . . .

Two months ago, I went down to the border in El Paso to reiterate my vision for an immigration system that holds true to our values, our heritage, and meets our economic and security needs. And this is an economic imperative. In recent years, one in four high-tech startups in America—companies like Google and Intel—were founded by immigrants. One in six new small business owners are immigrants. These are job creators who came here to seek opportunity and now seek to share it. This is our strength. This makes America special—we attract talented, dynamic, optimistic people who continually refresh our economy and our spirit.

But we have a system that allows the best and brightest to come study in America, then tells them to leave and set up the next great company somewhere else. We have a system that tolerates immigrants and businesses that break the rules and punishes those that follow the rules. We have a system that separates families and punishes innocent young people for their parents' actions by denying them the chance to earn an education, or contribute to our economy, or serve in our military.

These are the laws on the books. And even as I swore an oath to uphold them, I know very well the real pain and heartbreak that deportations cause. I know how concerned and angry many of you are. And I promise you, we are responding to your concerns and working every day to make sure we're enforcing our laws in the best possible way. I know how badly some people want me to bypass Congress and change the law on my own. And believe me, I'd like to solve these challenges on my own. But it's not how our democracy works.

Let's be honest. I need a dance partner, and the floor's empty. Five years ago, 23 Republican senators supported comprehensive immigration reform because they knew it was good for our economy. Today, they've walked away. Republicans helped write the DREAM Act because they knew it was good for our country. Today, they've walked away. Last year, we passed the DREAM Act through the House only to see it blocked by Senate Republicans. It was heartbreaking to get so close, then see politics get in the way. And that's all that's changed in the past few years. Not the circumstances—but the political winds. That's left states to come up with patchwork versions of reform that don't solve the problem. And you and I know that's not the right way to go.

So you have every right to keep the heat on me and the Democrats. And I know you will, believe me. But I ask you to remember who's been standing with you. Remember who we need to move. Because usually, as soon as I come out in favor of something, half of Congress immediately hates it—even if it was once their idea. So I need you to keep building a movement for change outside of Washington. One that they can't stop. One greater than this community, that bridges party lines, that unites business and labor, faith and law enforcement, and all who know America can't continue operating with a broken immigration system. And I promise you I will keep up this fight. Because Washington is way behind the rest of the country on this.

Glossary

bipartisan: involving the agreement or cooperation of two political parties that usually oppose each other's policies

remittances: money

Short-Answer Questions

1. How would you describe President Obama's tone in his speech to the National Council of La Raza? Please cite examples.

2. Explain President Obama's proposed solutions for immigration reform.

3. Why does President Obama start off his speech by talking about the accomplishments of his administration in regards to Hispanic progress? Please explain.

Barack Obama: Speech at the National Council of La Raza

Barack Obama:
Speech Announcing DACA

Author
Barack Obama

Date
2012

Document Type
Presidential/Executive; Speeches/Addresses

Significance
Protected immigrants who came to the United States as children from deportation

Overview

On the thirtieth anniversary of the 1982 *Plyler v. Doe* decision, in which the Supreme Court found it unconstitutional to withhold state funds from school districts educating undocumented immigrants, President Barack Obama announced the Deferred Action for Childhood Arrivals (DACA). DACA deferred the deportation of low-risk individuals for two years upon certain conditions. It did not, however, provide a path to citizenship. DACA targeted young people who had immigrated as children. DACA was an alternative to the failed DREAM Act, which sought to grant immigrant students temporary legal status, putting them on a path to citizenship. DACA symbolized what Obama called "America's patchwork heritage"—the idea that various ethnicities, religions, cultures, and races are what make the United States great and unique—and embodied the notion that young people should not be punished for trying to live the American dream in the only nation many of them had ever known.

Document Text

. . . These are young people who study in our schools, they play in our neighborhoods, they're friends with our kids, they pledge allegiance to our flag. They are Americans in their heart, in their minds, in every single way but one: on paper. They were brought to this country by their parents—sometimes even as infants—and often have no idea that they're undocumented until they apply for a job or a driver's license, or a college scholarship.

Put yourself in their shoes. Imagine you've done everything right your entire life—studied hard, worked hard, maybe even graduated at the top of your class—only to suddenly face the threat of deportation to a country that you know nothing about, with a language that you may not even speak.

548

The Schlager Anthology of Hispanic America

Protesters at a DACA rally in San Francisco (Pax Ahimsa Gethen)

That's what gave rise to the DREAM Act. It says that if your parents brought you here as a child, if you've been here for five years, and you're willing to go to college or serve in our military, you can one day earn your citizenship. And I have said time and time and time again to Congress that, send me the DREAM Act, put it on my desk, and I will sign it right away.

Now, both parties wrote this legislation. And a year and a half ago, Democrats passed the DREAM Act in the House, but Republicans walked away from it. It got 55 votes in the Senate, but Republicans blocked it. The bill hasn't really changed. The need hasn't changed. It's still the right thing to do. The only thing that has changed, apparently, was the politics.

As I said in my speech on the economy yesterday, it makes no sense to expel talented young people, who, for all intents and purposes, are Americans—they've been raised as Americans; understand themselves to be part of this country—to expel these young people who want to staff our labs, or start new businesses, or defend our country simply because of the actions of their parents—or because of the inaction of politicians.

In the absence of any immigration action from Congress to fix our broken immigration system, what we've tried to do is focus our immigration enforcement resources in the right places. So we prioritized border security, putting more boots on the southern border than at any time in our history—today, there are fewer illegal crossings

Barack Obama: Speech Announcing DACA

549

than at any time in the past 40 years. We focused and used discretion about whom to prosecute, focusing on criminals who endanger our communities rather than students who are earning their education. And today, deportation of criminals is up 80 percent. We've improved on that discretion carefully and thoughtfully. Well, today, we're improving it again. . . .

Now, let's be clear—this is not amnesty, this is not immunity. This is not a path to citizenship. It's not a permanent fix. This is a temporary stopgap measure that lets us focus our resources wisely while giving a degree of relief and hope to talented, driven, patriotic young people. . . .

Precisely because this is temporary, Congress needs to act. There is still time for Congress to pass the DREAM Act this year, because these kids deserve to plan their lives in more than two-year increments. And we still need to pass comprehensive immigration reform that addresses our 21st century economic and security needs—reform that gives our farmers and ranchers certainty about the workers that they'll have. Reform that gives our science and technology sectors certainty that the young people who come here to earn their PhDs won't be forced to leave and start new businesses in other countries. Reform that continues to improve our border security, and lives up to our heritage as a nation of laws and a nation of immigrants. . . .

And I believe that it's the right thing to do because I've been with groups of young people who work so hard and speak with so much heart about what's best in America, even though I knew some of them must have lived under the fear of deportation. I know some have come forward, at great risks to themselves and their futures, in hopes it would spur the rest of us to live up to our own most cherished values. And I've seen the stories of Americans in schools and churches and communities across the country who stood up for them and rallied behind them, and pushed us to give them a better path and freedom from fear—because we are a better nation than one that expels innocent young kids.

. . . This is the right thing to do for the American people. . . .

Here's the reason: because these young people are going to make extraordinary contributions, and are already making contributions to our society.

I've got a young person who is serving in our military, protecting us and our freedom. The notion that in some ways we would treat them as expendable makes no sense. If there is a young person here who has grown up here and wants to contribute to this society, wants to maybe start a business that will create jobs for other folks who are looking for work, that's the right thing to do. Giving certainty to our farmers and our ranchers; making sure that in addition to border security, we're creating a comprehensive framework for legal immigration—these are all the right things to do.

We have always drawn strength from being a nation of immigrants, as well as a nation of laws, and that's going to continue. And my hope is that Congress recognizes that and gets behind this effort.

Glossary

amnesty: a pardon for people who have been convicted of political offenses

immunity: protection or exemption from something

Short-Answer Questions

1. How does President Obama use identity when talking about undocumented young people? Please cite examples.

2. What benefits to border security does President Obama see to DACA and the DREAM Act?

3. How does President Obama compare DACA and the DREAM Act?

Barack Obama: Speech Announcing DACA

Marco Rubio:
Presidential Campaign Launch Speech

Author
Marco Rubio

Date
2015

Document Type
Speeches/Addresses

Significance
Presents Rubio, the son of Cuban exiles, as the ideal presidential candidate because he understands the plight of the common American and the true meaning of the American dream

Overview

After serving a full term in the U.S. Senate, Marco Rubio, a Republican, launched his presidential bid rather than seek reelection. The son of Cuban exiles, Rubio used his own experiences to connect with not only the Hispanic community but also others who were neglected by the government at the time. Rubio was critical of not only the Obama administration and Democratic policies but of presidential hopefuls within the Republican Party who wanted to bring the United States back to a mythical time of prosperity. Rubio argued that for the United States to progress, it must be forward thinking and limit the role of the federal government. The United States, he said, must focus on strengthening the family bond, uplifting the common American, and improving the country's moral standing with a stronger focus on religion.

Document Text

. . . I chose to make this announcement at the Freedom Tower because it is a symbol of our nation's identity as the land of opportunity. And I am more confident than ever that despite our troubles, we have it within our power to make our time another American Century.

In this very room five decades ago, tens of thousands of Cuban exiles began their new lives in America. Their story is part of the larger story of the American miracle. How, united by a common faith in their God given right to go as far as their talent and work would take them, a collection of immigrants and exiles, former slaves and refugees, became

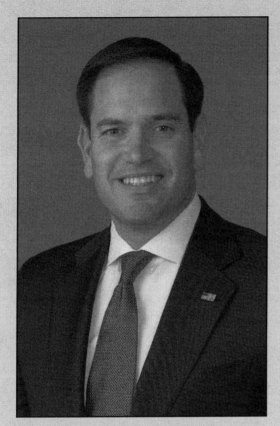

Marco Rubio (United States Senate)

one people, and together built the freest and most prosperous nation ever.

For almost all of human history, power and wealth belonged only to a select few. Most people who have ever lived were trapped by the circumstances of their birth, destined to live the life their parents had. But America is different. Here, we are the children and grandchildren of people who refused to accept this.

Both of my parents were born to poor families in Cuba. After his mother died when he was nine, my father left school to go work. My mother was one of seven girls raised by a disabled father who struggled to provide for his family.

When they were young, my parents had big dreams for themselves. But because they were not born into wealth or power, their future was destined to be defined by their past. So in 1956 they came here, to the one place on earth where the aspirations of people like them could be more than just dreams.

My father became a bartender. My mother a cashier, a maid and a Kmart stock clerk. They never made it big. But they were successful. Two immigrants with little money or education found stable jobs, owned a home, retired with security and gave all four of their children a life far better than their own.

My parents achieved what came to be known as the American Dream. But now, too many Americans are starting to doubt whether achieving that dream is still possible:

Hard working families living paycheck to paycheck, one unexpected expense away from disaster. . . .

Young Americans, unable to start a career, a business or a family, because they owe thousands in student loans for degrees that did not lead to jobs. . . .

And small business owners, left to struggle under the weight of more taxes, more regulations and more government.

Why is this happening in a country that for over two centuries has been defined by equality of opportunity?

Because while our people and economy are pushing the boundaries of the 21st century, too many of our leaders and their ideas are stuck in the twentieth century.

They are busy looking backward, so they do not see how jobs and prosperity today depend on our ability to compete in a global economy. So our leaders put us at a disadvantage by taxing, borrowing and regulating like it's 1999.

They look for solutions in yesterday, so they don't see that good-paying modern jobs require different skills and more education than the past. They blindly support an outdated higher education system that is too expensive and inaccessible to those who need it most.

And they have forgotten that when America fails to lead, global chaos inevitably follows, so they appease our enemies, betray our allies and weaken our military.

At the turn of the 19th century, a generation of Americans harnessed the power of the Industrial Age and transformed this country into the leading economy in the world. And the 20th century became the American Century.

Now, the time has come for our generation to lead the way toward a new American Century.

If we reform our tax code, reduce regulations, control spending, modernize our immigration laws and repeal and replace ObamaCare, the American people will create millions of better-paying modern jobs.

If we create a 21st century system of higher education that provides working Americans the chance to acquire the skills they need, that no longer graduates students with mountains of debt and degrees that do not lead to jobs, and that graduates more students from high school ready to work, then our people will be prepared to seize their opportunities in the new economy.

If we remember that family—not government—is the most important institution in society, that all life deserves protection, and that all parents deserve to choose the education that's right for their children, then we will have a strong people and a strong nation. . . .

This election is not just about what laws we will pass. It is a generational choice about what kind of country we will be.

Just yesterday, a leader from yesterday began a campaign for President by promising to take us back to yesterday.

But yesterday is over, and we are never going back. We Americans are proud of our history, but our country has always been about the future. Before us now is the opportunity to author the greatest chapter yet in the amazing story of America. . . .

Whether or not we remain a special country will depend on whether that journey is still possible for those trying to make it now:

The single mother who works long hours for little pay so her children don't have to struggle the way she has. . . .

The student who takes two buses before dawn to attend a better school halfway across town. . . .

The workers in our hotel kitchens, the landscaping crews in our neighborhoods, the late-night janitorial staff that clean our offices . . . and the bartenders who tonight are standing in the back of a room somewhere. . . .

If their American Dreams become impossible, we will have become just another country. But if they succeed, the 21st Century will be another American Century. This will be the message of my campaign and the purpose of my presidency. . . .

Glossary

Freedom Tower: building in Miami, Florida, that originally hosted Cubans as they fled communist Cuba following the 1959 Cuban Revolution

inevitability: certainty that something will happen

Short-Answer Questions

1. What problems does Rubio associate with hurting American progress? What are his solutions?

2. Rubio says, "We Americans are proud of our history, but our country has always been about the future." Explain what he means by that.

3. When talking about the "average American," Rubio says, "Whether or not we remain a special country will depend on whether that journey is still possible for those trying to make it now." What does he mean by this, and why is this important for U.S. progress? Explain.

Marco Rubio: Presidential Campaign Launch Speech

Denice Frohman: "Abuela's Dance"

Author
Denice Frohman

Date
2015

Document Type
Poems, Plays, Fiction

Significance
A writer's acknowledgment of her grandmother's struggles as a Hispanic American woman in another era

Overview

Award-winning poet Denice Frohman has won a reputation for her powerful works that represent her status as a queer person and a Hispanic American. Frohman, who is of both Puerto Rican and Jewish ancestry, earned a master's degree in education at Drexel University. She then worked for the Philly Youth Poetry Movement as a director and organizer. Her work as a poet and performer was recognized in 2013 when she won both the Women of the World Poetry Slam Championship and the Southern Fried Poetry Slam Championship. She is also a recording artist whose work appears in the album *Feels Like Home*.

Document Text

I creep into your room, Abuela.
Like an 8 year old on Christmas morning
up 3 hours too early,
but it's 1pm and you're still sleeping.

I decide to wake you.
Call me selfish, but
there's something left in you
that I need hold before you're gone.

As your eyes open, I wait
your face, trying to make sense of mine,
trying to translate me into something you've
spoken
before
And I know   it only takes about 22 seconds,

Denice Frohman in 2011 (Knight Foundation)

but I swear, it's long enough for me to fall in love again.

"Abuela, yo soy tu nieta. Recuerda?"
And there   your eyes widen like football fields,
as you reach for me in your back pocket, like a crumpled dollar bill
you forgot you had, showing me
that I have always been worth holding onto.

After we exchange short Spanish greetings,
I try to keep the conversation going,
but I'm not fluent,
this language, your language
was always bumpy road.
So I turn the radio on to fill the pot holes in my tongue
and we dance.

Let Celia Cruz lay the clues that stitch you back to me
the lyrics pulling themselves over the gaps in your seams
like a jacket covering the puddles in your memory lapses, synapses snapping,
and though your mind is a retired dancer with two left
feet,
your spirit is a 22 year old woman,
with legs that could wrap Christmas presents for days
and
hips that could make God want a lap dance.

Every chorus a question I ask like:
"Abuela, how did you feel when it was illegal to wave
your own flag?"
Every melody, a moment to capture your history like:
"Abuela, did you really walk 3 miles to school everyday?"

Every riff, a chance to end those sleepless nights once
and for all:
"Abuela, did you ever figure out how to stay in love?
I promise I won't tell a soul I know."

See when we dance,
we make corpses wanna boogie.
You in bed, moving your arms
conducting the skeleton of my body like a symphony

my hips, rocking back and forth, with a dip and
a twist,
kissing the accents in your favorite song's lips,
reaching for the dimple's in your memory
for me to take a picture with.

I can make you feel like when she was 22,
growing up in a poor Puerto Rican town
too high up to place on the map.
Abuela, do you remember you yet?

And I know this just amuses you, but the
truth is this was never just dancing.

You represent of part of me that people said I
could
never claim.

You give me the language to speak my identity
fluently,
for the first time

this was never just dancing.
And maybe it's because I'm the only one that can
get
to you,
the 22 year old in you, the joy, the smile
that forgets to show itself on most days.

Abuela, you make me feel useful.
You make me feel like I come from someplace, so
who needs maps any way,   I have you.

So go ahead Abuela, sleep—just not forever.
Because you and I have a lot more dancing left to
do.

Glossary

"Abuela, how did you feel when it was illegal to wave your own flag?": This is a reference to the law
known as Law 53, or La Ley de la Mordaza. Between 1948 and 1956, when the law was in force, it was
illegal to display or even possess a Puerto Rican flag.

"Abuela, yo soy tu nieta. Recuerda?": Literally, "Grandmother, I am your granddaughter. Remember?"

Celia Cruz: Cruz (1925–2003) was a Grammy and Latin Grammy Award–winning Cuban American
singer, most often associated today with salsa music. She also appeared in movies and on television and
received her own star on the Hollywood Walk of Fame. She had a long and formidable career, recording 37
studio albums between the 1950s and her death.

Short-Answer Questions

1. How does Frohman's relationship with her abuela help her connect to her own Puerto Rican heritage?

2. What parts of Abuela's history does Frohman bring up to spark her fading memories?

3. How does Frohman use dance as a metaphor for her Hispanic American experience?

Manuel Pastor: "Latinos and the New American Majority"

Author	**Significance**
Manuel Pastor	Summarized Hispanic Americans' complicated relationships with both the Democratic and Republican parties and speculated on the various ways they would influence politics in the decades to come
Date	
2016	
Document Type	
Essays, Reports, Manifestos	

Overview

The rapidly growing number of Hispanic Americans throughout the twentieth century led to no shortage of questions regarding how they might affect the American political landscape. Some speculated that their influence might resemble that of African Americans, who largely defected from the Republican Party starting in the 1930s as the Democrats increasingly identified as a party committed to social reform and the protection of civil rights. Others thought that the Republicans stood a good chance of wooing Hispanic supporters, particularly once the party moved in a markedly conservative direction in the 1980s, taking a stand against abortion rights and drug dealing. The question of how Hispanic Americans would align politically and affect future elections, particularly those involving future presidents, remained a topic of discussion and analysis into the twenty-first century.

Manuel Pastor, a professor of sociology and American studies and ethnicity, examines the issue in an article he wrote for the publication *Dissent* in 2016, a year that Donald Trump's candidacy for president upended American politics and led many to wonder how Latino voters would respond. Pastor takes into consideration Trump's vitriolic rhetoric about Mexican immigrants and identifies the increase in Latino naturalizations as a critical factor in the outcome of future elections. He nonetheless acknowledges that Hispanic Americans are not necessarily a monolithic bloc; differences of region, national origin, religious affiliation, and concerns over specific issues (such as immigration) have long informed where Hispanic voters fall on the political spectrum.

Hillary Clinton ultimately won approximately two-thirds of the Hispanic vote in 2016, a drop from the previous election in 2012 but nearly identical to the numbers seen in the presidential election of 2020. While such statistics seem to indicate a firm commitment to the Democrats on the part of Hispanic voters, room for variation still exists.

Pastor discusses the various ways Hispanics voters might influence politics in the future. (Flickr)

Document Text

Since the 1980s—dubbed the "Decade of the Hispanic"—every major election cycle brings the breathy declaration that the Latino vote will be decisive in selecting the next U.S. President. But after nearly every election, the post-mortem is "not this time," leaving many to wonder when and whether that "Hispanic" decade will ever come. . . .

How does the history of Latino politics illuminate its present?

First, while polls almost always suggest that Latinos rank immigration below other issues such as the economy and education, immigration has become a litmus test: threatening to deport family members is simply a non-starter. . . .

Second, Latino politics may have roots in community organizing and movement building, but it's also never been too far from the Democratic Party either. Such proximity is, for better or worse, likely to continue. The Republican Party has tried to be competitive . . . but its actual base has hardened in the form of Tea Party adherents and Trump aficionados fearful of demographic change. . . .

Third, pan-Latino identity, once the result of a sort of strained political imagination, is increasingly real. There are many reasons for this, including the advantage to Spanish-language media . . . of constituting a single group for purposes of efficient marketing. But Latino voters also sense the underlying racism in anti-immigrant appeals and Latino politicians see the power in collective numbers. . . .

Fourth, the growing numbers of those who identify as pan-Latino also increasingly identify as non-white. This was not foreordained: many assumed that Latinos could gradually assimilate, becoming more like Italian Americans rather than African Americans in terms of how they integrate into American society. Indeed, this was the political basis for the Republican project—widening the circle of whiteness to let another potentially anti-black group in. But demonizing a group of people can prompt them to reassess their political allegiances—and recent research suggests that the longer Latino immigrants live in the United States, the less likely they are to identify as white. . . .

All this should be good news for progressives. Latinos are movement-oriented and Democratic stalwarts, making them ripe for new forms of integrated voter engagement. . . . Moreover, getting it right on a single key issue—immigration—can open up a conversation with Latinos on many other issues, such as the economy and education as well as climate change. . . .

Unfortunately, both progressives and mainstream Democrats tend to be somewhat complacent, convinced that minority constituencies will come to them. . . .

This has often led to what some observers call "hispandering" by Democrats: dangling cabinet appointments, offering up Spanish-language one-liners, and listing things candidates have in common with our *abuelas*. . . . Of course, the Republicans have gone one worse, offering up candidates with Spanish surnames who promise not just to stall immigration reform but to actively deport neighbors and friends. . . .

While there are some hopeful signs, the general story is that the latent political power of Latinos goes underutilized and unrealized for a series of reasons. The first is the age of the population: the median age of Latinos is twenty-eight, versus for-

ty-three for non-Hispanic whites. . . . The second factor is, of course, citizenship: while Latinos constitute roughly 15 percent of all adults in the U.S. (and more than 17 percent of all residents), they are likely to form only 12 percent of all voting-age citizens in 2016.

You might assume that this fall-off from all adults to all potential voters happens because Latinos are such a large share of immigrants, particularly the undocumented—but that's only partly true. Yes, Latinos are about three-quarters of the undocumented and nearly 60 percent of all non-citizen immigrants. But the most striking fact is that Latinos are over half of the nearly 9 million individuals who are eligible to naturalize but have not yet crossed that threshold into civic participation. . . .

The larger question, especially for both progressives and mainstream Democrats, is what happens after the election. The Trump phenomenon masks the challenges ahead. The fact that his net favorability rating among Latinos is a startling negative 64 percent might help the Democratic Party secure the presidency, and the taint he will leave on the Republican Party is likely to scare away Latinos for a while. . . . But winning against Trump is not the same thing as devising a winning Latino strategy for the long run. . . .

So what do we need to do for a smarter future?

First, we need to really trust the emerging "New American Majority" so many are talking about. In the 2014 midterms, the president was advised to put off any further executive actions on immigration reform because of the likelihood that this might cause blue senators in red states to lose their jobs. They lost anyway—and in places like Colorado, activating the Latino vote through a commitment to immigration reform might have actually saved, not cost seats.

Second, while we need to accelerate naturalization, we also need to emphasize efforts to engage Latino youth. The millennial generation constitutes a whopping 44 percent of all Latino eligible voters, as compared to 35 percent of black voters and 27 percent of white voters. . . .

Third, securing that youth engagement will require articulating issues in a sharper way. The popularity of the insurgent Sanders campaign with young voters is mirrored by its success with younger Latinos. . . .

Fourth, we need to recognize the centrality of the black-Latino alliance—if only because the conservative and Republican project in this arena has been all about separation. . . . Putting more resources into inter-group organizing efforts, particularly in our urban areas and in the South, where the two groups live in close proximity, will be key.

Finally, we need to couple our attention to race and immigration issues with a focus on economic justice and economic growth. Latino poverty rates are roughly similar to those of African Americans, and both are suffering from an economy that has under-delivered on jobs and wages. While politically engaging Latinos requires that we tackle the challenges of immigration status, educational inequality, and housing insecurity . . . the broad working-class economic agenda that has been so central to progressive politics is clearly resonant and necessary. . . .

Glossary

abuelas: grandmothers

foreordained: predetermined, predestined

millennial generation: those born between the early 1980s and the late 1990s

Sanders campaign: the 2016 presidential campaign for the Democratic nomination of Vermont Senator Bernie Sanders, who lost the nomination to Hillary Clinton

Short-Answer Questions

1. What are some of the reasons Pastor cites explaining why the Republican Party has struggled to win over Hispanic voters since the 1980s? Why have the Democrats also fallen short in terms of securing Hispanic voters?

2. What steps does Pastor suggest to Democratic leaders for better organizing and motivating Hispanic voters in elections?

3. Pastor suggests that "the longer Latino immigrants live in the United States, the less likely they are to identify as white." Why might this be the case? How might this correlate with the level of enthusiasm among Latinos for participating in politics?

Donald Trump:
Speech on Immigration

Author
Donald Trump

Date
2016

Document Type
Speeches/Addresses

Significance
New York real estate magnate Donald Trump's comprehensive plan for overhauling America's immigration system, described in a speech given in Arizona in 2016

Overview

The presidential election of 2016 proved to be one of the most contentious in modern American political history, reflecting the growing divisions between voters based on class, race, region, education, and gender. The Democrats selected as their candidate Hillary Rodham Clinton, former First Lady, U.S. senator, and secretary of state during President Obama's first term. Long a fixture in U.S. politics, Clinton came to be viewed as controversial and unethical by many on the right, which rallied around an unconventional candidate for the Republican Party, real estate developer and reality show host Donald J. Trump.

Trump made immigration, specifically from Latin American countries, one of the central issues of his campaign. When Trump formally announced his plan to run for president in the summer of 2015, he spoke of Mexico in unfavorable terms: "They're sending people that have lots of problems, and they're bringing those problems with us. They're bringing drugs. They're bringing crime. They're rapists. And some, I assume, are good people." His remarks sparked controversy and anger, but he remained dogged on the campaign trail in the months that followed, insisting that the Obama administration, and by proxy Clinton, had much to answer for when it came to issues caused by immigration along America's southern border.

In a speech given in Phoenix, Arizona, in August 2016, Trump addressed a crowd from a state long dealing with problems involving border security and undocumented immigration. He took the opportunity to detail what he considered to be the many failings of Obama and Clinton regarding immigration and outline a comprehensive ten-point plan to curb the flow of undocumented immigrants and secure the southern border. He pledged a host of new laws and measures, including an impenetrable wall, should he win the White House in the election to be held three months later.

Donald Trump in 2016 (Gage Skidmore)

Document Text

... President Obama and Hillary Clinton have engaged in gross dereliction of duty by surrendering the safety of the American people to open borders. President Obama and Hillary Clinton support Sanctuary Cities, they support catch-and-release on the border, they support visa overstays, they support the release of dangerous criminals from detention—and they support unconstitutional executive amnesty.

Hillary Clinton has pledged amnesty in her first 100 days, and her plan will provide Obamacare, Social Security and Medicare for illegal immigrants—breaking the federal budget. On top of that, she promises uncontrolled low-skilled immigration that continues to reduce jobs and wages for American workers, especially African-American and Hispanic workers. . . .

Now that you've heard about Hillary Clinton's plan . . . let me tell you about my plan. . . .

Number One: We will build a wall along the Southern Border.

On day one, we will begin working on an impenetrable physical wall on the southern border. We will use the best technology, including above-and below-ground sensors, towers, aerial surveillance and manpower to supplement the wall, find and dislocate tunnels, and keep out the criminal cartels, and Mexico will pay for the wall.

Number Two: End Catch-And-Release

Under my Administration, anyone who illegally crosses the border will be detained until they are removed out of our country.

Number Three: Zero tolerance for criminal aliens.

According to federal data, there are at least 2 million criminal aliens now inside the country. We will begin moving them out day one. . . .

Beyond the 2 million, there are a vast number of additional criminal illegal immigrants who have fled or evaded justice. But their days on the run will soon be over. They go out, and they go out fast.

Moving forward, we will issue detainers for all illegal immigrants who are arrested for any crime whatsoever, and they will be placed into immediate removal proceedings. We will terminate the Obama Administration's deadly non-enforcement policies that allow thousands of criminal aliens to freely roam our streets. . . .

We're also going to hire 5,000 more Border Patrol agents, and put more of them on the border, instead of behind desks. We will expand the number of Border Patrol Stations. . . .

Number Four: Block Funding For Sanctuary Cities

We will end the Sanctuary Cities that have resulted in so many needless deaths. Cities that refuse to cooperate with federal authorities will not receive taxpayer dollars, and we will work with Congress to pass legislation to protect those jurisdictions that do assist federal authorities.

Number Five: Cancel Unconstitutional Executive Orders & Enforce All Immigration Laws

We will immediately terminate President Obama's two illegal executive amnesties, in which he defied federal law and the constitution to give amnesty to approximately 5 million illegal immigrants.

Hillary Clinton has pledged to keep both of these illegal amnesty programs—including the 2014 amnesty which has been blocked by the Supreme Court. Clinton has also pledged to add a third executive amnesty. . . .

In a Trump Administration, all immigration laws will be enforced. As with any law enforcement activity, we will set priorities. But, unlike this Administration, no one will be immune or exempt from enforcement—and ICE and Border Patrol officers will be allowed to do their jobs. . . .

Our enforcement priorities will include removing criminals, gang members, security threats, visa overstays, public charges—that is, those relying on public welfare or straining the safety net, along with millions of recent illegal arrivals and overstays who've come here under the current Administration.

Number Six: We Are Going To Suspend The Issuance Of Visas To Any Place Where Adequate Screening Cannot Occur

According to data provided to the Senate Subcommittee on Immigration and the National Interest, between 9/11 and the end of 2014, at least 380 foreign-born individuals were convicted in terror cases inside the United States. . . .

As soon as I enter office, I am going to ask the Department of State, Homeland Security and the Department of Justice to begin a comprehensive review of these cases in order to develop a list of regions and countries from which immigration must be suspended until proven and effective vetting mechanisms can be put into place. . . .

Number Seven: We will ensure that other countries take their people back when we order them deported. . . .

According to a report from the *Boston Globe*, from the year 2008 through 2014, nearly 13,000 criminal aliens were released back into U.S. communities because their home countries would not take them back. Many of these 13,000 releases occurred on Hillary Clinton's watch—she had the power and the duty to stop it cold and she didn't do it.

Those released include individuals convicted of killings, sexual assault and some of the most heinous crimes imaginable, who went on to reoffend at a very high rate.

Number Eight: We will finally complete the biometric entry-exit visa tracking system.

For years, Congress has required a biometric entry-exit visa tracking system, but it has never been completed.

In my Administration, we will ensure that this system is in place at all land, air, and sea ports. Approximately half of new illegal immigrants came on temporary visas and then never left. . . .

Number Nine: We will turn off the jobs and benefits magnet. . . .
Immigration law doesn't exist just for the purpose of keeping out criminals. It exists to protect all aspects of American life—the worksite, the welfare office, the education system and much else. . . .

I will enforce all of our immigration laws.

The same goes for government benefits. The Center for Immigration Studies estimates that 62 percent of households headed by illegal immigrants used some form of cash or non-cash welfare programs, like food stamps or housing assistance. . . .

Number 10: We will reform legal immigration to serve the best interests of America and its workers

We've admitted 59 million immigrants to the United States between 1965 and 2015.

Many of these arrivals have greatly enriched our country. But we now have an obligation to them, and to their children, to control future immigration—as we have following previous immigration waves—to ensure assimilation, integration and upward mobility. . . .

Glossary

amnesty: pardon, forgiveness

biometric entry-exit visa tracking system: a means of tracking the movement of immigrants through the recording of physical characteristics like fingerprints and photographs of a person's face

dereliction: neglect, disregard

detainers: requests from a criminal justice agency requesting a prisoner remain in custody or an alert be issued when the prisoner's release is pending

ICE: U.S. Immigration and Customs Enforcement, a federal agency tasked with protecting the United States from illegal immigration that might undermine national security

sanctuary cities: cities with an expressed or implied policy that disapproves of local law enforcement reporting someone's immigration status unless they are suspected of committing a crime

visa: entry permit

Short-Answer Questions

1. Based on his speech, what does Trump consider to be the failings of Barack Obama and Hillary Rodham Clinton regarding their handling of immigration?

2. In what ways does Trump describe illegal immigration as a threat to the safety and livelihoods of American citizens? How does he specifically refer to illegal immigrants from Latin American countries?

3. Much of Trump's speech seems to imply that illegal immigrants are more likely to engage in criminal behavior, but studies suggest that the opposite is true. Why might this be the case?

Donald Trump: Speech on Immigration

Donald Trump:
State of the Union Address

Author
Donald Trump

Date
2018

Document Type
Presidential/Executive; Speeches/Addresses

Significance
Trump's address reviewing the progress made by his administration since taking office and his future agenda, with much of the address devoted to proposed reforms to immigration

Overview

President Donald J. Trump gave his first and only State of the Union Address before a joint session of Congress in late January of 2018. He took the opportunity to highlight what he considered some of his administration's more notable accomplishments over the previous year since his inauguration, such as tax reform and job creation, and plans to overhaul the nation's infrastructure and repeal and replace the Affordable Care Act. Trump also devoted much of his speech to the issue of immigration, which had been a key plank in his platform while campaigning for president. He told personal stories of people directly impacted by the flow of migrants into the United States either illegally or by exploiting legal ambiguities. These individuals, who were present for the speech, included the parents of two teenage girls killed by members of MS-13, a criminal gang with a presence stretching across the United States and Central America, and an Immigration and Customs Enforcement (ICE) agent targeted for assassination by MS-13.

Having related these personal accounts, Trump shifted his focus to presenting a plan consisting of "four pillars" intended to overhaul immigration policies while maintaining a sense of bipartisanship. In broad terms, the pillars included citizenship for nearly two million undocumented children brought to the United States by their parents, measures to better secure the southern border, the cancellation of a visa lottery that awarded green cards to those seeking American citizenship regardless of their background, and restrictions on single immigrants being able to bring in large numbers of relatives. The proposals broadly served as the basis for H.R. 6136—Border Security and Immigration Reform Act of 2018, a bill introduced that June in the House of Representatives that failed to pass, showing how elusive changes to immigration law continued to be.

Official White House portrait of Donald Trump (Shealah Craighead)

Document Text

... Struggling communities, especially immigrant communities, will also be helped by immigration policies that focus on the best interests of American workers and American families.

For decades, open borders have allowed drugs and gangs to pour into our most vulnerable communities. They have allowed millions of low-wage workers to compete for jobs and wages against the poorest Americans. Most tragically, they have caused the loss of many innocent lives.

Here tonight are two fathers and two mothers: Evelyn Rodriguez, Freddy Cuevas, Elizabeth Alvarado, and Robert Mickens. Their two teenage daughters—Kayla Cuevas and Nisa Mickens—were close friends on Long Island. But in September 2016, on the eve of Nisa's 16th Birthday, neither of them came home. These two precious girls were brutally murdered while walking together in their hometown. Six members of the savage gang MS-13 have been charged with Kayla and Nisa's murders. Many of these gang members took advantage of glaring loopholes in our laws to enter the country as unaccompanied alien minors—and wound up in Kayla and Nisa's high school.

Evelyn, Elizabeth, Freddy, and Robert: Tonight, everyone in this chamber is praying for you. Everyone in America is grieving for you. And 320 million hearts are breaking for you. We cannot imagine the depth of your sorrow, but we can make sure that other families never have to endure this pain.

Tonight, I am calling on the Congress to finally close the deadly loopholes that have allowed MS-13, and other criminals, to break into our country. We have proposed new legislation that will fix our immigration laws, and support our ICE and Border Patrol Agents, so that this cannot ever happen again.

The United States is a compassionate nation. We are proud that we do more than any other country to help the needy, the struggling, and the underprivileged all over the world. But as President of the United States, my highest loyalty, my greatest compassion, and my constant concern is for America's children, America's struggling workers, and America's forgotten communities. I want our youth to grow up to achieve great things. I want our poor to have their chance to rise.

So tonight, I am extending an open hand to work with members of both parties—Democrats and Republicans—to protect our citizens of every background, color, religion, and creed. My duty, and the sacred duty of every elected official in this chamber, is to defend Americans—to protect their safety, their families, their communities, and their right to the American Dream. Because Americans are dreamers too.

Here tonight is one leader in the effort to defend our country: Homeland Security Investigations Special Agent Celestino Martinez—he goes by CJ. CJ served 15 years in the Air Force before becoming an ICE agent and spending the last 15 years fighting gang violence and getting dangerous criminals off our streets. At one point, MS-13 leaders ordered CJ's murder. But he did not cave to threats or fear. Last May, he commanded an operation to track down gang members on Long Island. His team has arrested nearly 400, including more than 220 from MS-13.

CJ: Great work. Now let us get the Congress to send you some reinforcements.

Over the next few weeks, the House and Senate will be voting on an immigration reform package.

In recent months, my Administration has met extensively with both Democrats and Republicans to craft a bipartisan approach to immigration reform. Based on these discussions, we presented the Congress with a detailed proposal that should be supported by both parties as a fair compromise—one where nobody gets everything they want, but where our country gets the critical reforms it needs.

Here are the four pillars of our plan:

The first pillar of our framework generously offers a path to citizenship for 1.8 million illegal immigrants who were brought here by their parents at a young age—that covers almost three times more people than the previous administration. Under our plan, those who meet education and work requirements, and show good moral character, will be able to become full citizens of the United States.

The second pillar fully secures the border. That means building a wall on the Southern border, and it means hiring more heroes like CJ to keep our communities safe. Crucially, our plan closes the terrible loopholes exploited by criminals and terrorists to enter our country—and it finally ends the dangerous practice of "catch and release."

The third pillar ends the visa lottery—a program that randomly hands out green cards without any regard for skill, merit, or the safety of our people. It is time to begin moving towards a merit-based immigration system—one that admits people who are skilled, who want to work, who will contribute to our society, and who will love and respect our country.

The fourth and final pillar protects the nuclear family by ending chain migration. Under the current broken system, a single immigrant can bring in virtually unlimited numbers of distant relatives. Under our plan, we focus on the immediate family by limiting sponsorships to spouses and minor children. This vital reform is necessary, not just for our economy, but for our security, and our future.

In recent weeks, two terrorist attacks in New York were made possible by the visa lottery and chain migration. In the age of terrorism, these programs present risks we can no longer afford.

It is time to reform these outdated immigration rules, and finally bring our immigration system into the 21st century.

These four pillars represent a down-the-middle compromise, and one that will create a safe, modern, and lawful immigration system.

For over 30 years, Washington has tried and failed to solve this problem. This Congress can be the one that finally makes it happen.

Most importantly, these four pillars will produce legislation that fulfills my ironclad pledge to only sign a bill that puts America first. So let us come together, set politics aside, and finally get the job done.

Glossary

bipartisan: two-party

ironclad: secure, unbreakable

MS-13: a criminal gang with a presence stretching across North and Central America

Short-Answer Questions

1. What portions of Trump's address deal specifically with concerns regarding security along America's southern border and illegal immigration across it?

2. As both a candidate and president, Trump was frequently criticized for employing divisive rhetoric in his speeches. Does that seem to be the case in this address? Why or why not?

3. What might have been the reasoning behind inviting individuals directly impacted by immigration and MS-13 to the State of the Union address? How might such a tactic be considered "political theater"?

Donald Trump: State of the Union Address

Alexandria Ocasio-Cortez: Response to Being Accosted by Ted Yoho

Author Alexandria Ocasio-Cortez	**Significance** Highlighted the issue of sexism, especially in Congress, and its tacit acceptance by the male establishment
Date 2020	
Document Type Speeches/Addresses	

Overview

In 2020, while walking up the steps of the Capitol, Rep. Alexandria Ocasio-Cortez (D-N.Y.) was accosted by Rep. Ted Yoho (R-Fla.), who uttered a sexist slur toward the New York representative. Despite being called out by Ocasio-Cortez, Yoho remained indignant, refuting the allegations on the grounds that he had a wife and daughters. In her speech to the House of Representatives, the Ocasio-Cortez pointed to the long-standing systemic nature of sexism among government and legislative officials. Ocasio-Cortez pointed to the long-standing systemic nature of sexism is the youngest woman elected to Congress, the first female member of the Democratic Socialists of America elected to Congress, a Latina, and a vocal champion of progressive issues.

Document Text

Thank you, Madam Speaker. And I would also like to thank many of my colleagues for the opportunity to not only speak today but for the many members from both sides of the aisle who have reached out to me in support following an incident earlier this week. About two days ago, I was walking up the steps of the Capitol when Representative Yoho suddenly turned a corner, and he was accompanied by Representative Roger Williams, and accosted me on the steps right here in front of our nation's Capitol. I was minding my own business, walking up the steps and Representative Yoho put his finger in my face, he called me disgusting, he called me crazy, he called me out of my mind, and he called me dangerous.

Alexandria Ocasio-Cortez
(Franmarie Metzler; U.S. House Office of Photography)

Then he took a few more steps and after I had recognized his comments as rude, he walked away and said, "I'm rude, you're calling me rude?" I took a few steps ahead and I walked inside and cast my vote, because my constituents send me here each and every day to fight for them and to make sure that they are able to keep a roof over their head, that they're able to feed their families and that they're able to carry their lives with dignity.

I walked back out and there were reporters in the front of the Capitol, and in front of reporters Representative Yoho called me, and I quote, "a f***ing b****." These were the words that Representative Yoho levied against a congresswoman. The congresswoman that not only represents New York's 14th Congressional District, but every congresswoman and every woman in this country. Because all of us have had to deal with this in some form, some way, some shape, at some point in our lives.

I want to be clear that Representative Yoho's comments were not deeply hurtful or piercing to me, because I have worked a working-class job. I have waited tables in restaurants. I have ridden the subway. I have walked the streets in New York City, and this kind of language is not new. I have encountered words uttered by Mr. Yoho and men uttering the same words as Mr. Yoho while I was being harassed in restaurants. I have tossed men out of bars that have used language like Mr. Yoho's and I have encountered this type of harassment riding the subway in New York City. This is not new, and that is the problem. Mr. Yoho was not alone. He was walking shoulder to shoulder with Representative Roger Williams, and that's when we start to see that this issue is not about one incident. It is cultural. It is a culture of lack of impunity, of accepting of violence and violent language against women, and an entire structure of power that supports that. Because not only have I been spoken to disrespectfully, particularly by members of the Republican Party and elected officials in the Republican Party, not just here, but the President of the United States last year told me to go home to another country, with the implication that I don't even belong in America. The governor of Florida, Governor DeSantis, before I even was sworn in, called me a "whatever-that-is." Dehumanizing language is not new, and what we are seeing is that incidents like these are happening in a pattern. This is a pattern of an attitude towards women and dehumanization of others.

So while I was not deeply hurt or offended by little comments that are made, when I was reflecting on this, I honestly thought that I was just going to pack it up and go home. It's just another day, right? But then yesterday, Representative Yoho decided to come to the floor of the House of Representatives and make excuses for his behavior, and that I could not let go. I could not allow my nieces, I could not allow the little girls that I go home to, I could not allow victims of verbal abuse and worse to see that, to see that excuse and to see our Congress accept it as legitimate and accept it as an apology and to accept silence as a form of acceptance. I could not allow that to stand, which is why I am rising today to raise this point of personal privilege.

I do not need Representative Yoho to apologize to me. Clearly, he does not want to. Clearly, when given the opportunity he will not, and I will not stay up late at night waiting for an apology.from a man who has no remorse over calling women and using abusive language towards women, but what I do have issue with is using women, our wives and daughters, as shields and excuses for poor behavior. Mr. Yoho mentioned that he has a wife and two daughters. I am two years younger than Mr. Yoho's youngest daughter. I am someone's daughter too. My father, thankfully, is not alive to see how Mr. Yoho treated his daughter. . . .

Now what I am here to say is that this harm that Mr. Yoho levied, it tried to levy against me, was not just an incident directed at me. But when you do that to any woman, what Mr. Yoho did was give permission to other men to do that to his daughters. In using that language in front of the press, he gave permission to use that language against his wife, his daughters, women in his community, and I am here to stand up to say that is not acceptable. I do not care what your views are. It does not matter how much I disagree or how much it incenses me or how much I feel that people are dehumanizing others. I will not do that myself. I will not allow people to change and create hatred in our hearts. And so, what I believe is that having a daughter does not make a man decent, having a wife does not make a decent man. Treating people with dignity and respect makes a decent man. . . .

Glossary

constituents: residents of an area served by an elected official

dehumanize: deprive of positive human qualities

incenses: makes very angry; enrages

Short-Answer Questions

1. How does Ocasio-Cortez frame sexism as systemic?

2. What arguments does Ocasio-Cortez make regarding politicians and their role in promoting sexism?

3. Why does Ocasio-Cortez call Yoho's invoking of his wife and daughters a "shield"? Please explain.

"Latinx LGBT Adults in the U.S."

Authors Bianca D.M. Wilson, Christy Mallory, Lauren Bouton, and Soon Kyu Choi for Williams Institute, UCLA School of Law **Date** 2021	**Document Type** Essays, Reports, Manifestos **Significance** Demonstrates the diversity and extent of LGBTQ+ representation among the U.S. Hispanic population

Overview

The report "Latinx LGBT Adults in the U.S.: LGBT Well-Being at the Intersection of Race" was created by scholars and researchers at the Williams Institute of the University of California at Los Angeles School of Law. The Williams Institute was founded in 2001 expressly to address the lack of scholarly research on the issues faced by LGBTQ+ Americans. The institute's mission is to bring rigorous scholarly study to the situation of sexual orientation and gender identity and to serve as a source of reliable information for laws and court cases that affect LGBTQ+ individuals.

Many of the reports issued by the Williams Institute are in the form of demographic studies, such as this one. The demographic reports give lawmakers and judges information they need to shape legislation that impacts the LGBTQ+ population. In addition to reports like this one, the Williams Institute files amicus briefs in court cases that give judges the information they need to make decisions. Briefs filed by the Williams Institute played significant roles in Supreme Court cases such as *Obergefell v. Hodges* (2015), which established marriage equality for same-sex couples.

Document Text

More than 11.3 million LGBT adults live in the U.S. They are a part of every community throughout the country, and they are diverse in terms of personal characteristics, socioeconomic outcomes, health status, and lived experiences. While LGBT people are similar to their non-LGBT counterparts in many ways, they also show differences that illuminate their unique needs and experiences related to sexual orientation and gender identity. . . .

KEY FINDINGS

Demographic Characteristics

• An estimated 2,253,000 U.S. adults self-identify as Latinx and LGBT. Among all Latinx adults, 5.6% identify as LGBT.

• Latinx LGBT adults in the U.S. are more likely to live in the West than in other regions: 38% of Latinx LGBT adults in the country live in the West, compared to 33% in the South, 18% in the Northeast, and 10% in the Midwest. . . .

• The Latinx LGBT adult population is younger than the population of Latinx non-LGBT adults. Sixty-five percent of Latinx LGBT adults are under age 35, compared to 45% of non-LGBT adults.

• Just over half (52%) of LGBT Latinx adults are women, and 48% are men.

• Among Latinx adults ages 25 and older, more LGBT than non-LGBT adults have a college education: 22% of Latinx LGBT adults have a college education, compared to 17% of Latinx non-LGBT adults.

• Overall, Latinx LGBT adults have served in the military at a rate similar to that for Latinx non-LGBT adults. However, when disaggregated by gender, a lower proportion of Latinx LGBT men (8%) served in the military compared to non-LGBT men (10%), but a higher proportion of Latinx LGBT women (3%) served in the military compared with non-LGBT women (2%).

• Although Latinx LGBT adults are more likely to report no religious affiliation than Latinx non-LGBT adults, many Latinx LGBT adults are religious. Thirty-eight percent of Latinx LGBT adults are Roman Catholic, 7% are Protestant, 2% are Muslim, and 26% have other religious affiliations.

• The vast majority of Latinx LGBT adults **(91%) and Latinx non-LGBT adults (90%) live** in urban areas.

• Latinx LGBT adults are more likely to live alone than non-LGBT adults: 15% of Latinx LGBT adults live alone, compared to 10% of Latinx non-LGBT adults.

• Among those who are married or cohabiting, about 70% of Latinx LGBT adults have a different-sex partner. Latinx LGBT women (73%) are more likely to have a different-sex partner than Latinx LGBT men (57%).

• Fewer Latinx LGBT adults (44%) than non-LGBT adults (57%) are raising children. . . .

Economic Characteristics

• Many Latinx adults experience economic insecurity.

• Nearly 40% of Latinx LGBT adults (37%) and non-LGBT adults (39%) live with a household income below $24,000 per year.

• Latinx LGBT adults are more likely to be unemployed (10% vs. 8%) and to experience food insecurity (32% vs. 25%) than Latinx non-LGBT adults.

• Latinx LGBT adults are less likely to live in low-income households—that is, below 200% of the federal poverty level (FPL)—than Latinx non-LGBT adults. . . .

Mental and Physical Health

• Fewer Latinx LGBT adults report fair or poor health than Latinx non-LGBT adults: 29% of Latinx LGBT adults and 31% of non-LGBT adults report their health as fair or poor.

• Nearly one-third (30%) of Latinx LGBT adults have been diagnosed with depression, compared to

16% of Latinx non-LGBT adults. Latinx LGBT women have the highest rates of depression (35%) compared with non-LGBT women (20%) and both groups of men. . . .

• Latinx LGBT adults are more likely to engage in high-risk health behaviors than Latinx non-LGBT adults. Among Latinx LGBT adults, 28% report current smoking and 8% report heavy drinking, compared to 16% and 3% of non-LGBT adults, respectively.

• More Latinx LGBT adults than non-LGBT adults report having mild or high disability, defined by the number of days that they experienced limitations due to poor health in the prior month. Among Latinx adults, 26% reported experiencing mild disability, defined as experiencing limitations because of poor health for 1–14 days in the past month; 11% reported high disability, defined as experiencing limitations because of poor health for 15–30 days in the past month. By comparison, 20% of Latinx non-LGBT adults reported mild disability, and 7% reported high disability.

• Compared to Latinx non-LGBT adults, Latinx LGBT adults had greater odds of being diagnosed with several serious health conditions, including asthma, diabetes, cancer, high blood pressure, and high cholesterol. . . .

Access to Health Care

• Latinx LGBT adults are more likely to have health insurance than Latinx non-LGBT adults: 28% of Latinx LGBT adults are uninsured, compared to 33% of Latinx non-LGBT adults. . . .

• Similar proportions of Latinx LGBT adults (60%) and Latinx non-LGBT adults (58%) have a personal doctor.

Discrimination and Stressful Events

• Latinx LGBT adults are more likely than Latinx non-LGBT adults to say they feel unsafe: 17% of Latinx LGBT adults said that they disagreed with the statement "You always feel safe and secure," compared to 11% of Latinx non-LGBT adults.

• Many Latinx LGBT adults reported experiences of discrimination and victimization. For example, 74% of Latinx LGBT adults reported having experienced everyday discrimination in the prior year (such as being treated with less courtesy than other people), 42% reported experiencing physical or sexual assault at some point as an adult, and 69% reported experiencing verbal assault or abuse at some point as an adult. Similar percentages of Latinx non-LGBT adults report experiencing discrimination and violence.

• Many Latinx LGBT adults also reported financial and job-related stress. For example, 62% reported not having had enough money to make ends meet in the prior year, 17% reported being fired or laid off in the prior year, and 30% reported experiencing a major financial crisis in the prior year. Latinx non-LGBT adults reported similar rates of financial and job-related stress.

Resiliency

• The majority (64%) of Latinx LGB adults and 40% of Latinx transgender adults reported feeling connected to the LGBT community.

• Less than half (43%) of Latinx LGBT adults reported feeling connected to the Latinx community.

• About two-thirds (68%) of Latinx LGBT adults reported feeling supported through their social circles. . . .

"Latinx LGBT Adults in the U.S."

Glossary

disaggregated: Separated into component parts. In this case, "disaggregated" means that, if you separate the results of the report by gender, you see a discrepancy that was not visible if you lumped males and females into a single category.

federal poverty level: A measure of income that is generated and used by the U.S. Department of Health and Human Services to judge eligibility for certain services and benefits. In 2021, the year this report was generated, the federal poverty level for one person was set at an annual income of $12,880.

Latinx: A term, coined around the year 2004, to refer to people of Hispanic origins. *Latinx* (usually pronounced "Latin-ecks") does not follow the gender binary of Spanish, which refers to men as *Latinos* and women as *Latinas*. As a result, *Latinx* can be applied to both women and men as well as non-binary and genderqueer individuals.

Short-Answer Questions

1. Where do most LGBT Latinx people live in the United States?

2. Generally speaking, are LGBT Latinx people healthier or less healthy than non-LGBT Latinx people?

3. Based on the statistics presented here, were LGBT Latinx people better off or worse off than non-LGBT Latinx people?

Latino GDP Report for 2021

Authors
Dan Hamilton, Matthew Fienup, David Hayes-Bautista, and Paul Hsu

Date
2021

Document Type
Essays, Reports, Manifestos

Significance
Outlined the remarkable progress made by Latinos living in the United States in terms of their growing demographic impact, economic contributions, and educational attainment

Overview

The Latino Donor Collaborative is a nonprofit, nonpartisan organization committed to promoting a positive view and representation of Latinos across the United States. Every two years the organization commissions the writing of a comprehensive report on the economic contribution of Latinos living in the United States. The report for 2021 revealed the continuing increase of Latino GDP (gross domestic product) by several billion dollars between 2010 and 2019—an increase that is 57 percent more rapid than the U.S. GDP as a whole. American Latinos on their own constitute a GDP comparable in size to that of France, the world's seventh-largest economy. Latinos also provided much fuel to drive the U.S. economy in the growth of participation in the American labor force, of which they accounted for 68.2 percent, and total consumption, which was measured as growing 123 percent faster compared to non-Latino consumption. From 2017 to 2019, the growth of real Latino GDP averaged 5.63 percent, roughly twice the rate of the entire U.S. economy. Accompanying the impressive gains made by Latinos to the health of the economy, the number of Latinos acquiring a bachelor's degree or above increased almost three times faster compared to non-Latinos.

While the report noted that the majority of Latinos continued to be concentrated largely in ten states, including Arizona, California, Florida, New York, and Texas, the three states with the fastest-growing Latino population were New Hampshire, North Dakota, and Vermont, all of which saw their Latino populations grow by 15 percent between 2015 and 2019. The report offered a generally optimistic analysis of Latino Americans' place in the Unites States, having successfully weathered decades of civil discord, economic upheaval, and various forms of oppression, to become an indispensable part of the U.S. population.

Document Text

. . . As a summary statistic for the economic performance of Latinos in the United States, the 2019 Latino GDP is extraordinary. The total economic output (or GDP) of Latinos in the United States was $2.7 trillion in 2019, up from $2.1 trillion in 2015, **and $1.7 trillion in 2010. If Latinos living in the U.S.** were an independent country, the U.S. Latino GDP would be tied for the seventh largest GDP in the world. Tied with France, the Latino GDP is larger even than the GDPs of Italy, Brazil or Canada. . . .

While impressive for its size, the U.S. Latino GDP is most noteworthy for its growth. Over the past 2 years, the growth of real Latino GDP averaged 5.63 percent, double the rate of the broader U.S. economy. Since 2010, real Latino GDP has grown 57 percent faster than real U.S. GDP and 70 percent faster than Non-Latino GDP. The growth of the U.S. Latino GDP even compares favorably on the world stage. From 2010 to 2019, the U.S. Latino GDP is the third fastest growing among the 10 largest GDPs, while the broader U.S. economy ranks fourth.

The $2.7 trillion U.S. Latino economy is both deep and wide. The U.S. Latino GDP's top industry sector is Education & Healthcare, totaling $446 billion or 16.4% of U.S. Latino GDP. This is followed by Professional & Business Services ($327 billion . . .) and Finance & Real Estate ($252 billion . . .). The Latino GDP is not only an engine of economic growth but also a broad foundation of support for the larger U.S. economy.

As noted in previous reports, the single largest component of Latino GDP is personal consumption. In 2019, Latino consumption stood at $1.85 trillion. U.S. Latinos represent a consumption market that is nearly identical in size to the entire economy of Texas. . . .

From 2010 to 2019, the number of people with a bachelor's degree or higher grew 2.8 times faster for Latinos than Non-Latinos. In addition to bettering themselves through educational attainment, working age Latinos are also significantly more likely to be actively working than non-Latinos. . . .

Because of its sheer size, the Baby Boom generation has dominated U.S. attention in business, politics and entertainment. Since 2010, this outsized generation has been turning 65 years old and retiring from the labor force and will continue to do so through the 2030s. . . .

While the Baby Boomers were capturing the public's attention, in its shadow, the Latino population grew dramatically from 1980 and 2010. Unsung and almost unnoticed, this Latino adult generation gathered the momentum necessary to create the world's 7th largest economy. . . .

Even less noticed are the children of this economically active generation, the Latino Post-Millennials, born between 1997 and 2020. These Latino children are beginning to enter the country's labor force and are doing so in ways that ensure a "slingshot effect" for the ongoing impact of Latinos in the United States. The timing of their entry into the labor force, the values they learned from their parents, and the tremendous strides in education they have made mean that their presence in the work force and the economy will be far more impactful in creating economic growth than the mere static numbers might suggest.

Just as a slingshot converts stored energy into a dramatic kinetic force, so the entry of Latino Post-Millennials into the vacuum created by the departing Baby Boomers will have an outsized impact on the U.S. labor force and economy and on the prosperity enjoyed by society at large. . . .

Whereas the U.S. had average annual real wage and salary growth of just 2.3 percent from 2010 to 2019, real wage and salary income growth for

Latinos averaged 3.5 percent. In five of the past nine years, Latino income growth has been at least double that of Non-Latinos. . . .

. . . From 2010 to 2019, the number of people with a bachelor's degree or higher grew 2.8 times more rapidly for Latinos than Non-Latinos. The number of educated Latinos rose by 73.1 percent during this time, while the number of educated Non-Latinos rose by only 26.5 percent. The annual gains in educational attainment by Latinos have been greater than 6 percent in each of the last six years. . . .

. . . With an accelerating recovery from the Financial Crisis and Great Recession, the growth of Latino home ownership accelerated rapidly beginning in 2014 and has remained high in each year since. Latino home ownership grew by seven percent in 2017 alone. Meanwhile the U.S. saw declining rates of homeownership through 2015. Although home ownership for the nation has begun to grow again, growth has remained below two percent in every year from 2015 to 2019. . . .

. . . From 2010 to 2019, Latinos added an average of more than 660,000 workers per year to the U.S. Labor Force. During that same time, Non-Latinos added an average of just over 510,000 workers per year. Over the entire period, the size of the Latino labor force increased by 25 percent while the size of the Non-Latino labor force increased just 3 percent.

One factor which drives Latino's strong contribution to the U.S. labor force is that Latinos have a younger median age than non-Latinos. In 2019, the Median Age for Latinos was 29.8 years. For non-Latinos, it was 40.8 years. Due to their age distribution, Latinos are adding substantial numbers of people to the critical category of working age adults, defined as ages 18 to 64. Meanwhile, Non-Latinos are experiencing a high concentration of population in the 55 and older age range, representing large numbers of near-retirees. . . .

According to Federal Reserve economists, the number of people retiring in the U.S. is forecast to peak in 2022 when close to 350,000 mostly non-Latino Baby-Boomers will retire each month. The U.S. faces a dangerous shortage of workers, a demographic crisis which threatens the country's ability to maintain even modest economic growth over the next two decades. Fortunately, Latinos are well on their way to rescuing the U.S. from this demographic time bomb, adding substantial numbers to the critical category of working age adults. . . .

Glossary

Baby Boom generation: Americans born between the years 1945 and 1960

consumption market: the sale of goods and services to people for their own consumption

GDP: gross domestic product, a measurement of the economic output of goods and services

median age: the age that divides a given population into two equal parts

Post-Millennials: Americans born near or after the year 2000

Short-Answer Questions

1. What "demographic time bomb" is identified in the report? What role might Latino Americans play in mitigating some of the worst effects of this crisis?

2. If the trends outlined in the report continue in the years to come, what sort of cultural and political changes might be anticipated?

3. What possible reasons account for the marked increase in the number of Latino Americans in the previous decade, and why they have proven so invaluable to the overall health and vitality of the United States?

List of Documents by Category

Cartoons, Images, Artwork

Casta Paintings
Codex Boturini
Codex Mendoza
Columbus Meets the Taíno
"Los Padrinos en los Funerales de Don Pedrito"
Louis Dalrymple: "School Begins"
Mexican American Marines in Vietnam
"National Boundary Line at Nogales"
Photograph of Mexican Agricultural Laborers
Universal Cosmography according to the Tradition of Ptolomy and the Surveys of America Vespucci and Others
"Zoot Suiters Lined Up outside Los Angeles Jail"

Essays, Reports, Manifestos

Aims and Purposes of the Latin-American Citizens League
Alexander von Humboldt: *The Island of Cuba*
Alurista and Rodolfo Gonzales: "El Plan Espiritual de Aztlan"
Álvar Núñez Cabeza de Vaca: *The Journey of Álvar Núñez Cabeza de Vaca*
Bartolomé de las Casas: *A Short Account of the Destruction of the Indies*
Bernal Díaz: *The True History of the Conquest of New Spain*
César Chávez: Plan de Delano
Christopher Columbus: Columbus Reports on His First Voyage
Constitution of the League of United Latin American Citizens
Crystal City Walkout Demands
David Reyes: "In Pursuit of the Latino American Dream"
"Decade of the Hispanic: An Economic Retrospective"
East LA Walkout Demands
El Plan de Santa Barbara: A Chicano Plan for Higher Education
Elsie Chavez Chilton: Working with the Civilian Conservation Corps near Las Cruces
Emma Tenayuca and Homer Brooks: "The Mexican Question in the Southwest"
Excerpts from the 1930 U.S. Census
Franciscan Friar Describes the Land and the People of New Mexico
Francisco Madero: Plan de San Luis Potosí
Frank del Olmo: "Latino 'Decade' Moves into '90s"
Frank Sotomayor: "Latinos: A Diverse Group Tied by Ethnicity"
Fray Antonio de la Ascension: A Brief Report of the Discovery in New Spain
Friar Junípero Serra: Response to the Revolt and Destruction of Mission San Diego
Guadalupe Vallejo Reminisces about the Rancho Period
Herman Badillo: "From Kennedy Democrat to Giuliani Republican"
Hernán Cortés: Second Letter to Charles V
Jesús Colón: "Greetings from Washington" (from *A Puerto Rican in New York*)
John G. F. Wurdemann: A Physician's Notes on Cuba
John L. O'Sullivan: "Great Nation of Futurity"

José Angel Gutiérrez: "The Thirty-Ninth MAYO Walkout: A Diary"

José Antonio Saco: "The Color Line"

José Vasconcelos: *The Cosmic Race/La raza cósmica*

Juan de Oñate: Letter about a Settlement in New Mexico

Juan Nepomuceno Cortina: Proclamation to the Mexicans of Texas, November 1859

Juan Nepomuceno Cortina: Proclamation to Texans, September 1859

Juan Seguín: *Personal Memoirs*

Latino GDP Report for 2021

"Latinx LGBT Adults in the U.S."

Leslie Sanchez: "The Emerging Latino Republican Majority"

Linda Chávez: "Toward a New Politics of Hispanic Assimilation"

Lionel Sosa: The Americano Dream: How Latinos Can Achieve Success in Business and in Life

Lorenzo de Zavala: *Journey to the United States of North America*

Manuel Gamio: Interview with Anastacio Torres

Manuel Gamio: Interview with Elías Garza

Manuel Gamio: Interview with Elisa Silva

Manuel Gamio: Interview with Isidro Osorio

Manuel Gamio: Interview with Juana de Hidalgo

Manuel Gamio: Interview with Juan Berzunzolo

Manuel Mier y Terán: Reports on the Divisions in Texas

Manuel Pastor: "Latinos and the New American Majority"

Marian M. George: *A Little Journey to Puerto Rico*

Memorandum by the American Ambassador in Mexico of a Conversation with the Mexican Minister for Foreign Affairs

Our Lady of Guadalupe: "The Apparitions and the Miracle"

Paul S. Taylor: Interviews with Mexican Americans in Nueces County, Texas

Paul S. Taylor: Sociological Observations of Mexican Americans in Nueces County, Texas

Pedro Albizu Campos: "Puerto Rican Nationalism"

Pedro Naranjo: The Pueblo Indians Call for War

Piri Thomas: "Brothers Under the Skin" (from *Down These Mean Streets*)

Plan de Ayala

"Plan of San Diego"

"Proclamation of Las Gorras Blancas"

Raúl Morín Discusses Mexican Americans in Military Service

Report of the Joint Fact-Finding Committee to the Fifty-Fifth California Legislature

Requerimiento

"Resolution on Racial Discrimination"

Richard Henry Dana Jr.: *Two Years Before the Mast*

Robert N. McLean: Protestant Religious Work among the Mexicans

Rodolfo "Corky" Gonzales: Arizona State University Speech

Samuel P. Huntington: "The Hispanic Challenge"

Selden C. Menefee and Orin C. Cassmore: *The Pecan Shellers of San Antonio*

Staff Report: Demographic, Economic, and Social Characteristics of the Spanish Surname Population of the Five Southwestern States—U.S. Civil Rights Commission, San Antonio, TX

Staff Report: Farm Workers—U.S. Civil Rights Commission, San Antonio, TX

Staff Report: A Study of Equality of Educational Opportunity for Mexican Americans in Nine School Districts of the San Antonio Area—U.S. Civil Rights Commission, San Antonio, TX

Susan Archuleta Looks Back at Jobs with the CCC and the National Youth Administration in Northern New Mexico

U.S. Commissioner General of Immigration Reports on Mexican Immigration

Virginia Escalante, Nancy Rivera, and Victor Valle: "Inside the World of Latinas"
Works Progress Administration Interviews with Hispanic Women in New Mexico, 1936–39
Young Lords Party 13-Point Program and Platform
"Youth Gangs Leading Cause of Delinquencies"

Legal

Delgado v. Bastrop
Hernandez v. Texas
Mendez v. Westminster
Plyler v. Doe
Serna v. Portales
Tzacoalco (Jalisco): Concerns about a Marriage

Legislative

Cuban Adjustment Act
DREAM Act
Father Ruiz: Statement before the U.S. Commission on Civil Rights
Henry B. González: Speech against the Chicano Movement
Joint Resolution on the Annexation of Texas
Requerimiento
Philip II: Spain Asserts Control over the Indians of Nueva Galicia
Platt Amendment
Proposition 187
Treaty of Guadalupe Hidalgo

Letters/Correspondence

Antonio López de Santa Anna: Message to the Inhabitants of Texas
Bishop Pedro Tamarón y Romeral Visits New Mexico
Christopher Columbus: Columbus Reports on His First Voyage
Elisha M. Pease: Letter to Texas Legislature on the "Cart War"
Fray Antonio de la Ascension: A Brief Report of the Discovery in New Spain
Friar Junípero Serra: Response to the Revolt and Destruction of Mission San Diego
Hernán Cortés: Second Letter to Charles V
Juan de Oñate: Letter about a Settlement in New Mexico
Stephen F. Austin: A Letter Describing the Texas Cause
Stephen F. Austin: Letter to George Fisher Describing the Occurrences in Texas
Tzacoalco (Jalisco): Concerns about a Marriage
Vernon D. Northrop: Letter to Secretary of State Regarding Puerto Rico

Poems, Plays, Fiction

Américo Paredes: "Alma pocha"
Américo Paredes: *George Washington Gómez: A Mexicotexan Novel*
Américo Paredes: "The Mexico-Texan"

List of Documents by Category

585

"Ballad of Gregorio Cortez"
"Corrido de Kiansis"
Daniel Venegas: *The Adventures of Don Chipote; or, When Parrots Breast Feed*
Denice Frohman: "Abuela's Dance"
"El Corrido Pensilvanio"
Hopi Creation Myth
José Antonio Villarreal: *Pocho*
Lorna Dee Cervantes: "Coffee"
"Los Sediciosos"
Luis Valdez: "Pensamiento Serpentino: A Chicano Approach to the Theater of Reality"
Origin Myth of the Acoma
Patricio Paiz: "En memoria de Arturo Tijerina"
Popol Vuh
Reyes Cárdenas: "If We Praise the Aztecs"
Rodolfo "Corky" Gonzales: "I Am Joaquín"
Sandra María Esteves: "Blanket Weaver"
Tato Laviera: "AmeRícan"

Presidential/Executive

Barack Obama: Speech Announcing DACA
Barack Obama: Speech at the National Council of La Raza
Donald Trump: State of the Union Address
Franklin D. Roosevelt: First Inaugural Address
Gerald Ford: Address to the Republican National Hispanic Assembly
Lyndon B. Johnson: Remarks at a Reception Honoring Henry González
Philip II: Spain Asserts Control over the Indians of Nueva Galicia
Ronald Reagan: Address to the Nation on United States Policy in Central America
Vernon D. Northrop: Letter to Secretary of State Regarding Puerto Rico

Speeches/Addresses

Alexandria Ocasio-Cortez: Response to Being Accosted by Ted Yoho
Barack Obama: Speech Announcing DACA
Barack Obama: Speech at the National Council of La Raza
Bill Richardson: Democratic National Convention Speech
Donald Trump: Speech on Immigration
Donald Trump: State of the Union Address
Father Ruiz: Statement before the U.S. Commission on Civil Rights
Fidel Castro: "History Will Absolve Me"
Fidel Castro: Speech at Presidential Palace
Franklin D. Roosevelt: First Inaugural Address
Gerald Ford: Address to the Republican National Hispanic Assembly
Henry B. González: Speech against the Chicano Movement
José Martí: "Our America"
Juan Nepomuceno Seguín: A Tejano Leader Calls for Support of the Texas Revolution
Luisa Moreno: "Caravans of Sorrow" Speech
Lyndon B. Johnson: Remarks at a Reception Honoring Henry González

Marco Rubio: Presidential Campaign Launch Speech
Reies López Tijerina: Interview after Martin Luther King's Assassination
Rodolfo "Corky" Gonzales: Arizona State University Speech
Ronald Reagan: Address to the Nation on United States Policy in Central America
Sonia Sotomayor: "A Latina Judge's Voice"
Sonia Sotomayor: Supreme Court Nomination Speech

Index

Volume numbers are indicated in bold before each page number.

A

Abascal, Salvador, **2:**350–51

Acheson, Dean, **1:**206

Acoma, **1:**3–5, **1:**25, **1:**27, **1:**64

Adams-Onís Treaty, **1:**78

Affordable Care Act, **2:**568

Agricultural Workers Organizing Committee (AWOC), **2:**380

Aguirre, Frederick P., **2:**477

Agustín, Juan, **1:**71

Aims and Purposes of the Latin-American Citizens League, **1:**224–26

Alexander VI, Pope, **1:**40

Alexander von Humboldt: *The Island of Cuba,* **1:**141–44

Alexandria Ocasio-Cortez: Response to Being Accosted by Ted Yoho, **2:**572–74

Alurista and Rodolfo Gonzales: "El Plan Espiritual de Aztlan," **2:**423–27

Alvara-do, Elizabeth, **2:**569

Álvar Núñez Cabeza de Vaca: *The Journey of Álvar Núñez Cabeza de Vaca,* **1:**47–49

American GI Forum, **2:**348

Américo Paredes:

"Alma pocha," **1:**294–96

George Washington Gómez: A Mexicotexan Novel, **2:**326–30

"The Mexico-Texan," **1:**291–93

Antonio López de Santa Anna: Message to the Inhabitants of Texas, **1:**122–24

Apache, **2:**395

Arce, Carlos H., **2:**482

Archuleta, Susana, **2:**309–11

Arizona, Hispanic population in, **2:**402–3, **2:**531, **2:**579

Arthur, Chester A., **2:**319

Ascension, Fray Antonio de la, **1:**67–69

Austin, Stephen F., **1:**95, **1:**109, **1:**113–15, **1:**119–22, **1:**125, **1:**150

Aztec Empire, **1:**3–5, **1:**16, **1:**20, **1:**24, **1:**30, **1:**44, **1:**46, **1:**50, **1:**57, **1:**60, **1:**63, **1:**77, **1:**81, **2:**388

B

Badillo, Herman, **2:**526–28

"Ballad of Gregorio Cortez," **1:**187–89

Baltasar, Juan, **1:**71

Barack Obama:

Speech Announcing DACA, **2:**548–51

Speech at the National Council of La Raza, **2:**545–47

Barber, Susan McSween, **2:**324

Bárbola, Magdalena, **1:**71

Bartolomé de las Casas: *A Short Account of the Destruction of the Indies,* **1:**54–56

Batista y Zaldivar, Fulgencio, **1:**250, **1:**253–54

Battle of Conception, **1:**125

Battle of San Jacinto, **1:**119, **1:**125, **1:**148

Battle of the Alamo, **1:**119, **1:**122–25

Bennett, Doug, **2:**465

Bernal Díaz: *The True History of the Conquest of New Spain,* **1:**30, **1:**60–63

Berzunzolo, Juan, **1:**265–69

Biden, Joe, **2:**540, **2:**543

Billings, John, **2:**429

Bill Richardson: Democratic National Convention Speech, **2:**538–41

Billy the Kid, **2:**322, **2:**324

bin Laden, Osama, **2:**541

Bishop Pedro Tamarón y Romeral Visits New Mexico, **1:**88–90

Black Panther Party, **2:**415, **2:**418

Blocker, William P., **2:**320

Bolívar, Simón, **1:**163

Bonney, William H. *See* Billy the Kid

Bonsol, Philip, **1:**257

Bouton, Lauren, **2:**575

Bracero Program, **2:**304, **2:**339–40, **2:**419

Bricken, Gordon, **2:**479

Brief Report of the Discovery in the South Sea, **1:**30

Brooks, Homer, **1:**238–39, **1:**241

Brown, Barbara Ledesma, **2:**477

Brownfield v. South Carolina, **2:**347

Brown v. Board of Education, **1:**227, **2:**347, **2:**354, **2:**357, **2:**419, **2:**464

Bucareli, Antonio María de, **1:**91–92

Burnet, David, **1:**117

Bush, George H.W., **2:**504

Bush, George W., **2:**504, **2:**529, **2:**538, **2:**540–41
Bustamante, Anastasio, **1:**116

C

Cabeza de Vaca, Álvar Núñez, **1:**30, **1:**47–49
California, **2:**303
    discrimination in educational system, **2:**419–22
    Hispanic experience in, **1:**175, **1:**197, **1:**200, **1:**206, **1:**217–18, **1:**243–45, **1:**265–66, **1:**271, **2:**349, **2:**365–66, **2:**472–84, **2:**502, **2:**508–11
    Hispanic population in, **2:**401–2, **2:**531, **2:**579
    Mexican territory of, **1:**102–5, **1:**107, **1:**109, **1:**140
    school segregation in, **2:**347, **2:**354–58
    Spanish colonial rule in, **1:**78, **1:**91
    Spanish exploration of, **1:**30, **1:**68–69, **1:**106
Calles, Plutarco, **1:**195, **1:**197
Campos, Pedro Albizu, **1:**206, **1:**231–34
Cárdenas, Reyes, **2:**493–94
Carranza, Venustiano, **1:**213
Carter, Jimmy, **2:**456, **2:**495–97, **2:**501
Cart War, **1:**110, **1:**145–47
Cass, Lewis, **1:**145
Cassmore, Orin C., **2:**331–34
Casta Paintings, **1:**85–87
Castillo, Bernal Díaz del, **1:**30, **1:**60–63
Castro, Daniel, **2:**482–83
Castro, Fidel, **1:**163, **1:**206, **1:**250–57, **2:**455, **2:**458
Castro, Maria Elena, **2:**482
Castro, Raúl, **1:**254
Cervantes, Lorna Dee, **2:**533–37
César Chávez: Plan de Delano, **2:**380–83
Charles V, **1:**20, **1:**44–46
Chávez, César, **2:**304, **2:**377, **2:**380–81, **2:**383, **2:**399, **2:**445
Chávez, Linda, **2:**504–5, **2:**507
Chiapas Massacre, **2:**533–37
Chicano Moratorium protest march, **2:**365
Chicano Movement, **2:**365, **2:**368, **2:**373–76, **2:**378, **2:**419, **2:**421, **2:**423, **2:**437, **2:**439, **2:**448, **2:**450, **2:**465, **2:**467, **2:**493
Chilton, Elsie Chavez, **2:**306–8
Chinese Exclusion Act, **1:**166, **2:**319–20
Choi, Soon Kyu, **2:**575
Christopher Columbus: Columbus Reports on His First Voyage, **1:**33–35

Ciprián, Juan, **1:**71
Civil Rights Act of 1957, **2:**414
Civil Rights Act of 1964, **2:**461–62
Clinton, Bill, **2:**538
Clinton, Hillary Rodham, **2:**559, **2:**562–67
Codex Boturini, **1:**4, **1:**16–19
Codex Mendoza, **1:**4, **1:**20–24
Cold War, **2:**378, **2:**485
Collins, Marjory, **2:**339–40
Colón, Jesús, **1:**297–99
Colorado, Hispanic population in, **2:**402, **2:**531
Columbus, Christopher, **1:**29, **1:**33–36, **1:**38, **1:**40
Columbus Meets the Taíno, **1:**36–37
Compean, Mario, **2:**432
Congress of Racial Equality (CORE), **2:**377
Constitution of the League of United Latin American Citizens, **1:**227–30
Coolidge, Calvin, **2:**312
Coronado, Francisco Vázquez de, **1:**30, **1:**50
Corral Verdugo, Ramón, **1:**212
"Corrido de Kiansis," **1:**179–81
Cortés, Hernán, **1:**29–30, **1:**44–46, **1:**57, **1:**60, **1:**62–63
Cortés, Luis, **2:**531
Cortez, Gregorio, **1:**176, **1:**178, **1:**187–89
Cortina, Juan Nepomuceno, **1:**151–58
Crawford, Edith, **2:**322
Cristero War, **1:**195, **1:**197
Cruz, Celia, **2:**557–58
Cruz, Ted, **2:**502
Crystal City Walkout Demands, **2:**432–34
Cuban Adjustment Act, **2:**455, **2:**458–60
Cuban Revolution, **1:**163, **1:**206, **1:**250, **1:**254–55, **1:**257, **2:**494, **2:**555
Cuevas, Freddy, **2:**569
Cuevas, Kayla, **2:**569
Cullen, Tom, **2:**352
curanderismo, **1:**190

D

DACA (Deferred Action for Childhood Arrivals), **2:**548–51
Dalrymple, Louis, **1:**166–68
Dana, Richard Henry, Jr., **1:**78, **1:**102–4
Daniels, Josephus, **2:**319–20
Daniel Venegas: *The Adventures of Don Chipote; or, When Parrots Breast Feed,* **1:**279–82
David Reyes: "In Pursuit of the Latino American Dream," **2:**477–80

590   The Schlager Anthology of Hispanic America

Davila, Bill, **2:**497

De Baca, Fernando, **2:**465

"Decade of the Hispanic," **2:**455–56, **2:**495, **2:**498, **2:**501, **2:**560

"Decade of the Hispanic: An Economic Retrospective," **2:**499–500

Declaration of Independence, **1:**293

Delano grape workers strike, **2:**377, **2:**379–83, **2:**456

Delgado, Antonio, **1:**145

Delgado v. Bastrop, **2:**358–60

Denice Frohman: "Abuela's Dance," **2:**556–58

Díaz, José Gallardo, **2:**341

Díaz, Porfirio, **1:**182, **1:**192, **1:**195, **1:**199, **1:**209–10, **1:**212–16, **1:**260, **1:**265, **1:**269

Diego, Juan, **1:**30, **1:**71, **1:**73–76

Doña Juana (Queen of Castille and León), **1:**42

Donald Trump:

Speech on Immigration, **2:**563–67

State of the Union Address, **2:**568–71

Don Pedrito. *See* Jaramillo, Don Pedro

DREAM Act, **2:**502, **2:**514–17, **2:**545, **2:**547–51

Du Bois, W.E.B., **2:**522

Dulles, John Foster, **1:**257

Durban, Dick, **2:**514

E

East LA Walkout Demands, **2:**419–23

Eisenhower, Dwight D., **1:**257

"El Corrido Pensilvanio," **1:**184–86

Elisha M. Pease: Letter to Texas Legislature on the "Cart War," **1:**145–47

El Plan de Santa Barbara: A Chicano Plan for Higher Education, **2:**435–38

Elsa Knight Thompson, **2:**393–94

Elsie Chavez Chilton: Working with the Civilian Conservation Corps near Las Cruces, **2:**306–8

Emma Tenayuca and Homer Brooks: "The Mexican Question in the Southwest," **1:**238–41

Emory, William H., **1:**134

Espinosa, Joe, **2:**362

Esqueda, Manuel, **2:**480

Esteves, Sandra María, **2:**451, **2:**453

Excerpts from the 1930 U.S. Census, **1:**202–4

F

Fabián, Juan, **1:**71

Father Ruiz: Statement before the U.S. Commission on Civil Rights, **2:**411–14

Felipe, Diego, **1:**71

Ferdinand II (King of Aragon), **1:**29, **1:**36, **1:**42

Ferdinand VII, **1:**221

Fidel Castro:

"History Will Absolve Me," **1:**206, **1:**250–54

Speech at Presidential Palace, **1:**254–57

Fienup, Matthew, **2:**579

Fisher, George, **1:**113

Flores, Pedro, **2:**491

Florida

Cuban immigration to, **2:**455

Hispanic population in, **2:**531, **2:**579

Spanish colonial rule in, **1:**47–48, **1:**78

Spanish exploration of, **1:**30

Foraker Act, **1:**169

Ford, Gerald, **2:**456, **2:**465–67, **2:**501

Fourteenth Amendment, **1:**260, **2:**354, **2:**358, **2:**360–61, **2:**363–64, **2:**461, **2:**464

Franciscan Friar Describes the Land and the People of New Mexico, **1:**50–53

Francisco Madero: Plan de San Luis Potosí, **1:**209–12

Frank del Olmo: "Latino 'Decade' Moves into '90s," **2:**495–98

Franklin D. Roosevelt: First Inaugural Address, **2:**315

Frank Sotomayor: "Latinos: A Diverse Group Tied by Ethnicity," **2:**481–84

Fray Antonio de la Ascension: A Brief Report of the Discovery in New Spain, **1:**67–69

Friar Junípero Serra: Response to the Revolt and Destruction of Mission San Diego, **1:**91–94

Frohman, Denice, **2:**556–58

G

Gadsden Purchase, **1:**110, **1:**182, **2:**393

Gaitan, Maria Elena, **2:**472, **2:**474, **2:**476

Gallegos, Bert, **2:**465

Gamboa Solis, Jorge, **2:**536

Gamio, Manuel, **1:**195–201, **1:**265–69, **1:**271–73, **1:**275–77, **1:**279

Garcia, Hector P., **2:**348

Garcia, Pilar, **1:**257

Garza, Elías, **1:**272

Garza, Reynaldo, **2:**519

General Colonization Law of 1824, **1:**95

George, Marian M., **1:**169–72

Gerald Ford: Address to the Republican National Hispanic Assembly, **2:**465–67

Giuliani, Rudy, **2:**526–27

Glavecke, Adolph, **1:**152
Gonzales, Rodolfo "Corky," **2:**378, **2:**384–85, **2:**388, **2:**423, **2:**425, **2:**439, **2:**441–42
Gonzales, Sabino, **2:**324
González, Henry B., **2:**369–73, **2:**375–76
Gonzalez, Yolanda, **2:**483
Grajales, Juventino, **2:**330
Great Depression, **1:**206, **1:**238, **1:**242, **1:**260, **1:**291, **2:**303, **2:**305–6, **2:**309–10, **2:**312, **2:**314–15, **2:**318–19, **2:**326–28, **2:**330–31, **2:**334, **2:**365
Guadalupe Lopez Méndez, **2:**535–36
Guadalupe Vallejo Reminisces about the Rancho Period, **1:**105–7
Guevara, Ernesto "Che," **1:**254, **2:**417, **2:**494
Gutierrez, Felix, **2:**482
Gutiérrez, José Ángel, **2:**428–29, **2:**431–34
Gutierrez, Nancy, **2:**472

H

Harding, President Warren G., **1:**259
Harper, W.D., **1:**190
Hatch, Orrin, **2:**514
Hayes-Bautista, David, **2:**579
Henderson, Donald, **1:**235
Henry Arthur McArdle, **1:**120
Henry B. González: Speech against the Chicano Movement, **2:**373–76
Herman Badillo: "From Kennedy Democrat to Giuliani Republican," **2:**526–28
Hernán Cortés: Second Letter to Charles V, **1:**44, **1:**44–46
Hernandez, Pete, **2:**347, **2:**361–62, **2:**364
Hernandez v. Texas, **2:**347–48, **2:**361–64
Herrera, Gregorio, **2:**323
Herrera, Trinidad, **2:**323
Hidalgo, Miguel, **1:**293
Hitler, Adolf, **2:**349, **2:**352
Holmes, Oliver Wendall, **2:**347–48
Homestead Act, **1:**110
Hoover, Herbert, **2:**304
Hoover, J. Edgar, **2:**411
Hopi, **1:**3–4, **1:**12–15, **2:**395
Hopi Creation Myth, **1:**4, **1:**12–15
Houston, Sam, **1:**125, **1:**148
Howe, Julia Ward, **1:**245
Hsu, Paul, **2:**579
Huerta, Dolores, **2:**304
Hull, Harry E., **2:**312–14

Humboldt, Alexander von, **1:**141–44
Huntington, Samuel P., **2:**522–25

I

Illinois, Hispanic population in, **2:**531
Immigration Act of 1924, **1:**259, **2:**319, **2:**419
Immigration Act of 1965, **2:**458, **2:**460
Immigration Reform and Control Act (IRCA), **2:**456
immigration to the United States, **2:**508–11, **2:**514–17, **2:**548–51, **2:**571
 from Central America, **1:**205
 from Latin America, **2:**419, **2:**563
 Latino, **2:**455
 from Mexico, **1:**175–76, **1:**195–96, **1:**199, **1:**202, **1:**205–6, **1:**259–60, **1:**265, **1:**267–69, **1:**273, **1:**276, **1:**279, **2:**312, **2:**326, **2:**330, **2:**522
Inca, **1:**50, **1:**77
Isabella I (Queen of Castile), **1:**29, **1:**36

J

Jaramillo, Don Pedro, **1:**190–91
Jarrin, Jaime, **2:**497
Jefferson, Thomas, **2:**447
Jesús Colón: "Greetings from Washington" (from *A Puerto Rican in New York*), **1:**297–99
Jim Crow laws, **1:**259
Jiménez, José, **2:**415
John G. F. Wurdemann: A Physician's Notes on Cuba, **1:**130–32
John L. O'Sullivan: "Great Nation of Futurity," **1:**127–29
Johnson, Lyndon B., **2:**335, **2:**348, **2:**369–70, **2:**372, **2:**458–59
Johnson-Reed Immigration Act. *See* Immigration Act of 1924
Joint Resolution on the Annexation of Texas, **1:**133–36
Jones, Joseph, **2:**358
José Angel Gutiérrez: "The Thirty-Ninth MAYO Walkout: A Diary," **2:**428–31
José Antonio Saco: "The Color Line," **1:**99–101
José Antonio Villarreal: *Pocho,* **2:**365–68
José Martí: "Our America," **1:**163–65
José Vasconcelos: *The Cosmic Race/La raza cósmica,* **1:**220–23
Juan de Oñate: Letter about a Settlement in New Mexico, **1:**64–66

592   The Schlager Anthology of Hispanic America

Juan Nepomuceno Cortina:
> Proclamation to Texans, September 1859, **1:**151–54
>
> Proclamation to the Mexicans of Texas, November 1859, **1:**155–58

Juan Nepomuceno Seguín:
> A Tejano Leader Calls for Support of the Texas Revolution, **1:**125–26
>
> *Personal Memoirs,* **1:**148–50

Juárez García, Benito Pablo, **1:**163, **1:**216, **2:**381, **2:**383, **2:**386, **2:**399

K

Kansas
> Hispanic experience in, **1:**176, **1:**179–81, **1:**200, **1:**270, **2:**303
>
> Spanish colonial rule in, **1:**77

Kennedy, John F., **1:**246, **2:**369, **2:**371–72, **2:**395–96

Kennedy, Robert, **2:**501

K'iche,' **1:**3, **1:**7–8, **1:**10

Kiley, Barbara, **2:**508

King, Martin Luther, Jr., **2:**377–78, **2:**393–96, **2:**399, **2:**451

Kissinger, Henry, **2:**487

Ku Klux Klan, **1:**245

L

La Alianza, **2:**393, **2:**396

la Ascensión, Antonio de, **1:**30

Lair, John B., **2:**429

Lange, Dorothea, **2:**366

Lara, Severita, **2:**429

las Casas, Bartolomé de, **1:**30, **1:**54–56

Las Gorras Blancas. *See* "Proclamation of Las Gorras Blancas"

Lasso de la Vega, Luis, **1:**73–76

Latino GDP Report for 2021, **2:**579–82

"Latinx LGBT Adults in the U.S.," **2:**575–78

Lau v. Nichols, **2:**461

Laviera, Abraham "Tato," **2:**489–92

League of United Latin American Citizens. *See* LULAC

Lemus, Pedro, **1:**114

Leslie Sanchez: "The Emerging Latino Republican Majority," **2:**529–32

LGBT Adults, Latinx, **2:**575–78

Lincoln County War of 1878, **2:**322

Linda Chávez: "Toward a New Politics of Hispanic Assimilation," **2:**504–7

Lindsay, John, **2:**527

Lionel Sosa: The Americano Dream: How Latinos Can Achieve Success in Business and in Life, **2:**512–13

Longoria, Felix, **2:**348

Lopez, Omar, **2:**543

Lorenzo de Zavala: *Journey to the United States of North America,* **1:**116–18

Lorna Dee Cervantes: "Coffee," **2:**533–37

"Los Padrinos en los Funerales de Don Pedrito," **1:**190–92

"Los Sediciosos," **1:**192–94

Louis Dalrymple: "School Begins," **1:**166–68

Luisa Moreno: "Caravans of Sorrow" Speech, **1:**242–45

Luis Valdez: "Pensamiento Serpentino: A Chicano Approach to the Theater of Reality," **2:**445–50

Lujan, Manuel, **2:**466

LULAC (League of United Latin American Citizens), **1:**205–6, **1:**224, **1:**227–30, **1:**283, **1:**290, **2:**326, **2:**348, **2:**358

Lyndon B. Johnson: Remarks at a Reception Honoring Henry González, **2:**369–72

M

Madero González, Francisco Ignacio, **1:**209–11, **1:**213–15

Magón, Ricardo Flores, **1:**265

Malcolm X, **2:**378, **2:**395–96

Mallory, Christy, **2:**575

Manuel Gamio:
> Interview with Anastacio Torres, **1:**199–201
>
> Interview with Elías Garza, **1:**269–72
>
> Interview with Elisa Silva, **1:**276–78
>
> Interview with Isidro Osorio, **1:**195–98, **1:**260
>
> Interview with Juana de Hidalgo, **1:**273–75
>
> Interview with Juan Berzunzolo, **1:**265–68

Manuel Mier y Terán: Reports on the Divisions in Texas, **1:**95–98

Manuel Pastor: "Latinos and the New American Majority," **2:**559–62

Marco Rubio: Presidential Campaign Launch Speech, **2:**552–55

Marcos de Niza, Friar. *See* A Franciscan Friar Describes the Land and the People of New Mexico

Marcus, David C., **2:**354

Marian M. George: *A Little Journey to Puerto Rico,* **1:**169–72

Mariscal, George, **2:**397

Martí, José, **1:**110, **1:**163, **1:**253

Index   593

Martinez, Lupe, **1:**184
Marx, Karl, **2:**350, **2:**447
Masferrer Rojas, Rolando Arcadio, **1:**257
Maximilian I, **1:**260
Maya, **1:**3–11, **1:**77, **2:**449
MAYO (Mexican American Youth Organization) *See* Mexican American Youth Organization (MAYO)
McCain, John, **2:**540–41
McCarty, Henry. *See* Billy the Kid
McCormick, Paul, **2:**354
McLean, Robert N., **1:**262–65
McSween, Alexander, **2:**322, **2:**324
McWilliams, Carey, **2:**352
Memorandum by the American Ambassador in Mexico of a Conversation with the Mexican Minister for Foreign Affairs, **2:**319–21
Mendez, Sylvia, **2:**355
Mendez v. Westminster, **1:**227, **2:**347, **2:**354–58, **2:**419
Mendoza, Antonio de, **1:**4, **1:**20
Menefee, Selden C., **2:**331–34
Mexican American Marines in Vietnam, **2:**443–44
Mexican-American Unity Council, **2:**375
Mexican-American War. *See* U.S.-Mexican War
Mexican American Youth Organization (MAYO), **2:**428, **2:**432
Mexican Farm Labor Program. *See* Bracero Program
Mexican Farm Worker's Act of 1942, **2:**419
Mexican Revolution, **1:**182, **1:**192–93, **1:**195, **1:**199, **1:**209, **1:**213, **1:**220, **1:**265, **1:**273, **1:**278, **2:**445, **2:**494
Mexican Workers, mass deportations of, **2:**303
Mexica people, **1:**16–19
Mickens, Nisa, **2:**569
Mickens, Robert, **2:**569
Mier y Terán, Manuel, **1:**78, **1:**95–98
Mina, Francisco Javier, **1:**222
Minerva Delgado v. Bastrop Independent School District, **1:**227
Minnow, Martha, **2:**520
Miranda, Emelio, **2:**324
Miranda, Felipe, **2:**324
Miranda, Jose Deloros, **2:**323–324
Miranda, Lorencita, **2:**322–25
Mireles, Antonia, **1:**152
Missouri Compromise, **1:**133
Moctezuma. *See* Montezuma II
Montaño, Otilio, **1:**213
Montejano, Rudy, **2:**480
Montezuma II (Aztec emperor), **1:**45–46, **1:**62

Morales, Alejandro, **2:**479
Moreno, Luisa, **1:**206, **1:**242–45
Moreno, Mario, **2:**369–70
Morín, Raúl, **2:**335–38
Morris, W.T. "Brack," **1:**187
Mount, Julia Luna, **2:**472–73
Mountjoy, Dick, **2:**508
Musharraf, Pervez, **2:**541

N

NAACP (National Association for the Advancement of Colored People), **1:**227, **2:**326
Naranjo, Pedro, **1:**81–83
Narváez, Panfilo de, **1:**47
National Boundary Line at Nogales, **1:**182–83
National Council of La Raza (NCLR) *See* UnidosUS
National Farm Workers Association (NFWA), **2:**380
National Labor Relations Act, **2:**410
National Youth Administration (NYA), **2:**306, **2:**309
Native Americans. *See* Acoma, Aztec Empire, Hopi, Inca, Maya, Mexica people, Pueblo people, Taíno
Navajo, **2:**395
Nevada, Hispanic population in, **2:**531
New Hampshire, Hispanic population in, **2:**579
New Mexico
    discrimination in educational system, **2:**461–64
    Hispanic experience in, **2:**306, **2:**308, **2:**322–23, **2:**337, **2:**394–95, **2:**411, **2:**473, **2:**538
    Hispanic population in, **2:**402, **2:**531
    Hispanic women's experience in, **2:**322–25
    indigenous peoples in, **1:**4, **1:**52, **1:**83
    Spanish colony in, **1:**30, **1:**50–51, **1:**53, **1:**64–66, **1:**77–78, **1:**81, **1:**88–90
New York
    Hispanic experience in, **1:**117, **1:**172, **1:**242, **1:**297–99
    Hispanic population in, **2:**531, **2:**579
North Dakota, Hispanic population in, **2:**579
Northrop, Vernon D., **1:**206, **1:**246–47, **1:**249
Nunez, Ricardo, **2:**466
Nuyorican movement, **2:**389, **2:**451, **2:**489, **2:**492
NYA (National Youth Administration) *See* National Youth Administration (NYA)

O

Oaxaca, Fernando, **2:**465
Obama, Barack, **2:**502, **2:**518, **2:**538–42, **2:**545–47, **2:**552, **2:**563

Obergefell v. Hodges, **2:**575

Ocasio-Cortez, Alexandria, **2:**502, **2:**572–74

Oklahoma, Hispanic experience in, **2:**303

Oñate, Juan de, **1:**64–66, **1:**77, **1:**88

Origin Myth of the Acoma, **1:**4, **1:**25–28

Osorio, Isidro, **1:**195–98, **1:**260

O'Sullivan, John L., **1:**109, **1:**127–29

Our Lady of Guadalupe: "The Apparitions and the Miracle," **1:**73–76

P

Paiz, Patricio, **2:**397–400

Palacios Rubios, Juan López de, **1:**40

Paredes, Américo, **1:**187, **1:**291–92, **1:**294–96, **2:**326

Paredes, Domingo Martinez, **2:**445

Pastor, Manuel, **2:**559–62

Patricio Paiz: "En memoria de Arturo Tijerina," **2:**397–400

Paul S. Taylor:

>Interviews with Mexican Americans in Nueces County, Texas, **1:**287–90

>Sociological Observations of Mexican Americans in Nueces County, Texas, **1:**283–86

Pease, Elisha M., **1:**145–47

Pedro Albizu Campos: "Puerto Rican Nationalism," **1:**231–34

Pedro Naranjo: The Pueblo Indians Call for War, **1:**81–84

Pennsylvania, Hispanic experience in, **1:**176, **1:**184–86

Perez, Jame O., **2:**480

Philip II: Spain Asserts Control over the Indians of Nueva Galicia, **1:**57–59

Philippine-American War, **1:**166

Photograph of Mexican Agricultural Laborers, **2:**339–40

Piri Thomas: "Brothers Under the Skin" (from *Down These Mean Streets*), **2:**389–92

Plan de Ayala, **1:**213–16

"Plan of San Diego," **1:**206, **1:**217–19

Plan of San Luis Potosí, **1:**213

Platt, Orville H., **1:**174

Platt Amendment, **1:**110, **1:**173–74

Plyler, James, **2:**468, **2:**471

Plyler v. Doe, **2:**468–71, **2:**548

Polk, James, **1:**110

Polo, Marco, **1:**35

Poor People's March on Washington, **2:**393–94

Pope Leo XIII, **2:**382

Popol Vuh, **1:**3, **1:**7–11, **2:**449

Power, Ramon, **1:**232

Prince, Ronald, **2:**508

"Proclamation of Las Gorras Blancas," **1:**159–62

Proposition 187, **2:**502, **2:**508–11, **2:**522

Ptolemy, **1:**38

Pueblo people, **1:**4, **1:**52, **1:**77, **1:**81, **1:**83–84, **1:**88

Puerto Rican nationalism, **1:**206, **1:**246, **2:**417

Puig Casauranc, Jose Manuel, **2:**320

R

Ramirez, Cristina, **2:**472–74

rancho period. *See* Guadalupe Vallejo Reminisces about the Rancho Period

Raúl Morín Discusses Mexican Americans in Military Service, **2:**335–38

Reagan, Ronald, **2:**456, **2:**485–88, **2:**502, **2:**504

Reies López Tijerina: Interview after Martin Luther King's Assassination, **2:**393–96

Reno, Janet, **2:**519

Report of the Joint Fact-Finding Committee to the Fifty-Fifth California Legislature, **2:**349–53

Republic of Texas, **1:**111–13, **1:**119–23, **1:**125–26, **1:**133–36, **1:**145, **1:**148

Requerimiento, **1:**40–43

"Resolution on Racial Discrimination," **1:**235–37

Reyes, David, **2:**477, **2:**479–80

Reyes Cárdenas: "If We Praise the Aztecs," **2:**493–94, **2:**498

Reynolds, A.R., **1:**182

Rice, Ben H., Jr., **2:**358–60

Richard Henry Dana Jr.: *Two Years Before the Mast,* **1:**102–4

Richardson, Bill, **2:**538–39, **2:**541

Riebe, Loren, **2:**483

Rio Chaviano, Alberto del, **1:**253

Rivera, Nancy, **2:**472–73, **2:**475

Robert N. McLean: Protestant Religious Work among the Mexicans, **1:**262–64

Robinson, Jackie, **2:**347

Rocha, Pedro, **1:**184

Rodolfo "Corky" Gonzales:

>Arizona State University Speech, **2:**439–42

>"I Am Joaquín," **2:**384–88

Rodriguez, Evelyn, **2:**569

Ronald Reagan: Address to the Nation on United States Policy in Central America, **2:**485–88

Ronstadt, Linda, **2:**496

Roosevelt, Franklin D., **2:**304, **2:**306, **2:**310, **2:**312, **2:**315–18
Roosevelt, Theodore, **1:**110
Rubio, Marco, **2:**502, **2:**552–55
Ruiz, Ralph, **2:**411–14
Ruiz Ferro, Julio Cesar, **2:**535

S

Saco, José Antonio, **1:**78, **1:**99–101
Salvatierra v. Del Rio Independent School District, **2:**358
Samuel P. Huntington: "The Hispanic Challenge," **2:**522–25
Sánchez, Gabriel, **1:**36
Sanchez, Leslie, **2:**529–32
Sand Creek Massacre, **2:**536
Sanders, Bernie, **2:**562
Sandra María Esteves: "Blanket Weaver," **2:**451–53
Santa Anna, Antonio López de, **1:**113, **1:**119–24, **1:**133
Schreiter, Oscar, **2:**351
Scott, Robert H., **2:**342
Second Continental Congress, **1:**293
Seguín, Juan Nepomuceno, **1:**125–26, **1:**148–50
Seguin Bexar, John N., **1:**126
Selden C. Menefee and Orin C. Cassmore: *The Pecan Shellers of San Antonio,* **2:**331–34
Serna, Diana, **2:**429
Serna, Judy, **2:**461
Serna v. Portales, **2:**461–64
Serra, Junípero, **1:**78, **1:**91–94
Seven Cities of Gold, **1:**50
Sherman, Gene, **2:**341–44
Short Account of the Destruction of the Indies, **1:**30
Silva, Elisa, **1:**276–79
Sinarquist movement, **2:**349, **2:**351–53
slavery
　　in the American South, **1:**57, **1:**78, **1:**109, **1:**122, **1:**137
　　in Cuba, **1:**99, **1:**101, **1:**130, **1:**141, **1:**143
　　in Jamaica, **1:**141
　　in Mexico, **1:**109, **1:**116
　　in Spanish colonies, **1:**40, **2:**513
　　in Texas, **1:**95, **1:**109, **1:**116, **1:**133, **1:**135
SNCC (Student Nonviolent Coordination Committee), **2:**377
Sonia Sotomayor:
　　"A Latina Judge's Voice," **2:**518–21
　　Supreme Court Nomination Speech, **2:**542–44

Sosa, Lionel, **2:**512–13
Soto, Hernando de, **1:**30
Sotomayor, Celina, **2:**543
Sotomayor, Frank, **2:**481–84
Sotomayor, Juan, **2:**543
Sotomayor, Sonia, **2:**502, **2:**518–21, **2:**542–44
Souza, Pete, **2:**543, **2:**546
Spanish-American War, **1:**78, **1:**110, **1:**166, **1:**169, **1:**173, **1:**206, **1:**234, **1:**249
Spanish Empire, **1:**3–4, **1:**8, **1:**10, **1:**29–30, **1:**52, **1:**54, **1:**56–57, **1:**59–60, **1:**63, **1:**77, **1:**82–83, **1:**88, **1:**234
Staff Report:
　　A Study of Equality of Educational Opportunity for Mexican Americans in Nine School Districts of the San Antonio Area, **2:**404–7
　　Demographic, Economic, and Social Characteristics of the Spanish Surname Population of the Five Southwestern States, **2:**401–3
　　Farm Workers— U.S. Civil Rights Commission, San Antonio, TX, **2:**408–10
Steinbeck, John, **1:**245
Stephen F. Austin:
　　A Letter Describing the Texas Cause, **1:**119–21
　　Letter to George Fisher Describing the Occurrences in Texas, **1:**113–15
Stirling, Matthew W., **1:**25
Susan Archuleta Looks Back at Jobs with the CCC and the National Youth Administration in Northern New Mexico, **2:**309–11

T

Taíno, **1:**30, **1:**36–37
Tamarón y Romeral, Pedro, **1:**78, **1:**89–90
Tato Laviera: "AmeRícan," **2:**489–92
Taylor, Paul S., **1:**283–90
Tenayuca, Emma, **1:**238–39, **1:**241
Tenochtitlan, **1:**4, **1:**20, **1:**24, **1:**29, **1:**44, **1:**46, **1:**57
Texas
　　Anglo-Hispanic culture in, **1:**109
　　annexation of, **1:**110, **1:**135–36
　　discrimination in educational system, **2:**428–34, **2:**468–71
　　discrimination in legal system, **2:**348, **2:**361–64
　　Hispanic experience in, **1:**148, **1:**151, **1:**155, **1:**179, **1:**181, **1:**184, **1:**190, **1:**193, **1:**268, **1:**271, **1:**283–84, **1:**287–88, **1:**293, **2:**331–32, **2:**408–14

Hispanic experience in education, **2:**404–7
Hispanic population in, **2:**401–3, **2:**531, **2:**579
Mexicans in, **1:**147, **1:**154–55, **1:**157, **1:**192–93, **1:**288–89, **1:**292
Mexican territory of, **1:**78, **1:**95–98, **1:**109, **1:**122
school segregation in, **2:**358–60
segregation in, **1:**227, **1:**240, **1:**244
Spanish colonial rule in, **1:**78
Spanish exploration of, **1:**49–50
Texas independence. *See* Republic of Texas
Texas-Mexico border, **1:**217, **1:**265
Thomas, Clarence, **2:**520
Thomas, José, **2:**392
Thomas, Piri, **2:**389–92
Thompson, Elsa Knight, **2:**393
Tijerina, Arturo, **2:**399
Tijerina, Reies López, **2:**393–96, **2:**399
Torano, Maria Elena, **2:**456, **2:**496–97
Torres, Anastacio, **1:**199, **1:**260
Tovilla Cristiani, Homero, **2:**536
Travis, William B., **1:**125
Treaty of Guadalupe Hidalgo, **1:**110, **1:**137–40, **1:**151, **1:**155, **1:**175, **1:**182, **1:**224, **2:**354, **2:**393, **2:**395–96
Treaty of Paris (1898), **1:**110, **1:**174, **1:**234
Treviño, Armando, **2:**430
Treviño, Eddie, **2:**430
Treviño, Jacinto, **2:**399
Treviño, Mario, **2:**429–30
Truman, Harry, **1:**231, **1:**246
Trump, Donald J., **2:**502, **2:**559, **2:**561, **2:**563–71
Truxillo, Charles, **2:**524
Tyler, John, **1:**133
Tzacoalco (Jalisco): Concerns about a Marriage, **1:**70–72

U

UCAPAWA (United Cannery, Agricultural, Packing, and Allied Workers of America), **1:**235, **1:**242
Undesirable Aliens Act, **2:**312
UnidosUS, **2:**499, **2:**545, **2:**547
Universal Cosmography according to the Tradition of Ptolomy and the Surveys of America Vespucci and Others, **1:**38–39
Urquizu, Jose, **2:**351
U.S. Civil War, **1:**209, **1:**238, **1:**265
U.S. Commissioner General of Immigration Reports on Mexican Immigration, **2:**312–14

U.S. Commission on Civil Rights, **2:**401–14
U.S.-Mexico War, **1:**78, **1:**110–12, **1:**133, **1:**137, **1:**145, **1:**175, **1:**182, **1:**184, **1:**190, **1:**202, **1:**206, **2:**354, **2:**393, **2:**423

V

Valdez, Luis, **2:**445, **2:**447, **2:**449–50, **2:**496
Valenzuela, Fernando, **2:**497
Valeriano, Antonio, **1:**30, **1:**73
Valle, Victor, **2:**472–73, **2:**475
Vallejo, Guadalupe, **1:**105–7
Vallejo, Ygnacio, **1:**106
Vasconcelos, José, **1:**220–23, **2:**441
Venegas, Daniel, **1:**279–81, **1:**283
Ventura Novo, Esteban, **1:**257
Vermont, Hispanic population in, **2:**579
Vernon D. Northrop: Letter to Secretary of State Regarding Puerto Rico, **1:**246–49
Vespucci, Amerigo, **1:**38–39
Vietnam War, **2:**378, **2:**397–98, **2:**417, **2:**434, **2:**443–44
Vilhein, José, **1:**117
Villa, Francisco "Pancho," **1:**213, **2:**386, **2:**399
Villa, Ray, **2:**480
Villarreal, José Antonio, **2:**365–68
Vizcaíno, Sebastían, **1:**67
Voting Rights Act of 1965, **2:**456
Voting Rights Act of 1975, **2:**498

W

Wald, Patricia, **2:**520
Waldseemüller, Martin, **1:**38
Warren, Earl, **2:**341, **2:**361–62
Washington, George, **2:**378
Williams, Roger, **2:**572–73
Wilson, Bianca D.M, **2:**575
Wolff, Jacob, **1:**36
Works Progress Administration, **2:**306–7, **2:**310, **2:**331
Interviews with Hispanic Women in New Mexico, 1936–39, **2:**322–25
World War I, **1:**184, **1:**199, **1:**227, **1:**259, **1:**287, **1:**290, **2:**303, **2:**326
World War II, **1:**238, **1:**246, **2:**304, **2:**339–41, **2:**347–49, **2:**485
experience of Mexican Americans in, **2:**335–38
Wounded Knee Massacre, **2:**536
Wurdemann, John G.F., **1:**130–32

Index   597

Y

Yarborough, Ralph, **2:**369, **2:**371
YLP. *See* Young Lords Party 13-Point Program
Yoho, Ted, **2:**572–74
Young Lords Party 13-Point Program and Platform, **2:**415–18
"Youth Gangs Leading Cause of Delinquencies," **2:**341–44

Z

Zapata, Emiliano, **1:**213
Zapata Salazar, Emiliano, **2:**494
Zavala, Lorenzo de, **1:**116–18
Zeremeno, Manuel, **2:**351
"Zoot Suit" (play), **2:**496
"Zoot Suiters Lined Up outside Los Angeles Jail," **2:**345–46
Zoot Suit Riots, **2:**304, **2:**341–43, **2:**345–46, **2:**349, **2:**351, **2:**353, **2:**399, **2:**496, **2:**498
Zuñiga, Gaspar de, **1:**64